Wisdom With Understanding is Better Than Rubies

Laurine Karon Greenberg
Fine Arts Collection

INDIA
FOOD AND COOKING

INDIA

The ultimate book on Indian cuisine

FOOD &
COOKING

PAT CHAPMAN

NEW HOLLAND

First published in 2007 by New Holland Publishers (UK) Ltd
London · Cape Town · Sydney · Auckland

Garfield House, 86-88 Edgware Road, London W2 2EA, United Kingdom
www.newhollandpublishers.com

80 McKenzie Street, Cape Town 8001, South Africa
Unit 1, 66 Gibbes Street, Chatswood, NSW 2067, Australia
218 Lake Road, Northcote, Auckland, New Zealand

ISBN 978 184537 619 2

Senior Editor: Clare Sayer
Production: Hazel Kirkman
Design: bluegumdesigners.com
Photography: Stuart West
Map: Stephen Dew
Illustrations: Tula Antonakos and Roger Hammond
Editorial Direction: Rosemary Wilkinson

10 9 8 7 6 5 4 3

Reproduction by Pica Digital PTE Ltd, Singapore
Printed and bound in Malaysia by Times Offset (M) Sdn.Bhd.

Contents

Introduction 6

1 | Indian cuisine 7

India today 8
Indian history 8
The regions of India 33
   map of India 34

2 | The Indian kitchen 43

Tools and equipment 44
Herbs and spices 46
Essential ingredients 56
Basic preparations and recipes 59

3 | Recipes of India 63

Starters, snacks, soups & salads 65
Poultry 89
Meat 109
Fish & shellfish 133
Vegetables 155
Lentils 197
Rice & bread 205
Chutneys & pickles 223
Desserts & sweet treats 237
Drinks 249

Index 253
Acknowledgements 256

Introduction

India is an ancient country with many races, many facets and many regional cooking styles which have evolved over thousands of years. They have in common a use of spices, the combinations of which are found nowhere else on earth, resulting in fascinating, diverse, sensual, colourful and addictive dishes. Not surprisingly, Indian food has become one of the world's most popular foods, which we neatly call curry.

I am a devotee of the word, indeed I have written several books with 'curry' in their titles. But I admit the word cannot sum up Indian cuisine. Some Indians feel it demeans their food, citing curryhouses where all dishes taste the same. When Indian food is cooked correctly, nothing could be further from the truth; every Indian dish tastes different, and every one superb. And the whole meal is made up of many components, only one or two of which may be curry, if by that we mean an ingredient in a spicy sauce. Indeed the term curry only applies to four recipes in this book.

To understand any cuisine fully, we need to establish how ingredients, methods and regional characteristics evolved and *India: Food and Cooking* begins by tracing India's amazing culinary journey over the millennia. Reading this and that reference book I found scant information and not one chronologically complete work on the subject. I felt I was a detective seeking information. The clues were there; and finding a missing link, for example where and when a particular spice or ingredient first became used was thrilling. I hope you enjoy that chapter as much as I enjoyed writing it.

India: Food and Cooking is first and foremost a recipe book, for which I have been fortunate enough to travel all over India collecting material from anyone wanting to talk food. The result is 200 recipes which provide the reader with the widest range of ingredients, tastes, flavours and methods, including the principal signature dishes of each of India's nine main and five minor culinary regions. They enable the reader to produce authentic-tasting, delicious food for self, friends and family. Some recipes may be familiar and some not, and the latter are intended to extend the reader's repertoire.

I hope you enjoy them all.

1 Indian cuisine

India today

Mainland India is located north of the equator on a 1.2 million square mile 'peninsula', extending from the freezing Himalayas to the searing tropical south. The Andaman and Nicobar Islands in the Bay of Bengal and Lakshadweep in the Arabian Sea are also part of India (see map on page 34).

At slightly more than one-third the size of the United States, India is the seventh-biggest country in the world. It has the world's fastest-growing population with a teeming 1.1 billion people. It has numerous aboriginal tribes, whose population alone exceeds 80 million, though most of the Indian population stems from three main genetic races. Most Indians are rural labourers or shantytown dwellers, on or below the poverty level, scraping by on insufficient, cheap food. By contrast, India boasts more dollar multimillionaires than any other nation and 100 million middle-class, professional and white and blue-collar workers can afford proper roofs over their heads, mod. cons. and three decent meals a day.

India has 26 federal states, 8 religions, 18 languages, all having their own script and style, and about 1500 dialects. It has several main culinary styles with numerous variations (see page 33).

Indian food is as complex as all its other attributes. It began its development thousands of years ago. At a time when Britain was covered in ice and populated with individuals in bearskins and wode, whose main activities included picking berries and clubbing to death anything live, including each other, India was already cooking refined spicy food.

To understand how India and its food evolved, we need to go on an exciting journey back to the beginning.

Indian history

In his book *Journey of Man*, genetics expert Spencer Wells estimates that homo sapiens first arrived in India about 60,000 years ago by migrating along the coastal route from Africa. Known as *Brachycephalic* (broad-headed) *Negroids*, they were stone-tool-making hunter-gatherers who used fire. Their direct tribal descendants are found to this day in the east and south Indian hills and in the Andaman Islands, still speaking their original languages.

Nisadas

About 20,000 years ago, the next racial group to enter India were Austrics or Nisada and they settled in the north-eastern Himalayan foothills. Wild rice probably originated there, and at some point the Nisada learnt to cultivate it by building irrigated rice-terraces, the successors of which are still around today. Nisada tribal descendants survive in the same area today, identified by their medium build, very dark skin, long heads, flat noses and their pre-Sanskrit languages. No tangible food remains have survived from that time but much can be deduced from today's words in those languages. For example, the ancient Nisada made oil from mustard seed, sugar from sugar cane and jaggery from palm sap. They used citric fruit, pumpkin, aubergine, banana and melon. They did not breed cattle or produce dairy products. Charred bones tell of the ancient diets of two tribes still resident in Bihar; the ancestors of the Chandalas ate dog and the ancestors of the Punjisthas, the original domesticators of the elephant, certainly ate elephant flesh.

Mongoloids (Nagas)

Another tribal group, the Mongoloids or Nagas from Central Asia, entered India via Mynamar and Bangladesh and settled in north-east India at around the same time as the Nisadas. Their diet included rice, fish, vegetables and occasionally meat. No dairy or wheat was eaten, and it seems that alcoholic beverages were popular, as was betel nut. It was indigenous to Bengal, and the habit of chewing it to aid digestion gave rise to paan, popular all over India to this day. The majority of today's Bengalis are of Nisada descent, but a significant number of tribal Nagas still dwell in the

Bengali Himalayan lowlands, and still use their own Indo-Mongoloid language of Mon-Khmer origin. Nagas are distinguished physically by a yellow skin colour, oblique eyes, high cheek bones, sparse hair and medium height.

Proto-Mediterranean Dravidians

The next racial group to arrive in north-west India and one of great importance were known as Dravidians, who came from the southern Mediterranean. Today they are distinguished by their dark skin colour, their angular facial bone structure and large teeth. By 9000BC Dravidians had established fields and huts in north-west India. Wild animals, which until now had been hunted and eaten, became fenced, bred for milk, meat and

Red saris drying in the sun give a splash of colour to Jodhpur's ancient blue and white houses

leather and were put to work as 'beasts of burden'. Sheep and goats were domesticated from the woolly *ovis* family, pig from wild boar and domestic cattle from the *aurox* or *bovidae* family, which includes water buffalo, gaur and yak. The flashy Indian native red jungle fowl *gallus gallus* or in Indian, 'bahn morog', was bred into the fatter and larger domesticated chicken. Ducks, geese and peacocks were also penned and bred for meat and eggs. Wild dogs chose to become domesticated camp followers for easy fodder and adoration. In return they offered their services on guard duties and as herders, though no use was found for wild cats or monkeys. The Dravidians were originally wheat-eaters, and they brought with them their knowledge of cultivating grain. This enabled them to cultivate the indigenous pulses and when they inherited the Nisada rice-terraces, rice became a further Dravidian staple. Cooking meat was confined mostly to roasting, specifically on spits over fire. Simple soups and stews were heated by placing hot stones into animal-skin water containers. The Dravidians knew how to tap palm trees to create the alcoholic beverage, toddy. Remnants of all these items have been found in excavated pots.

India's earliest known farming village was discovered in 1974 at Mehrgarh alongside the river Indus, now in Pakistan. It was populated between 7000 and 2000BC. Excavations have revealed grinding stones which prove the use of wheat and barley, and pottery cooking vessels used for boiling and stewing, which clearly improved upon the earlier skin-bag technique. Charred bone remains show that that they cooked meat by grilling. We know that contemporary Mesopotamia or Sumeria (the Fertile Crescent, now Iraq) was growing garlic, onions, broad beans, peas, lentils, leeks, radishes and turnips, and it is inevitable that Mehrgarh grew these items too. India's unique black rock salt (kala namak) was indigenous to the land-locked hills of the Indus area, and although there seems to be no evidence, it is likely that it was in use at this time. We do know they used mustard and sesame seeds. Cave-finds from as early as 6000BC indicate that coriander was also in use. Cumin was certainly used in Mesopotamia; the Sumerian word is 'gamun' which is undoubtedly the root of the later Persian word, 'kermun' and the even later Roman word 'cuminus', although first written mention of cumin in India was not until 300BC.

The Indus Valley Civilization

By 3500BC probably over a thousand Dravidian villages and trading posts were strung out along the length of the river Indus. The innovation that changed history, or rather invented it, was writing. Mesopotamian Sumerian scholars inscribed hiero-glyphic word-pictures, later called *cuneiform*, on clay tablets. Thoughts and inventions were committed to script rather than memory. Above all, events were recorded and the prehistoric era was over. Shortly after this Egypt independently became literate with her own script. The Chinese remained in isolation until after 300BC. But by 3000BC they too had become literate, and they had mastered herbal medicine. Legend has it that the emperor Shen-Nung discovered tea in 2737BC when he was in the southern Chinese province of Yunnan and a few leaves accidentally fell into water he was boiling. Containing caffeine, it immediately became popular and was pronounced *tê* in Chinese. Tea was also indigenous to Assam, though it is doubtful that the Indian Mongoloid tribes of the time learned to boil water, let alone make tea, and we must assume that the process did not reach India until much later. Once it did it was called Cha-i-khitai, which evolved into the Hindi name Char.

By 2500BC two vast walled cities, Mohenjo-Daro and Harappa, had been established on the Indus, each with a population in excess of 40,000. Called the Indus Valley Civilization, it lasted for a thousand years with its own script, yet its existence remained unknown until the 20th century, its remains buried and forgotten. Excavation reveals that the cities had grids of streets around which were brick-built blocks of housing, complete with under-floor running water and lavatories with drainage and ventilation. Among the public build-ings were vast temple buildings, meeting halls and the Great Baths. Numerous excavated factories and craft shops have yielded wonderful artefacts and remnants of cotton and wool garments.

Long-distance trade between India, Egypt and Sumeria by land and sea had become an important way of exchanging ideas and goods. Raw materials and value-added items such as garments, artefacts, precious items and foodstuffs became interchanged. The Indus Valley people were not only farmers, they were competent and efficient hunters and fishermen as evidenced by the finding of numerous slings, knives and fish hooks. The meat stews of Mehrgarh had not been forgotten. Hand stone-roller-grinders, the design of which is still found all over India, confirm the use of spices. Summer crops of fish, vegetables and fruit were, and still are, harvested and dried for use in the harsh winters. Fruit and vegetable remains found in pots and pottery illustrations prove that banana, date, gourd, pomegranate and coconut were in use. Carbonized mustard seeds have been found, as have the remains of wheat, barley and India's most important lentil, gram (chana dhal), at the huge, impressive granaries.

Egyptians pioneered flour milling for their unleavened bread. Later they learned to use yeast for the fermentation process required for brewing beer and for leavening dough. To bake their bread they created the side-entry charcoal-fired clay oven. Indus Valley traders had seen the Egyptian ovens and granaries and were impressed by small, sleek creatures patrolling the grain stores, their role – to kill the rodents. Egypt's indigenous feral cat was so revered, it had not only been domesticated millennia before, it had also been elevated to god-status. Cats, granaries and ovens soon became the norm in the Indus Valley. A small metre-high clay oven variant seems to have been invented in India at the same time. Instead of having a side-entry, this egg-shaped vessel's entry hole was at the top, which was narrower than its centre point. It was the ancestor of today's tandoori oven. Its base had a small air hole, below which was placed an even earlier invention, charcoal. At this stage the oven was only used for bread-making, something fundamental to daily existence. Easily transported, this oven was probably specifically invented to enable travelling traders to make their daily bread at their campsites. Corroborative evidence exists in the form of oven remains found all along ancient trade routes. At more formal staging posts, remains of braziers and bones suggest that cooked meats and fish were sold at street stalls.

By 2000BC Egypt had pioneered egg-hatcheries with incubators to breed geese, duck and hens. When the courtiers entombed Tutankhamun, they included food and drink items he would need for his onward journey; jars of wine, pickled eggs and pots of spices including the indigenous aniseed, cumin and nigella.

The Aryans

Prior to 1500BC, a group of tribal nomads had migrated from central Asia to a region which became known as the land of the Aryans (meaning 'superior beings'), which later became Iran.

Some stayed put and were to form the world's first empire a thousand years later. One branch moved to the Caucasus to become known as Indo-Europeans. By 1500BC another Aryan branch entered the Indus Valley, and most of India's contemporary population are descended from them. They brought with them their Sanskrit language and war chariots drawn by horses, animals that struck terror into the Dravidians, who had not seen anything like them before. Neither had they seen such vast herds of cattle as those that Aryan farmers brought with them.

Beef and milk were Aryan necessities, as were cream, butter and yogurt. Yogurt is milk into which bacteria are introduced. Then the mixture is left to rest at a constant temperature to induce fermentation, souring and coagulation. Nomadic tribes carried their water and spare milk in horse-leather or goatskin pouches. It is conceivable that wild bacteria created the first yogurt, and trial and error led to its controlled production and enjoyment. It is called 'dahi' in Hindi, but the word we know originated from a Turkestan Hun word from around 100AD, 'yogurmak', (to blend).

The Aryans also brought the pomegranate to India. Native to Iran, where it is still the national

A vibrantly colourful group of Rajasthani women make their way up a steep hill

fruit, it resembles a large apple. Indeed its name derives from the Latin, 'poma-granata', apple with many seeds. Pomegranate was certainly used in pre-biblical times. Intriguingly, it is widely believed to be none other than Adam's forbidden 'apple' in the Old Testament. Owning pomegranate was considered to be an Aryan prosperity symbol. Their staple was barley, used on its own in gruel or mixed with honey, or baked as cakes. Prior to encountering the Dravidians, the Aryans did not use spices, salt, rice, wheat, wild meat, fish, garlic and onion.

Despite the fact that they were learning new skills and ingredients, writings from 1000BC indicate that the pale-skinned (described by historians as 'wheaten'), fine-boned Aryans despised the Dravidian's cultured ways and lack of military skill. They felt themselves superior to the dark-skinned, coarser-featured Dravidians, whom they called

demons. It was probably because of this total incompatibility that the Dravidians gradually drifted away from north India. Most took up residence in the south, where they were largely left to their own devices from then on (see page 39).

The Aryans on the other hand spread eastwards to take control of north India. A few eventually reached Bengal where they encountered impenetrable forests, unbearable humidity, mosquito-infested swamps and rivers prone to regular flooding. They also encountered the aboriginal Mongoloids, who by now called themselves Banga, or 'beautiful'. This name was not enough to prevent the Aryans from despising them, as they had the Dravidians. Matters were not helped by the fact that Banga diet consisted of fish, eel and snake and many forbidden wild meats, all cooked in fish oil or mustard oil. Indigenous vegetables such as gourd, coconut and plantain including its flower were eaten, as were leafy vegetables such as colcasia. Alcoholic beverages were rife. Even so some Aryans stayed and mixed with the Banga to become known as Vratya, introducing ingredients such as pulses, aubergine and yogurt, which soon became firmly established in Banga cuisine. Integration at that stage was minimal as is proved by today's Bengali vocabulary. Only 2% of words have Sanskrit roots.

The Aryans who remained in the Indus Valley had no use for anything Dravidian and their infrastructure and buildings were simply left to decay and become buried. The Aryans' main concern was to impose Sanskrit and Vedic pressures upon the population. From 1200BC, the first of four Vedas, meaning 'knowledge', were written in Sanskrit, leading to the establishment of the Hindu religion, with the worship of the cow and the proscription of beef-eating as its fundamental dogma. The complicated caste system was created and Ayurvedic medicine, literally 'life-knowledge', was developed. Ayurvedic philosophy states that the Indian meal must have six rasas (tastes): sweet, salty, bitter, pungent, sour and spicy. Sanskrit writings also included secular details. For example, to purify foul water, it must be boiled in copper vessels, exposed to sunlight, filtered through charcoal, and cooled in earthen vessels. Remains of legumes such as peas have been found in the Indus Valley dating back to at least 2500BC, and this is confirmed by Sanskrit writings detailing the use of lentils such as masurah (masoor), mugda (moong), masah (urid), mansaka (moth) and kullata (gram). These were added to soup and several 'new' rice varieties came into the diet. Rice was always boiled either in water or milk, and the process of making clarified butter (ghee) was in use by then. Coriander, sesame, mustard, cumin, long-pepper, onion and garlic had been in use for thousands of years already. By 700BC there

is recorded use for the first time of round peppercorn, ginger and turmeric. Being indigenous to south India, and therefore undiscovered until the arrival there of the Dravidians, it indicates that trading had become established between north and south. These notations about pepper are the first recorded use of a spice for its piquancy. There were no rules restricting the consumption of alcohol and barley, many plants and grass were distilled and enjoyed, it seems by all.

As time went by, records about cooking became more detailed. By 300BC court physician Sushruta wrote in his *Sambuita Sustrastbanaum* that meat was prepared in various ways: roasted on spits, cooked with milk and ghee, seasoned with spices, ground and made into balls, and minced. But most intriguing of all, he describes a further technique as meat spread with a honey-coloured spicy paste and cooked in the clay oven, the Indian invention referred to earlier (see page 11), and in Sushruta's Sanskrit words called 'kavan kunndu' (fire-container). Could 'kunndu' be the derivation of the Hindi word 'tandoor'? The paste 'kunndu pachitam' (fire-paste) 'spread on meat' sounds remarkably like a marinade described by someone who does not cook. The contents of this marinade are unclear, but to achieve the colour as described, it could well contain yogurt to assist in tenderizing the flesh, plus such spices as garlic, cumin, coriander, pepper and turmeric plus salt and indeed honey itself. Up to now the tandoor had only been used to cook bread. For the first time we know that spiced meat and probably poultry too was cooked in the tandoor.

The Persians
The ancient Iranians also have a claim to the derivation of the word 'tandoor'. It could have derived from their words 'tata', meaning 'hot', and 'andar', meaning 'inside'. However, it was the Egyptian-designed side-entry oven that was used in ancient Iran where it is still called the 'tonir', and their

bread 'nane lavash'. A millennium later the side-entry oven migrated westwards to become the Turkish pitta oven, which itself evolved into the Italian pizza oven.

As for the distinction between the names Iran and Persia, the country originated as Iran, the home of the Aryans (see page 11). The word 'Persia' derived from the Greek word for Iran's western province 'Fars', or 'Parsis' and was not applied until after the Greek conquest of Iran and of its empire by the Greek king Alexander the Great in 334BC. The country retained this name until 1935, when it reverted back to Iran.

Back in 1500BC, life for the Ayrans who had remained in Iran was troubled by wars and skirmishes until belief in a new religion unified the population. Zoroastrism worshipped natural gods, such as sun and sky, earth, wind and fire to whom sacrifices were made. The date of its foundation by the prophet Zoroaster is unknown, but was probably before 1000BC. From that point on the nation became literate, made intricate artefacts and developed their own civilization. Iran's greatest monarch, Cyrus, focussed on expansion. In 550BC he defeated Iran's western neighbour, the former Assyria (once Mesopotamia) and annexed that territory to Iran. In 532BC he took control of north-west India and proclaimed his territory as the world's first empire. His successor, Emperor Darius, extended the territory further east. Iranian cuisine also emerged using indigenous ingredients such as spinach, pistachio, almond, pomegranate, saffron and rosewater. Rice was not indigenous and probably arrived there by trade after the Aryans first encountered Dravidian cultivation terraces. But it soon became the Iranian staple. Their word for rice was 'rijzah'. The Tamil word 'arisi' derived from this, meaning literally to 'separate', referring to the process of splitting the grain from the husk. The Iranian word also became the derivation for the Latin word 'oryza' and the modern Italian word, 'riso', hence the word 'risotto'. Today, there are over 7,000 varieties of rice, and it is the staple of over two-thirds of the world's population. Biriani (see pages 211, 213 and 214) derives its name from the Persian word 'berenji', a type of long-grain rice. It was the Moghuls, themselves of Persian ancestry who developed the dish into the classic biriani. Rice and meat and/or vegetables, cooked together in a pan until tender, became known as 'polo' or 'polou'. It eventually evolved into Turkish Pilav, Greek Pilafi, Spanish Paella and Indian Pullao (see pages 208 and 209).

The Greeks

Greek civilization slowly grew from a series of independent warring states, such as Athens, Troy, Crete and so on, which came together from around 900BC as a unified power. They traded with Iran, Egypt and Assyria (formerly Mesopotamia) and by 600BC it is recorded that they used olive oil, herbs, and wine in their cooking. In India at the same time, two religions were founded largely as an antithesis to the multi-god Hinduism, animal slaughter and the caste system: Buddhism by Gautama Buddha and Jainism by Mahavirawas. Strict vegetarianism was required, although later Buddhists were allowed meat under certain restrictions. Jains went further and forbade the eating or killing, accidentally or deliberately, of any creature. The Jataka, the Buddhist 'bible', describes all aspects of life, including food. Specifically it mentions the use of asafoetida instead of garlic and onion, believed to be an aphrodisiac. It also mentions wheat-flour cakes (presumably flat-bread) cooked in clay ovens, described using the Iranian word 'tonir'.

Between the 5th and 4th centuries BC, and in rather more secular terms, Assyria's king Sardanapalus introduced the first cooking competition, the prize being a lifetime's worth of gold. Archestratus wrote the first Greek cookbook, called *Hedypathia* (Pleasant Living). Another Greek, Athenaeus, describes a pot specifically designed with appropriate-sized compartments enabling the simultaneous boiling of peacock, goose and hen's eggs. He makes no mention of why this needed to be done, nor about the different timings each egg-size would require. Greek historian Herodotus described the transport of ingredients on elephants, camels and horses on his travels between the Fertile Crescent, Asia and Egypt. He also stated that India 'is a vast desert-land full of gold, fantastic tribes of men and giant ants'.

In 327BC, flush with victories, Alexander took his army into north-west India. The Greeks found none of Herodotus' gold (it was and still is in the southern state of Karnataka where they did not go) and no giant ants but they did find numerous warring tribes, whom initially they conquered in a series of vicious battles. They also found the banana, and its Indian name 'pala' passed into classical Greek. One Greek legacy was the importation of grapes and wine into the Punjab. Vineyards have remained there ever since.

The Greek empire was now at its peak and held a trade monopoly from India to Spain. Alexander would have carried on to south India, but after their first defeat his troops had become war-weary and wanted to go home and Alexander chose to go with them. The last word went to the Persians. Following the decline of the Greeks a new Persian empire emerged, its people known as Parthians. Between 247BC and 224AD it existed alongside Rome, during which time Persian cooking became more sophisticated. Imports originally from China, such as apricot (zardaloo) and plum and Arabian sultanas and raisins had become locally grown. Certain Persian savoury dishes have always combined sweet and sour with fruit and meat, a classic example of which is Faisanjan, duck with pomegranate and almonds. This dish never reached India, but the concept did with the arrival of the Parsees from Persia in Gujarat in the 12th century (see page 20). The Persians were also partial to sweets made from syrup, wheat flour and ghee, which later became adopted by the Arabs.

Arabs

From at least 2000BC pagan, nomadic tribes from Arabia had gained the mastery of the deserts in which they lived, by transporting goods between various civilizations. To this end they domesticated the camel, invented the caravan (groups of traders and load-carrying camels) and the dhow, ocean going ships, built to the same design to this day. By 300BC, the Nabatean tribes from Aqaba and Petra were accomplished sailors. Finding their trading profits somewhat reduced by Alexander's Greek monopolies, they pioneered new sea routes to southern India in their dhows. The Chinese had already pioneered long-distance sea routes in their junks and located clove, mace and nutmeg (Indonesia) and cinnamon (Sri Lanka) which they traded in south India, specifically in the city of Cochin (meaning China-town), where fishing nets of Chinese design are still in use. In return the Chinese purchased garlic, ginger, pepper, coconut and betel nut.

Mauryan Empire

After the departure of the Greeks, battle commenced between numerous minor rulers. By 305BC a Hindu king, Chandragupta Maurya, was the ultimate victor. He created India's first true empire with territories including all of today's Pakistan and India north of the Vindhya mountain range. His son Ashoka expanded the empire into south and east India. Despite his achievements, or maybe because of them, Ashoka, tired of the bloodshed of war, converted from Hinduism to Buddhism. This led to violent disagreement amongst his Aryan-Hindu-Brahmin courtiers and to the decline of the empire after Ashoka's death in 231BC.

Once again the nation was rife with minor wars until one incursion of significance came from outside India. By 130BC the Kushans controlled all territories from the western part of the Ganges Valley and the Arabian sea outlet of the river Indus

to Afghanistan and Uzbekistan. By 50AD King Kanishka had expanded the Kushan dynasty to include all of northern India. To celebrate, he had records made of court life. For the first time we read that clove, nutmeg, mace, cinnamon and cassia, previously imported into India by Chinese maritime traders, were now being cultivated along with India's indigenous mustard, pepper, turmeric, garlic and ginger and long-established coriander and cumin. The records stated that meat was fried in ghee to which cumin, yogurt, pomegranate and black salt (kaka namak) were added. The most interesting use of nutmeg is in the following recipe of the time: '*Pound betel leaves, cardamom, sandal-*

wood, and many spices including nutmeg into a paste, form it onto a thin reed-like skewer and allow it to dry. Then remove the skewer and ... smoke it!'

The Silk Road (or Spice Route)

The greatest Kushan ambition was to connect their central Asian land-routes with those of Egypt, Arabia, Persia and India, with the objective of increasing Kushan prosperity. The Chinese were also keen to link their routes to central Asia. It necessitated creating new roads and hostels across 2,000 miles of inhospitable snow-bound mountain passes and searingly hot deserts. By 100BC the route, or routes, were open for business, extending

All over India acres of fresh red chillies are dried in the searing sun, then ground to create chilli powder

over 7,000 miles from eastern China to the Mediterranean. Having achieved this, the Kushan kings set their sights on trade with Rome. Meetings with Kushan ambassadors including one with the Emperor Hadrian (of the wall fame) in about 120AD are recorded by Roman historians. In its heyday, goods took at least two years to travel the entire route, changing hands many times, and in the process enjoying extensive price mark-ups. By the 1200s the route, in some disrepair, was rebuilt after which trade continued thriving until the Portuguese

maritime successes of the 16th century (see page 28). From that point trade slowly declined until it literally trickled out in the 19th century. Ironically it was not until the 18th century that a German archaeologist gave the route the name it is now best known by, the Silk Road, although it was known earlier as the Spice Route.

In 100BC China commenced trading on the route with exports which included paper, furs, bronze artefacts, gunpowder, compasses, lacquered goods, ceramics and cast-iron goods. China had by then invented the process of casting whereby molten iron was poured into sand moulds. This enabled them to build the first cast-iron ovens and woks. Cast-iron karahis appeared in India at this time. Ironically, silk exports were minimal in the early days of trading along the route.

Chinese food exports included fruits, such as oranges, peaches and apricots, and vegetables in dried or seed forms, spices, tea and, most unexpectedly, rhubarb, indigenous to Tibet, for use as a purgative. From Persia China imported rice, saffron, almonds, pistachio nuts and, equally unexpectedly, spinach, which was used in ancient Iran as an antidote to hangovers! From India China imported buffaloes, lions, peacocks, elephants, cotton, herbal medicines, incense, muslin, opium, silver, sandalwood, coconuts, ginger, garlic, spices, kohlrabi cabbage, cucumbers, onions and sugar.

China was desperate for horses, which could not be bred there due to a calcium deficiency in all organic matter including water. Arab horses were prized above all. Also from the Arabs, China imported camels, wool, tapestries, glass, frankincense, myrrh, cumin, coriander and sesame. Raw materials such as ivory, coral, jade and lapis lazuli were imported into China, made into artefacts and exported back to the West. Less tangible exchanges included knowledge, philosophy and religion. Buddhism reached China by travelling down the Silk Road.

The Romans

By 50AD the Romans had expanded their empire as far as Persia. Here, it seems, they encountered silk for the first time in the form of silk banners recovered from Parthians (Persians) they defeated in battle. The Romans now controlled almost the entire Mediterranean; all except its eastern end where they were obliged to trade with the Arabs, a people the Romans were never destined to conquer. They loathed the Arabs and their trading monopoly, the secrets of which the Arabs protected with their lives. Certainly no Roman was ever allowed to traverse the onerous Arabian deserts. True, the Romans were trading with the fledgling Kushan Silk Road, but their conquest of Egypt enabled them to establish a route which by-passed both Arabs and Kushans. The Romans travelled by land down the Nile valley then by sea along the Indian coast to establish a trading post at Arikamedu (south of Madras), where they traded with Indian and Chinese merchants. The arrival of Parthian silk in Rome heralded an astounding demand; every wealthy Roman woman was desperate to wear it. But initially only limited amounts were exported from China. This was to change so rapidly that by 200AD silk represented 30% of all goods being dispatched down the Silk Road and the Romans were obliged finally to trade with this route.

At first the Romans exported low-value goods. Inventories of the time specified human exports such as jugglers, acrobats and slaves, who were bought at the markets of the Roman Orient. Slave trading, incidentally, continued on the Silk Road at centres such as Bukhara and Khiva until the mid-nineteenth century. It was the relentless lust for oriental luxuries and especially Chinese silk that ultimately drained Rome of its wealth and gold and by 400AD made inevitable the decline of the Roman Empire.

In the meantime, Rome had captured Britain in 44AD and they brought their spices and Roman recipes with them. For the first time, Britain got to taste garlic, onion, ginger, cassia, saffron, coriander, honey, wine, salt and pepper. All were very valuable, but none more so than the last two. Both were issued as rations to the troops, who promptly used them for barter. Salt was so important that the word 'salary' derives from it, as did the phrase '*he's not worth his salt*' meaning he is not worth paying. Pliny (62 to 114AD) described pepper as the most important spice of all, and Apicius, the celebrated Roman gourmet food writer, used it in nearly all his recipes. Pepper was used in place of money at times, and Alaric the Visigoth demanded 1.3 tons as part of the payment he required to lift his blockade of Rome in

408. Not long after that, the Romans left Britain and the use of spice there was forgotten.

Indian Kingdoms

Following the decline of the Kushan empire, India again saw the rise of several smaller kingdoms which changed hands and territory quite regularly. Eventually, a family of wealthy merchants, the Guptas, acquired land by any means. By 320AD they came to power under Chandra Gupta. Eventually their empire included direct or indirect rule of most of India and Ceylon. Though it only lasted for two hundred years, the Gupta period is known as India's 'golden age'. Hinduism, education and the arts were nurtured. India's most famous poet, Kalidasa, wrote for the court and the celebrated Ajunta cave-paintings were created. Chinese traveller Fa Hian noted that whilst Indian peasants were vegetarian, largely eating roots, stalks, leaves, flowers and fruits, this was certainly not the case with the rich, who enjoyed meat dishes cooked with spices, especially cardamom. Fa Hian went on to say that they also regularly ate breads and rice dishes, along with milk (from bizarre sources such as elephant). Honey had been replaced by sugar cane. Alcoholic beverages were widespread. Three meals a day were now the norm.

For a thousand years from the 500s, many invaders entered India using the Khyber pass as their route. First contenders were the central Asian Mongol Huns whose empire by 520 already extended from Persia to Afghanistan. They took over the Gupta territory, though their rule was short-lived, and had declined by 600.

Muslims

We return to Arabia for the next significant event. Mohammed was born in 570, and grew up in the busy trading city of Mecca. Aged about 40, he had a vision in which he was called to be a prophet by God (Allah). By 622 Mohammed's preachings led to the formation of the Islamic religion, with its followers known as Muslims. It not only had the effect of unifying the Arabs; it gave them the confidence to venture out of their deserts in the name of conquest. The collapse of Rome and the Huns left the perfect vacuum for the Muslim Arabs to fill and by 700, as they spread out from Mecca they established an empire that would eventually stretch from Spain and Morocco to the Chinese border. By 712 the Muslims had conquered the Hindu kingdom of Sindh (now Pakistan). By 736 they had reached the banks of the river Jamuna, where they founded a new city that they named Dhillika. It was the first city of Delhi.

Muslims ate wheat and meat, with a proscription on pork. After conquering the Turkestan tribes, the Muslims found that the Turks had long-since invented the Kebab (see pages 73 and 77), meaning 'cooked meat'. They had also perfected the technique of marinating meat before grilling it and the method of pounding flavoured meat and shaping it over skewers, originally their swords. Shish, incidentally, is the Turkish word for 'skewer'. The Arabs created the Kafta, a round meat-ball, which became India's Kofta. The Muslims brought these kebab techniques into India and India invented many more. From India, the Muslims acquired the taste for native rice and lentils. Popular dishes were Persia's Birianis and Pullaos, and rice cooked with lentils – Kitchri (see page 208) in those days a Punjabi speciality. The Samosa (see page 84) probably also originated in the ancient Middle East, where thin stuffed pastries called Borek have been formed into various shapes and deep-fried for many centuries. Only triangles reached India. The Arabic word for sweet is 'hulw' and by the 7th century Arab hulv was a cooked mixture of date, sugar and milk. Later they incorporated the Persian sweet-making techniques of frying syrup and wheat flour in ghee. The Arabs took their hulv to India, where it became Halva (see page 239), made from sugar, butter ghee and vegetables, fruit or semolina. So important is halva to India that cooks who specialize in it are called 'halvais'.

At around 1000, the Afghan Mahmud of Ghazni arrived in India and observed that despite the efforts of his Muslim predecessors, Hinduism prevailed. He set about destroying Hindu temples and pursuing a policy of the rigorous persecution of Hindus.

Parsees

In around 1100, and far away in Persia, another people being subjected to Islamic persecution, because of their Zoroastrian religion, was forced to flee Persia or die. They sailed from the Gulf to Gujarat. The story goes that when priests asked for asylum, the king produced an overflowing bowl of milk and said 'my country is full; there is no room for you.' The priests added a sprinkling of sugar, saying 'Sire, the milk does not spill, yet we have sweetened it.' This so impressed the king that they were allowed to settle there. They became known as Parsees (the word deriving from Persians), and were left to their own religious beliefs. In the 12th century Gujarat was invaded by Muslims, though their rule did not last long. They were benign to the Parsees, who lived in Gujarat for a further five hundred years, during which time they developed a unique culinary repertoire of their own. As we have seen, certain Persian dishes combine sweet and sour with fruit and meat. The Parsees adopted this concept, and added piquant and savoury tastes to it. Dhansak (mutton cooked with lentils and aubergines, see page 114) and Kolmino Patio (hot, sweet and sour prawns, see page 140) are classic examples. Parsees have no culinary taboos, and they love eggs, all meats and fish. The Parsees, in turn, influenced savoury Gujarati cooking, with one of their flavours – sweet.

The south

After 8,000 years of continuous settlement in north-west India, the Dravidians found themselves in the invidious position of having to leave or be marginalized by the Aryans (see page 11). By 1000BC most meandered into south India. Being hot and inhospitable, infested with malarial mosquitoes and teeming with wild animals, it was unoccupied by all but a few tribes. The Dravidians began farming there by planting their beloved rice, mustard seed and pulses. Native to the area but new to the Dravidians were the indigenous coconut, ginger, turmeric, curry leaf and India's original piquant spice, peppercorns. These ingredients soon became integral; one simple dish originated from this time with all of them was Milagu-tannir (see page 67), the Tamil translation of which means 'pepper-water'. An Anglicized version of this dish achieved 20th-century celebrity when it became the tinned soup, Mulligatawney from Heinz. By around 700BC, the south had become the centre of Hinduism, and it remains so to this day.

From 300BC Tamil literature called Sangams tell us that early Tamils ate spit-roasted wild boar, which were fed on rice and kept apart from sows to improve flavour. A Tamil roasted rabbit dish served with millet rissoles is mentioned in the Sangams and still exists to this day. They also ate iguana and parrot. Rasams and Sambar (see pages 68 and 204) were around by 400BC. Fish (meen) and fisherman (meenavar) entered the Tamil language at that time. Kari in Tamil means 'pepper', and writings from c300AD tell that a dish cooked with pepper was called Thallikari or just Kari. Later this evolved into a spicy stew, which is found in Tamil Nadu to this day under the same name, Kari or Kuri or Turkari (see pages 164 and 196). Strict Hindu Dravidians proscribed the consumption not only of the cow but horse, duck, chicken and all wild animals and birds. Meat-eating ceased to become the norm. In any case the temperatures of the south made the digestion of meat and thick heavily-sauced meals very hard, and cooking techniques veered to thin-sauced, light, vegetarian meals. As ever all over India, alcoholic beverages flowed freely in the homes and taverns and to this end, from the earliest days a tribe, the Thiyas, has always specialized in toddy-tapping.

Over the next centuries, warring north Indian kingdoms changed hands frequently, but the central Indian Vishauna mountains acted as a sufficient barrier to leave the south largely uninvaded. Southern rulers came to the fore. The Cholas ruled Tamil Nadu on and off from the 1st century BC until the 12th century AD. Other dynasties included the Pallavas, Pandyas and Chalukyas. Small sects of immigrants came to south India by sea; a group of Jews first arrived in the Konkan area after 200BC following Greek persecution, and a second group arrived in the Goa area after 70AD following the Roman destruction of their Jerusalem temple. They fled again to south India's Cochin in the 1560s, following Muslim then Portuguese persecution. Their Kosher cuisine was barely Indianized, in that it used few spices, but one item of interest is the Filowri (see page 83) – a variation of Egypt's Felafel. The first Christian came too; St Thomas the Apostle is said to have landed in Kerala in 52AD to found the 'Syrian' Church at Muziris (Cranganore). His language was Syriac Aramaic, his converts known as Syrian Christians. To this day they eat spicy offal, chicken, duck, fish, shellfish, beef and wild boar.

Many very elaborate Hindu temples were constructed all over south India, and still remain in daily use. From the beginning, religious festivals dominated the temples. Pongal is a four-day festival celebrating the harvest. Diwali is celebrated in November. Tamil New Year falls in mid April, coincidentally the date of the Buddhist new year. Food is closely associated with festivals at which time the temples have always cooked for the masses, dispensing it liberally to all-comers. The first Dravidian arrivals planted wheat, but it was not suited to the south's climate, whereas rice was. Once introduced to the south, its use evolved in ever more sophisticated ways, such as in Dosa (see page 80) – the south Indian pancake made from thin, fermenting rice and lentil-flour batter. It was on record as being made by the 6th century at the Brahmin temple in Udipi, a small Karnataka town a few miles north of Mangalore, as festival food for thousands of worshippers. Also from Karnataka hails the traditional Kootoo (see page 167) – a hot and sour mixed vegetable dish containing sesame, chilli, tamarind and coconut. Eleven hundred years ago it was called Melogra, at which time it contained pulses, greens and mixed vegetables. The first mention of Parpata (Papadom) was around 500BC. Buddhist writings tell how they were made by women specialists who had spent a lifetime learning their skill. The method is identical to this day; made near Madras (Chennai), each papadom is made by hand, from an oily, lentil-flour dough ball, which is slapped by hand, in a trice, into a thin flat disc, and laid out on huge trays to dry in the sun. Until very recently, papadoms were virtually unknown outside south India, apart from one area; Rajasthani 14th-century records tell that papad-makers travelled in the raja's retinue. Rajasthan has enjoyed papadoms (called kheladas) ever since.

Brahmins (monks) recorded a considerable amount of detail about food and many preparations appear in temple records. The *Manasoolasa*, a cookbook written by the holy man Somesvara in 1127AD specifically for use by 'royal households' tells of 'vataka', made of green beans soaked to remove their skins, then ground to a paste and shaped as a ball then deep-fried. Today it is called Vada.

The first record of Jalebi (see page 242) – syrup-drenched, crisp spirals, was from the 1450 writings of the south Indian scholar Jinasura who tells that they were served then as the penultimate sweet item before the arrival of the concluding curds (yogurt) and rice. Another writer a century later described jilabi (sic) as something which '*looks like a creeper, tasty as nectar*'. The word itself derives from the ancient Persian word 'zalibaya' and it is probable that it originated there many centuries earlier.

Indian food has always been eaten with the right hand. In the south all parts of the fingers can be used, like a scoop. In the north this is considered vulgar and only the tips of the fingers are used, with bread used as the scoop. At some unrecorded time, but probably at the beginning of south Indian civilization, a unique disposable plate was utilized on which to serve their food. They used (and still do) the large, waterproof, oblong, fleshy leaves of the banana tree which grow up to 2.5 m (8 ft) in length. When used as plates, for a sadya (feast) precise rules apply; only the end section is used and its narrow part faces left. Servings begin on the bottom left half of the leaf on which is placed chopped yellow plantain. Next come deep-fried jaggery-coated banana-chips, then plain ones, then papad. Top left are placed lime and mango pickles, Thoran, Aviyal, Kootoo, Tukari, Pachadi and Kichudi. Only when these are all served may one eat, after which the rice is served bottom centre, and Sambar and Kalan is poured on to the rice. When all is eaten, a dessert such as Payasam or Jalebi is served on the leaf. After this comes Rasam and a little curd. But the conclusion is even more clever. The leaf is simply folded up and discarded; no washing-up, no ecological damage, no cost, and all this from 2,500 years ago.

Very little has changed to this day in south Indian culture and cuisine, despite the odd incursions by Muslims from about 800. Unlike those in the north, they were largely ineffective, though the Moplah tribe, descended from early Muslim maritime traders, married Keralan women, converted them to Islam and introduced a meat-eating cuisine. Kuttichara is whole goat stuffed with chickens inside which are eggs. Being fishermen, Meen Moplah Biriani (see page 211) uses mixed seafood but could equally use mutton, chicken, egg or fish and Arikadaka is mussels and rice flour,

Street markets are where you will find the freshest produce. The seller splashes water on her wares, which include aubergines, gourds, beans and herbs

cooked in-shell. One effective Islamic incursion was in the 14th century when Hyderabad became Muslim-ruled, and this was reinforced by the subsequent placement of Moghul royal relatives as Hyderabadi Nizams (see page 31). Other than that rule, the Moghuls never had effective control of south India. We can therefore say that her culinary roots go back nearly 3,000 years, making it India's oldest, virtually unaltered cuisine.

Indian Muslims

Back in the north, in 1206 a Muslim sultan took Delhi and established the Delhi Sultanate and with it control of northern India. In the same year, several thousand miles away, a far more celebrated warrior, Genghis Khan (meaning the 'universal ruler') was enthroned as Mongol emperor. With his terrifying, unyielding cavalry he gained control of all land north of the Himalayas from China to Poland. Although nomadic and avid raw-meat-eaters (including horse and camel), the Mongols installed a considerable level of culture. In need of material goods and with the Silk Road in some decline, Genghis' grandson Kublai Khan re-established it in the late 1200s. However, not for the first time, the Himalayas proved to be the barrier that prevented a Mongol takeover of India at that time although for two centuries uncoordinated Mongol raiding parties caused frequent havoc in the Punjab. In 1398, the Mongols under Timur-the-lame (Tamerlane) decided the time had come to take India. Timur led his army from his capital Samarkand into India via the Khyber Pass and destroyed Delhi. This was the end of the Delhi Sultanate, though Muslims remained in full control of most of north India.

Moroccan traveller Ibn Battuta who lived in India between 1325 and 1354 describes Delhi Sultanate banquets of meats including whole stuffed sheep, poultry, sparrow (kunjshakka) and breads, sweets and rice dishes. Paan originated in Bengal (see page 33), is uniquely Indian and is eaten to aid digestion. Battuta says of Paan '*the banquet concludes with paan, available to any citizen, native or stranger, at no cost*'. Battuta gives the first written reference to Khitchri (see page 208), rice with moong lentils. '*The munj* [moong dhal] *is boiled with rice and then buttered. This is what they call Kishri, and on this they breakfast every day*'. He also notes barley was stored in the thick cavity-walls of the Delhi fort, and was used to feed Indian horses. However, barley's main use was to produce an alcoholic beverage called 'fuqqa' which was served in pewter tankards, despite the Koran's prohibitions.

The next century saw the establishment of the world's newest religion. Sikhism's founder, Guru Nanak Dev, was born in the Punjab in 1469. He rejected both the punitive persecution being imposed upon the Punjabis at the time by Islam and the multi-god, caste system of the Hindus in favour of one god. Sikhs remain a staunch but tiny minority in India to this day.

The Great Moghuls

In 1483 a minor ruling family near Samarkand gave birth to a son, whom they called Babur. Bamber Gascoigne in his book *The Great Moghuls* said of Babur 'his credentials could hardly be improved upon'. His father was descended from Timur, and his mother from Genghis. Babur became king at the age of eleven when his father died. At fourteen he began a series of conquests. Babur was cunning, daring, and undoubtedly lucky and proved to be an astute general. At just eighteen he ruled from Samarkand to Kabul. But his target was India, and after five attempts he finally took Delhi in 1526. With just 12,000 soldiers, he pulled off the impossible by defeating an army ten times greater than his own, albeit with the advantage of a new weapon imported from the West, the flintlock gun. Babur marched into Delhi and declared himself sultan. He then waited for retaliation. To his surprise there was none. To the indigenous Indian population, the fact that Babur was not of the Hindu religion, and that he was not even Indian, did not bother them. For several hundred years, they had had a succession of Muslim rulers, so another was 'de facto'. He would probably be no worse than his predecessors. Babur set about empire-building. He cleverly did so without dethroning any of the incumbent Hindu maharajas and princes, who were allowed autonomy in their own states, providing they accepted Babur as ruler, and paid their taxes directly to him.

The seeds of the Moghul empire were sown. The court spoke Persian, and in that language Moghul meant Mongol, literally 'savage uncivilized barbarian'. Not surprisingly, this was not something Babur wished to be associated with, and the word Moghul was not applied until the 1660s.

Babur died in 1530 and was succeeded by his son Humayan, who consolidated the rule until his death in 1556. History repeated itself in that Babur's grandson Akbar also came to the throne at a tender age (fourteen). Akbar reigned for 50 years, during which time he expanded the empire to include Afghanistan and Bengal. So enormous was the wealth the taxes yielded, it enabled everything the Moghuls did to be magnificent. Akbar's army, consisting of 100,000 men, 10,000 camels and 1,000 war elephants, was invincible. Moghul rule, though austere for their subjects, created a lifestyle unmatched anywhere else on earth before or since. Their courts were highly civilized, if at times quite violent. They built for their own protection and enjoyment forts, palaces, landscaped gardens, mosques and mausoleums which were unparalleled, as is witnessed by India's most famous landmark and arguably the world's most outstanding building, Agra's Taj Mahal. Their cities were bigger than their counterparts in Europe. Agra was bigger than London, a fact not unnoticed by visiting English ambassadors. Akbar's opulence at court was displayed in his magnificent robes, oversized jewels, elephant jousting, massive parades, and luxury in everything he did, especially in the huge harem.

In the interest of security and privacy, the emperor, his wives and children lived inside the innermost part of each fort, the harem. No other male was allowed in. Akbar had three close wives; one Muslim, one Christian and one Hindu; if one religion was the wrong choice, at least one of the others would assure Akbar's entry to heaven! In addition the harem contained 100 eunuchs guarding innumerable children and as many as 1,000 women. Despite popular perception, most were not sexual partners but were tailors, dress-makers, musicians, puppeteers, dancers and nurse-maids. Just to be sure, one of the eunuchs' duties was to ensure that any item that might be used sexually was neutralized; carrots and cucumbers for example were always cut into little pieces. Besides Akbar and probably the entire harem were more interested in alcohol and drugs than sex.

Nearly all the Moghuls ignored Islamic drinking prohibitions. Babur loved wine, arrak and bhang (cannabis). Humayan was addicted to alcohol and opium, indeed his accidental death, where he broke his neck falling down stairs, resulted from this addiction. Akbar preferred bhang, whilst of the great emperors yet to come, Jehangir drank day and night, Shah Jehan drank a little and only Aurangzeb abstained.

As for their food, the Moghuls simply did to their cooking what they did to their architecture, art, warfare and lifestyle; they perfected it. There were dozens of court chefs, from different Indian regions. They were given status, time and money to work at their craft. The harem and the court amounted to 2,000 mouths, all of which had to be fed. But the few chefs who cooked for the emperor himself were la crème de la crème, although their every action was scrutinized and recorded by petty officials including poison-testers. Historian Abdul Fazl in 1590 in his *Ain-i-Akbari* chronicled Akbar's court life and food. Classical Moghul dishes such as

Korma, Roghan Gosht, Pasanda and numerous others have not been bettered since. Traditional Pasanda was developed because the emperor's teeth were in a state of decay. In consequence, meat had to be tender enough to break up with the fingers, thus avoiding the need for a knife. Young meat such as calf or kid was always used. In 1590 Abdul Fazl gives a Khitchri recipe: '*Take 5 seer each, rice, split dal and ghee, and ⅓ seer salt. This gives seven dishes.*' Since one seer equalled 900g (2 lb), Fazl's recipe would have fed 140 not seven!

Korma probably derived from the Persian 'Koresh', a ghee-based mild stew. The Moghuls indianized it, using cream, yogurt and ground almonds, saffron and aromatic spices. It was said that if a chef could cook a Korma he could cook for the Moghul court. If he could cook two dozen variations he would be 'king of the kitchens', and cook for the emperor's table. Roghan Josh Gosht is an astoundingly aromatic meat (gosht) dish, perfected in Kashmir. There are two possible derivations of the word 'Roghan'. In Kashmiri, it means 'red'. However in Persian it means 'clarified butter'. 'Josh' means 'heat', which describes the intense but slow heat required to get the most from this dish. The alternative meaning for 'Josh' is 'juice'. The fact is that none of these meanings is incorrect. The dish did originate in Persia as a slow-cooked meat dish. Much later, when the Moghuls retreated to the cool of the Kashmir mountains to escape the heat of the summer, it acquired highly aromatic spices, such as brown cardamoms, saffron and cloves. It also became red with the use of alkanet root (ratin jot) and a strange indigenous plant called 'maaval' which was called 'cockscomb' by the British because it resembles that bodily piece of the male chicken!

Ice was one thing that was available in abundance in the Kashmiri mountains. Runners carried large blocks of ice from the Himalayas to wherever the Moghuls were in residence at their lowland courts of Agra, Delhi and Lahore. By keeping the blocks huge, they were able to travel far. On arrival the blocks were smaller, but the emperors regarded them as a basic court necessity to keep their rooms cool. 16th-century Indian air-conditioning was achieved by having man-made waterfalls trickling down serrated walls in every room in the Moghul household and the now cooler air was circulated by fan-pulling servants (punkah wallahs). Ice was only fed into the waterfall of the room where the emperor was present. There was no shortage of punkah wallahs, nor ice, and it is not surprising that Moghul chefs got hold of it. They already made a spicy sweet cream. It did not take much evolution to mixed crushed ice with the spiced cream mixture. No stirring took place, and the mixture was put into special conical moulds (which enabled the item to slip easily out of the mould before serving). The moulds were then packed in ice-filled boxes and the cream froze solid to become known as Kulfi (see page 248).

A short distance from Agra is the city of Fatephur Sikri, built by Akbar, yet abandoned 14 years later for want of a decent water supply. It remains intact, and one can explore the entire fortress including the once private inner-sanctum of its harem. There are two places of special interest here. One is the harem kitchen, which still carries the smoke-stains of the last cooking done there in the 16th century. Nearby is a vast alfresco chess board (India invented chess) where Akbar sat playing the game with servants dressed as the chess pieces making the moves on the board. His 'opponent' would be one of his inner court advisors, who were careful enough never to win. There were nine permanent advisors, known as Akbar's navrattan or 'nine jewels'. Each was at the top of his profession: vizier, general, imam, poet, musician, philosopher, artist, Akbar's biographer and one other, which legend has it was his head chef. Maybe it was he who created the delightful Moghul vegetable dish, Navrattan Korma (see page 174) containing nine colourful ingredients.

Akbar's son Jehangir succeeded in 1605 and made Srinagar his Kashmiri summer headquarters, which he called 'heaven-on-earth'. There he created the beautiful Shalimar gardens with thousands of flowers, and spectacular fountains that splash into ponds where Jehangir kept royal carp, allegedly with gold rings in their noses. Their descendants are still there today, healthy as ever, but without the gold rings. Jehangir died aged just 48 in 1627 as a result of his addiction to both alcohol and opium.

Shah Jehan succeeded him and is best-known for his opulent life-style. The emperors enjoyed displaying their wealth, no one more than him. At his court banquets, solid gold, life-sized models of spices such as cloves and cardamoms were dispersed in the food being served. This was no act of generosity however, because woe betide the syco-phantic courtier who did not immediately return the item to the emperor with grovelling thanks. The concept of actually eating gold and silver was also invented by the Moghuls. It was in the form of edible silver or gold foil leaf, 'vark', pronounced 'varak'. It was made from a nugget of either pure gold or silver which was hammered between leather pads by craftsmen, until it was in small sheets thinner than paper. The concept remains unchanged, with sheets placed on top of such dishes as birianis, kormas and halvas, as an inter-esting edible garnish. It is vegan, has no flavour, and of course it was a major talking point, the more so because the Moghuls claimed vark to be an aphro-disiac. It was one of several ingredients said at one time or another to increase desire or lust. The Moghul must-have aphrodisiac list was devoid of logic and probably effectiveness, but for what it is worth, as well as vark it included aniseed, coriander, garlic, ginger, honey, almonds, pistachio nuts, carrot and turnip.

Even for the richest country on earth, the ulti-mate overspend came with the building of the Taj Mahal as a mausoleum for Shah Jehan's wife Mumtaz who died in her twenty-first childbirth. He was not sufficiently disconsolate over losing his wife to miss the opportunity to hold the Taj Mahal's inaugural party. Legend tells us it was held in moon-light with all the guests dressed in white. All food served had to be white, served on mother-of-pearl or silver platters. The highlight was a famous all-white Korma (see page 121), no doubt garnished with silver vark.

Shah Jehan next commenced to build an iden-tical Taj Mahal in black marble on the opposite bank of the River Jamuna, the remains of which exist to this day. This was the last straw for his son Aurangzeb, who correctly predicted that his father's spending would bankrupt the empire if allowed to continue. Aurangzeb imprisoned him and took the throne in 1658. Shah Jehan went blind and was imprisoned for eight years, during which he was asked what dish he would like to eat. It was called Shah Jehan's Last Stew, and was allegedly served every day until his death. The rather austere Aurangzeb reigned until 1707, after which the empire fell into terminal decline.

The Europeans

During the Moghul period a new and irresistible force was preparing to change the world. The north Europeans were coming. To understand why, we need to return to Rome, whose decline occurred because the gold reserves of the Romans became exhausted in their lust for luxuries such as silk, perfumes and spices (see page 18). When Rome finally collapsed, control of the Mediterranean Sea went to those with the most effective navy; Genoa in the west and Venice in the east, ensuring them the monopoly of north European trade. The Arabs took over lands from Spain to Egypt and Iran and eventually India. Most significantly they now owned the ports of the eastern Mediterranean. Venice was as much the beneficiary as the Arabs, who as always relied on their ability to navigate their deserts. Between them they created astonishing price-fixing. Price was also inflated by Arabian tall stories. The exact origin of most spices was a well-guarded secret, and their acquisition was made to sound perilous. When the Greek historian Herodotus visited Arabia, he was regaled with tales by Arab traders. Frankincense grew on trees guarded by swarms of tiny, venomous flying serpents. Cassia grew in a large lake, protected by huge, screeching, winged bats and to prevent being eaten alive by the monsters, cassia-gatherers had to disguise themselves with cattle-hides. Cinnamon, wrote Herodotus, was used exclusively by gigantic vultures as their nest material, which they built on a precipitous mountainside, held in place by mud. The Arabs fed the birds with ox carcasses, which being very heavy, caused the nests to collapse to the valley floor, where waiting gatherers scooped up the cinnamon and ran. Those not quick enough were eaten alive by the enraged vultures. Believed or not, stories such as this were fostered for two millennia simply to inflate prices to unrealistic levels.

To take just one price example, pepper at its south Indian source grows, then as now, as a virtually wild, inexpensive and prolific plant. By the time it had changed hands along the Spice Route through a succession of middlemen, pepper had assumed such value that in Roman times it was as viable as cash (see page 18). In 12th-century London, one pound of pepper would purchase several sheep, and it was used to pay taxes and rents. For example it was a week's mooring fee for a Venetian merchant ship in London docks. Price thus precluded the use of spices by the masses. They were luxuries only afforded by aristocrats in their court cooking and so valuable that the court housekeeper had to account for them. She presented her spice list for each meal to the lady of the manor, the spice-cupboard key-holder, who signed off the list as a receipt; it evolved into the word 'recipe'.

No one paid more for spices than the Europeans on the edge of the known world and it was a source of deep annoyance to them. The way to break the monopolies was to find new routes. In the early 15th century the Portuguese monarch was persuaded to finance adventurous mariners to explore the African coast to find a route to India. The prizes promised to be great, for both king and captain. It took a sailor called Columbus decades to convince the rival Spanish monarch that the enormous wealth of fabled India and China lay just a few thousand miles across the unexplored Atlantic. In 1492 he 'discovered' land, never realizing that another continent, later called America, and another ocean, the Pacific, lay between him and his spices. Alarmed that the Portuguese would soon follow them, the Spanish demanded that the Pope decree them the sole occupational rights to the New World they were in the process of discovering. In 1494, the Pope did indeed issue such a decree, drawing a line down the map, which should have handed all New World lands to Spain. As luck would have it, the line passed right through a land yet to be discovered.

The Portuguese

In 1498 the Portuguese reached India via Africa and soon set up a permanent base at Gowapuri, renamed Goa, until then a minor Arab port, in a largely Hindu area. They defeated the incumbent sultan in the name of Christianity and all Muslims were killed or persecuted. A state of peace had existed between the Muslims and Hindus, mainly because of the former's importation of Arab horses, required by the latter for their cavalries. The Portuguese were quick to supply horses to the Hindus. In 1500 Portuguese captain Cabril accidentally pioneered a transatlantic route. The prevailing winds and tides took his ship *Coelho* to a landfall in Brazil. To his amazement, he discovered that it was on the Portuguese side of the papal decree line. He claimed Brazil for Portugal, and in the process speeded up Portuguese journey times to and from India. Further bases were established in Africa's Mozambique and Angola. By 1522 the

Portuguese had located the source of all spices, had circumnavigated the world, and had begun to amass enormous wealth as their trading activities displaced those of the Spice Route.

In culinary terms, the Portuguese left an indelible mark; Goan food is unique and is not found anywhere else in India. A century earlier the Portuguese had literally followed their noses to the island of Madeira. The strong fragrance of fennel on the prevailing westerlies allegedly led them there, and they named the port Funchal, from their word 'funcho', fennel! They introduced the spice to India, though it should be said that it never displaced the indigenous similar-flavoured aniseed. This explains why both are called 'saunf'. For their own comfort the Portuguese also introduced European bread rolls and loaves. Though rice remains important to Goa, bread still takes precedence, and is eaten with most meals. The Portuguese also introduced cakes, pasties, pies, cheese, beef, pork, sausage making and wine. From Brazil, edible 'discoveries' which were soon introduced to Goa included tomato, potato, pineapple, guava, certain squashes, cashew and most importantly, the chilli. Belonging to the nightshade family, the tomato and the potato were not accepted by Moghuls, Indians and British alike, because they believed them to be deadly poisonous. It was not until American missionaries reintroduced them to India in the 19th century that both became accepted. This explains the absence of tomato and potato in many traditional recipes which predate the discovery of the 'New World'. Not so chilli, which, although also a member of the nightshade family, became immediately accepted. When they first discovered the chilli in Brazil, the Portuguese thought its piquancy was the work of the devil, and they called both the natives and the chilli 'Diaboles'. Chilli does not appear in any Portuguese traditional recipes. The Portuguese discovered the mango in Goa and exported it to Brazil. Later they reimported new varieties back into Goa, which they grafted onto the indigenous Goan varieties to create some of India's best, largest and lushest mangoes. These include Alfonso, Costa, Malcurada, Fernandino, Xavier, and Monserrat, and small sour varieties pickled in brine (chepnim), or in oil (miscoot). The Alfonso is arguably today's favourite Indian mango.

The Goan population were soon converted to Christianity by Jesuit priests whose brutality and fearful 'inquisition' made even the Muslims quake. It was hardly surprising that rulers all over India felt uneasy about the Portuguese. Other than allowing their diplomats to attend court, a stand-off existed between them and the Indian rulers. Yet despite a long-term ambition to get their hands on India's wealth, the Portuguese did not attempt to take the country. Had they done so, the fledgling Moghul empire may never have become established.

The British

In 1608 the newly-formed English East India Company's representative William Hawkins landed in Gujarat and discovered a well established Moghul India. His mission was to establish direct trading between England and India. The fourth Great Moghul, Jehangir, had just succeeded to the throne and so Hawkins journeyed to Agra to request an audience with him. There he discovered to his disgust that the Portuguese were not only ensconced at court, but gave the impression of having the close ear of the emperor. And they had no reason to help the 'Company' to become trading rivals.

Whether or not Jehangir's advisors were influenced by the Portuguese, they certainly treated Hawkins as unimportant. It was not helped by the pathetic baubles Hawkins had bought as gifts for the emperor, richer by far than the British King James. Hawkins became a subject of derision. He was kept waiting for three months for an appointment to see Jehangir. But as luck would have it he had one advantage; he could speak Persian, the

Moghul court language, and something which the Portuguese never bothered to learn. Since he was under no pressure to return to England, Hawkins persisted, and eventually was given an audience, albeit with a minor court official of no higher rank than himself. He must have impressed that official, because he was subsequently allowed several private audiences with Jehangir, who it seems was so fascinated with Hawkins' descriptions of his travels that they drank alcohol together. Despite that, the Portuguese saw to it that it did not lead to permission to trade. Since the Portuguese controlled the seas around India, the first essential was to wrest that control from them.

On his eventual return to England, the message Hawkins gave King James was to send a war-fleet, and rather better presents for the emperor who had everything. The advice was heeded. Flush with their 1588 Armada success, the English knew their ships and cannons were more manoeuvrable than their Spanish and Portuguese counterparts. A fleet was dispatched in 1612 and, sure enough, it had no difficulty in defeating the Portuguese ships off Surat. A new ambassador, Sir Thomas Roe, a better-educated, more sophisticated man, was dispatched to India. There he found a Jehangir so impressed with the British maritime victory that he met Roe without delay. The Moghuls had never been a maritime power, which made their coasts vulnerable. Jehangir was only too pleased to water down Portuguese influence. Their religious fanaticism had reached the stage where even the all-powerful Moghuls were concerned that their Muslim faith would be undermined. In Roe, like Hawkins, he found a pragmatic ally, with no overt religious convictions, just a desire to trade. The emperor frequently summoned Roe to attended court. Roe described typical court feasts of '*fifty dishes of meats and rice of all types and a spicy venison dish as the most savoury I have ever tasted*', almost certainly a reference to Dopeyaja or Do Peeaza (see pages 103 and 113). On one occasion

Jehangir sent an elk to Roe's residence, and on another occasion he sent a wild boar, requesting return of the tusks.

By 1618, the precious licences were granted, and the long-desired base at Surat was established. The Company rapidly outgrew their trading post at Surat, and in 1640 easily obtained permission to establish a second post at the tiny coastal town of Madras, on the south-east coast. The Dutch had been in India in a minor way for the same length of time as the British, but they represented no real threat to them. The French were a different matter. They did not arrive until 1664, but before long they had captured Madras. The story of the rivalry between the French and British in India, fascinating though it is, has no place here. Suffice to say that it was Clive of India who ousted the French from Madras and Calcutta, and gained control of Mysore from its Muslim ruler Tippu Sultan. Called the Tiger, Tippu had made the mistake of siding with the French against the British during Napoleonic times. It cost him his life, and brought Muslim rule to an end in Mysore. Tippu Sultan had one culinary addiction; he loved oranges. Had it not been for Clive, it is conceivable that Napoleon would have been emperor of India. As it was the English permitted the French to remain ineffectually in one tiny corner of south India, Pondicherry in Tamil Nadu. Similarly in the 17th century the Dutch had a toehold in south India. The Dutch, French and even the Danish aspired to oust the British from India. All failed.

It was a fortuitous time for the British. By then the Moghuls were in serious decline. In the twelve years following Aurangzeb's death in 1707, five emperors came and went. Muhammed Shah was the fifth and during his reign a Turkish ruler, Nadir Shah, ransacked Delhi, massacred its population, and removed to Persia much of the Moghul treasure-trove including the legendary jewel-encrusted Peacock Throne. This was followed by a number of tribal wars which culminated in the battle of Panipat in 1761. Although a weak Moghul emperor was the victor, he next had to face a nationwide mutiny from his army, who had not been paid for the two previous years, and quite reasonably demanded remuneration. As Moghul rule fragmented, new autonomous royal courts developed.

One was the Nizam, in Hyderabad. Muslims had taken control of Hyderabad in the 14th century and during Moghul times, a royal relative was despatched to consolidate this far-distant enclave. While Tippu consorted with the French, Hyderabad's 18th-century Nizam wisely chose to side with the British, which accounted for his court's survival and subsequent immense wealth. The 1930s Nizam was the richest royal on earth. His palace dining-table seated 100. One feature of that table was the solid silver electric-powered model train, which ran a circuit around the table. Its purpose was to deliver drinks to each diner. In 1962 India deposed her royals and the Nizam took umbrage and his fortune and retired in Australia. In the south-central part of India, Hyderabad, now called Andrah Pradesh, is still India's largest state, with a mainly Muslim population. Consequently, this is a meat-eating cuisine, which from the 1300s has specialized in Kebabs and Koftas, and above all Birianis (see page 214). The cuisine is also one of India's hottest, as indicated by Baigan ka Salan (aubergine curry, page 158), Mirchi ka Salan (Hyderabadi chilli curry, page 174) and Chowgra (yogurt-based vegetable curry, page 163).

Another autonomous court, established in the 16th century, was that of the rich royals of Lucknow in north India, the Nawabs of Avadh, who were again blood-relations of the Moghuls. Sadly, despite conscientious early rule, the last Nawab's love of the good life led to a reputation for debauchery, and the dynasty's demise by the mid 1700s.

Lucknow, being Muslim, enjoyed meat, but its cooking became unique. One process was called Dum Pukht (see page 104) which literally means 'containing-the-steam'. The technique originated in ancient Persia. A pot was filled with meat and spices. A tightly-fitting lid was sealed with chapatti dough. A hole was dug in the soil and white-hot charcoal was placed in its bottom. Next the sealed pot was surrounded with hot coals, buried in the sand and left undisturbed to cook for a few hours. The magical moment came when the lid was opened in front of the diners, releasing all those captured fragrances. Covered pit cooking has been the norm all over India for centuries, but it was the Moghuls who named the technique Dum Pukht. The story of its royal patronage in Lucknow is entertaining. Rumour had it that Nawab Wajid Ali Shah was visiting the construction site of a new palace. A huge pot of food for the workers was literally just being unsealed as the Nawab passed by. The aromas captivated him so much that his court chefs were trained to perfect the technique. One learned work of the time, the *Guzashta Lucknow* by philosopher Abdul Hamil Sharar, said '*the most important activity in human life is eating. As any community or nation progresses, its diet is the most salient guide to its refinement*'!

What effect did the Europeans have on Indian food? Only the Portuguese changed it and then only in their Goan territory. The other Europeans had no effect on it whatsoever, although there is some Dutch culinary influence in today's Sri Lanka. The French left a love of baguettes and an almost unadulterated French cuisine with no spicing in their Pondicherry enclave. Despite the many reforms the British bequeathed India during their glittering Raj period, the one thing they had no impact on was Indian food. Members of a Buddhist tribe called the '*Mogs*', which can still be found in Assam, became household cooks for Raj families, and between them and their British memsahibs they created Anglo-Indian food. Kobiraji (egg-battered fried chicken, page 91) is one such recipe. When the British left India in 1947, this way of spicing their otherwise bland food soon became virtually extinct. The only British culinary legacy is to be found in a plethora of their former institutions such as Indian clubs and public schools which serve food unchanged to this day – unspiced food, something which Indians say you eat only when you are sick!

Modern India

Over a period of 10,000 years and more the principal regional cuisines of India have developed. In chronological order they are south Indian, Bengali, Punjabi, Gujarati, Rajasthani, Maharashtran, Parsee, Moghul, Kashmiri, Hyderabadi, Lucknowi and Goan (see page 33–42).

Our culinary almost journey ends here.

When India's independent democracy cut away the powers of their royals in 1962, the days of the lavish courts went too. The ex-maharajas still live well in their palaces, with more servants than they can count, but they are no longer willing or able to finance and pioneer new things, including the culinary arts. Most of their palaces have been handed to the state for new uses such as hotels or museums, or simply been left to decay. It could have meant the end of the great chef and Indian culinary innovation.

Fortunately, three developments took place. Indian restaurants took off in the West, and nowhere faster than in Britain. In 1950 there were six in the whole nation; by 2000, there were 8,500. The media decided that curry had become the nation's favourite. Secondly, the arrival of television captivated new audiences and brought the world into their living rooms. And thirdly, the world itself became accessible in the form of cheap travel. India was an early beneficiary. The big cities already had a sprinkling of luxury hotels, but it was not an industry. India's aptly named business Moghuls reacted in style and grasped the nettle. In the 1960s, India's most famous hotel, the Taj Mahal Bombay, engaged three new bright young directors with the brief to create a luxury hotel group. They took out leases on several ex-royal palaces including Udaipur's Lake Palace and Jaipur's Rambagh Palace, and more importantly they started a national hotel-building programme which continues to this day. The Oberoi group commenced their own expansion plans, and the well-heeled Indian Tobacco Company formed a new division which they called the Welcom Group, which by the 1980s had an impressive portfolio of hotel properties and a linkage with Sheraton. The tourists poured in and these luxury hotels were as opulent as any palace they replaced. But it was not just the lobby and the bedrooms that glittered. Up to that point the Indian food available at the existing hotels was, according to the Taj Group's Camelia Panjabi 'sub-standard, lazily cooked and doing nothing for India'. Her aim was to recreate regional, authentic Indian classic and home dishes, in new restaurants throughout the Taj group. New restaurants require new chefs and the Taj group's rigorous chef-apprentice scheme encouraged initiative and innovation from all its trainees. It is now the envy of India, turning out a succession of world-class chefs. The other hotels followed with their own restaurants and training schemes. Centuries-old word-of-mouth recipes have been written down for the first time. Moving forward, some modern chefs have sympathetically evolved new techniques and recipes, without losing sight of all the techniques and tastes that have developed over the centuries, proving that in the hands of masters, even an ancient cuisine can develop.

As for India's new restaurants, they were an eye-opener, not only for the tourists, but for Indians, most of whom were introduced for the first time to the wealth of dishes that are their own regional Indian food.

The regions of India

There is no single Indian cuisine. In a land mass larger than Europe, there is as much variety, if not more than is to be found across Europe. India's food has always been dictated by history and geography. As one passes from region to region, the changes can be subtle, even unnoticed. But when you compare Kashmiri cuisine with Keralan cuisine, or Bengali with Punjabi, each thousands of miles apart, the differences are huge. But one thing unique to India in all its regions is the use of spices.

This chapter examines the major characteristics of India's regional cuisine, from north to south. Ironically this leaves the longest-established cuisine (south Indian) until last. For information on the dishes of a particular region, refer to the index at the back of the book.

Extreme north
Kashmir

Kashmir is India's most northerly state, located in the Himalayas thousands of feet above sea level. As the final ice age retreated some 10,000 years ago, tribes moved into the harsh, cold mountains. But it was not until around 1200AD that Muslims entered the area. At partition in 1947 Kashmir was split between India and Pakistan, leading to conflict. On both sides of the border most Kashmiris are meat-eaters (even Hindu Kashmiris) whose rich sauces and ghee help to combat the cold. The Moghuls built a summer retreat in the 16th century and brought with them aromatic spices, such as cardamom, cinnamon, clove and aniseed – spices used in Kashmir's most celebrated dish, Korma. The Kashmiri Muslim wedding feast, the Wazwan, is remarkable. Traditionally, it must contain exactly 36 different dishes, including chutneys and accompaniments. At least seven mutton dishes must be served. The number of guests is expected to exceed 500, and only rams are cooked, with all parts used. Lotus, apples, saffron and rice but not wheat are specifically Kashmiri.

The north-east
Bengal

Ten states currently make up India's north-east, and nine, still populated by tribes, are unremarkable in culinary terms. The exception is the largest state, West Bengal. Prior to partition, East Bengal was part of the group, but this is now mainly Muslim Bangladesh. Bengali cuisine is India's second oldest-established. Mustard oil and seeds and the aromatic nigella seeds have been around in Bengali cuisine for thousands of years, as has the spice mixture unique to Bengal, Panch Phoran (see page 62). Contrary to popular belief, West Bengal is a prosperous, booming industrial, very fertile agricultural state and it is one of India's major culinary areas. Bengalis like sour tastes as seen in Dal Doyi Jhol (lentil and yogurt soup), and, thanks to the Portuguese, they were the first to make Paneer. Their unique dishes include Chachchori Morog (stir-fried mild chicken curry), Rezala Morgh (rich-tasting hot chicken) and Kalia (a thin red sauce). Aubergine were indigenous and Baigan Burtha is the smoky puréed version. Niramish is a remarkable vegan curry. Bengalis have a sweet tooth and they adore their sweet chutneys. J. A. Sharwood, a Victorian Raj merchant, exported sweet Bengali mango chutney into Britain in the 1800s, and it is now a major feature at the curry-house. It is not eaten in this form in India, but its basis was Bengali Choti, mature sweet mango pickle. In the 19th century, Bengal became famous for its sweets and sweetmeats.

North central
Punjab, Haryana, Himachal Pradesh and Uttaranchal

For the purposes of this book, the north central area includes at its most northerly point Himachal Pradesh. This area, as its name suggests, is in the foothills of the Himalayas. It is not a state with a particular culinary reputation although the very best basmati rice comes from here; Dehradun

INDIA
STATES AND CULINARY REGIONS

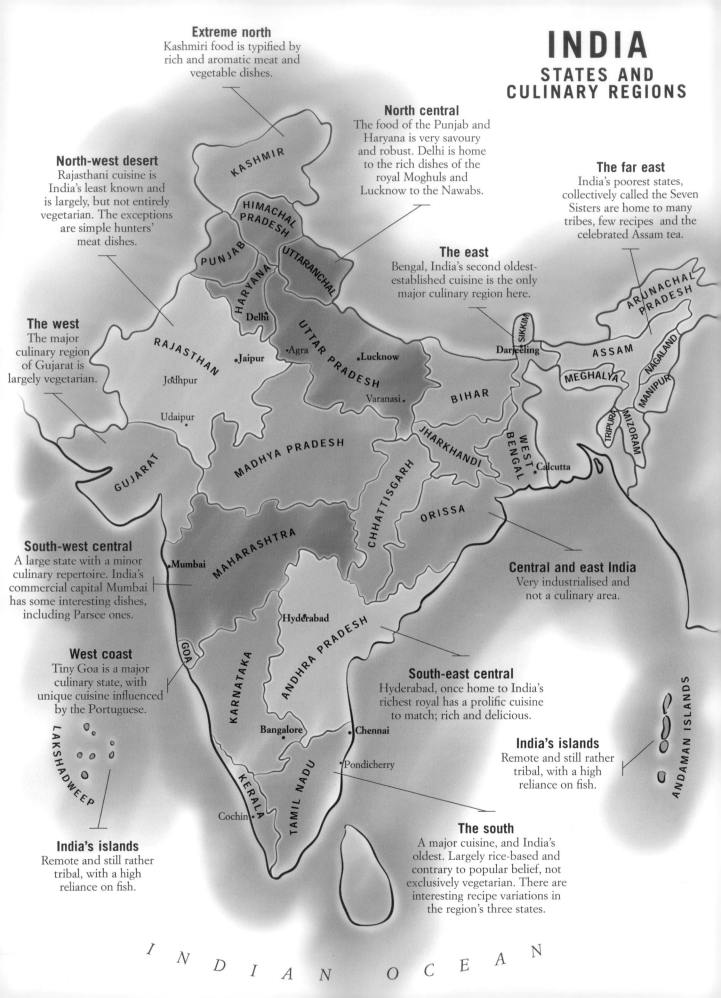

Extreme north
Kashmiri food is typified by rich and aromatic meat and vegetable dishes.

North central
The food of the Punjab and Haryana is very savoury and robust. Delhi is home to the rich dishes of the royal Moghuls and Lucknow to the Nawabs.

The far east
India's poorest states, collectively called the Seven Sisters are home to many tribes, few recipes and the celebrated Assam tea.

North-west desert
Rajasthani cuisine is India's least known and is largely, but not entirely vegetarian. The exceptions are simple hunters' meat dishes.

The east
Bengal, India's second oldest-established cuisine is the only major culinary region here.

The west
The major culinary region of Gujarat is largely vegetarian.

South-west central
A large state with a minor culinary repertoire. India's commercial capital Mumbai has some interesting dishes, including Parsee ones.

Central and east India
Very industrialised and not a culinary area.

West coast
Tiny Goa is a major culinary state, with unique cuisine influenced by the Portuguese.

South-east central
Hyderabad, once home to India's richest royal has a prolific cuisine to match; rich and delicious.

India's islands
Remote and still rather tribal, with a high reliance on fish.

India's islands
Remote and still rather tribal, with a high reliance on fish.

The south
A major cuisine, and India's oldest. Largely rice-based and contrary to popular belief, not exclusively vegetarian. There are interesting recipe variations in the region's three states.

KASHMIR
HIMACHAL PRADESH
PUNJAB
HARYANA
UTTARANCHAL
Delhi
RAJASTHAN
Jaipur
Agra
UTTAR PRADESH
Lucknow
Jodhpur
Varanasi
BIHAR
Udaipur
SIKKIM
Darjeeling
ARUNACHAL PRADESH
ASSAM
MEGHALYA
NAGALAND
MANIPUR
TRIPURA
MIZORAM
WEST BENGAL
Calcutta
GUJARAT
MADHYA PRADESH
CHHATTISGARH
JHARKHANDI
ORISSA
Mumbai
MAHARASHTRA
GOA
KARNATAKA
ANDHRA PRADESH
Hyderabad
Bangalore
Chennai
Pondicherry
LAKSHADWEEP
KERALA
TAMIL NADU
Cochin
ANDAMAN ISLANDS

I N D I A N   O C E A N

Basmati is to rice what Krug or Dom Perignon is to champagne.

South-west of Himachal Pradesh is Punjab, which like Kashmir was another state split into two after partition, with western Punjab and the Moghul city of Lahore in Pakistan. Food knows no boundaries, and Punjabi food is identical in both the Punjabs. It is one of India's major culinary styles, which began to evolve from early in the first millennium AD. It is perhaps the best known Indian food because the original curry restaurants in the developed world based their menus on Punjabi cuisine. Dairy farming is a major Punjabi industry and its prolific wheat crops earn it the title 'the granary of India' and parathas and puris are staples. The food is very savoury and fenugreek leaf (methi) and mustard leaf (rai) are virtually staples. Robust curries like Punjabi Keema, Methi Gosht, Aloo Ghobi Methi and Sag Paneer are typical.

South of Punjab is Haryana, meaning 'green land'. Its crops include oilseeds, spices, all types of grain, peas and beans and much else. Haryana was once part of the Punjab, as its culinary repertoire shows, but one recipe from Haryana is Mattar Valor (pea and green bean curry, see page 172).

Delhi (Moghul cuisine) and Uttar Pradesh

Almost surrounded by Haryana is Delhi, the small state containing India's capital city. Delhi has no cuisine in its own right; it was during the 16th century that Indian food was taken to its supreme culinary heights in the Moghul capital city of Delhi. The French may believe they invented 'haute cuisine', but they were pipped to the post by Moghul chefs, who did to Indian food what the French chef Varenne did to French cooking a century later; they perfected sauces using garlic, butter and cream with the addition of something uniquely Indian; a marriage of spices. They created supremely aromatic curries with sensual sauces like Classic Korma, Pasanda, Rhogan Josh Gosht and Raan (roast lamb). The standard curryhouse has

based some of its formula on mild, rich, creamy dishes such as these, albeit lacking the subtlety of the real thing.

East of Delhi is the largely Muslim state of Uttar Pradesh, with Moghul Agra and its Taj Mahal in the west and the river Ganges flowing through its length. Of culinary importance is Lucknow, now an Indian army city, and one which is of immense historical importance especially during the time of the Nawabs, who came to royal prominence as the Moghuls declined. One legacy is Nawabi cuisine. Lucknow, being Muslim, enjoys meat, but its cooking is unique. Flavours are spicy, aromatic and subtle and the food is luxurious. One process is called Dum or Dum Pukht. It means slow-cooking by steaming the curry or rice dish, in a handi or round pot, whose lid is sealed into place with a ring of chapatti dough. The resulting dish is opened in front of the diners, releasing all those captured fragrances (see page 31).

North-west desert
Rajasthan

Rajputs, or king-warriors, believed to be direct ancestors of Alexander's Greeks (see page 14) settled in the state now called Rajasthan, the land of the kings, from around 600AD. Rajasthan is arguably India's most colourful state, renowned for its palaces and forts, charismatic cities and sparse jungles and lakes, making it India's top tourist state. Ironically, Rajasthani cuisine is India's least known, and tourists are unlikely ever to try it.

In the far west is the Thar desert, where it is not unknown for rain to be absent for years. Consequently no wheat, rice or root vegetables grow there, and such harsh conditions result in Rajasthan's unique cuisine being largely but not entirely vegetarian. Specialized crops that do grow in this region include kair or ker (a small berry), sangri (Rajasthani string-bean, see page 186), guar (cluster beans) and bhajra (millet). Indeed there is a popular millet porridge called Bhajra Khichadi, often eaten with pure ghee alone. Raabri is a traditional Rajasthani millet soup. Gram is made into rissoles or sauces akin to the dishes of neighbouring Gujarat, although lacking the sweet taste so beloved by Gujaratis (see Gujarat below). Other lentils used are mooth, moong and the indigenous arhar dahl. Other than south India, Rajasthan is the only state to make papadoms (there called kheladas). A unique salad is Papad Methi Dana Subzi, where papadoms are cooked with sprouted fenugreek seeds then cooled. Marwari cuisine is found in and around Bikaneer, Jodhpur and Jaisalmeer and uses all these ingredients along with asafoetida in preference to garlic and sweetish local chillies. Some Marwari dishes are too hard to replicate without a lifetime of practice. For just one example they peel, core and dry whole karela (bitter gourds), then stuff them with a mixture of fenugreek seeds and leaves, fried to become crunchy, and finally they bake them to completion. Sour tastes from amchur (dried mango power) are popular as are pickles and rai (mustard seed and/or leaf).

Camels and cattle are beasts of burden, and they are a source of milk. Hunting is still a way of life providing wild meat and poultry, cooked on the spot, examples of which are Jungli or Lal Maas and Sufaid Mas, red, very hot curries and white, mild curries respectively. Where there is sufficient water, leaf vegetables, small gourds and mushrooms are cherished.

The west
Gujarat
South of Rajasthan and extending to the Arabian sea is Gujarat. In the seventh century, descendants of the Huns, the Gurjaras, settled in western India and named their lands Gujarat after their tribe. Today's Gujarat is a largely Hindu, prosperous, agricultural and industrial state and it is India's diamond state. Though not on the main tourist trail, Gujarat has its share of fine monuments and architecture and its art and crafts are renowned with

gorgeous items such as gold and silver embroidery (jari), patterned silk with tie-dyed thread (patola), tie-dyed cloth (bandhani), perfumes and wood-carving. Gujarati land is very fertile. Non-edible crops include cotton and tobacco. Cash crops include banana, chana (gram lentil), cumin, mango, millet, peanut, rice, sugar cane and wheat. So with all this pedigree, it is perhaps not surprising that Gujarat is a major culinary region, with a unique and abundant indigenous cuisine. Gujarat is home to more vegetarians (about 70%) than anywhere else in India, and their food is also India's least spicy. Despite its long Arabian Sea coastline, fish does not prevail. No other Indian state makes a greater variety of pickles than Gujarat.

Prime ingredients in savoury dishes are yogurt and gram flour, with a little sugar added. The penchant for sweet tastes is a result of the Parsee influence (see page 20). Khadi is just one dish showing Gujarati adoration of these ingredients. This soup-like dish, often served with with gram flour dumplings also called Kari or Khadi, may have been the very dish which gave curry its name. It has a yellow gravy made with turmeric, lentils, spices and yogurt. Pakora or Bhaji also originated in Gujarat. Other dishes of note are Ravaiya (stuffed baby aubergine) and Sevian Tamatar (wheat vermicelli noodles, a rare Indian ingredient). Bombay Mix, the general name for crunchy spicy nibbles made from a deep-fried spicy gram flour dough and originated in Gujarat, where they are known as Murukus. Sev is the very fine vermicelli-sized version.

Not all Gujaratis are Hindus or vegetarians. As a result of ancient Muslim occupations, there remains a small group of Gujarati meat-eating Muslims, called the Bohris Community. One of their dishes is the outstanding Gosht Tikkea Malai ke Bohris (baked marinated beef, see page 115). In this dish cubes of best beef are marinated in cream, garlic and ginger. They are coated with breadcrumbs and baked.

Central and east India
Madhya Pradesh and Orissa

In the centre of India is the vast state of Madhya Pradesh. It is heavily industrialized, and the city of Bhopal, which came to fame when its chemical processing plant exploded, the resultant gas escape killing and maiming thousands, contains India's only diamond mine. By contrast, many aboriginal and primitive tribes live off the beaten tracks. Madhya Pradesh is not renowned for its cuisine. However, it is home to several ex-maharajas, including one practising cook-gourmet, the ex-maharaja of Sailana, whose city is virtually on the Rajasthan border. One true Madhya recipe is Osaman, a sweet and spicy dhal water beverage.

South-east of Madhya Pradesh and south of Bengal is Orissa. Its unspoilt beaches on the Bay of Bengal see few tourists and are now under threat from an industrial revolution that is sweeping aside Orissa's historic sculptured buildings, and handicrafts. The seaboard city of Puri (no relation to the bread) is one of India's most holy pilgrimage destinations. Tribes have existed in the inner jungles for 20,000 years. Orissa has never had a culinary heritage, but three typical Orissan recipes are Charu (tamarind consommée), Bhoona Murgh (mild, dryish chicken curry) and Baigan Burtha (smoky aubergine purée).

South-west central
Maharashtra including Mumbai (Bombay)

By mediaeval times a kingdom of some sophistication had become occupied by the Marathas, Hindu warriors of mean repute. Today's large state of Maharashtra is located in central India's table-land, the Deccan plains. At its north are the Vidayah and Satpura mountain ranges, and the Western Ghats separate the Deccan from the state's 600-mile-long coastline on the Arabian Sea. Maharashtran or Marathi food was developed over the centuries as a minor cuisine. It is mild and delicately spiced and uses tamarind and fresh coconut. The Maharashtran climate is perfect for viticulture and supports two grape crops a year. One brand of method-champagne is widely exported under the name Omar Khyam.

Mumbai (Bombay) is the vibrant, buoyant, commercial centre of India, with some of the highest property prices in the world, contrasting with some of the most appalling poverty. It is celebrated for its prolific movie industry, Bollywood, and pricey restaurants, including home-delivery pizza, which all contrasts horribly with the ubiquitous shantytowns, and street-begging. Bombay was the creation of the British and as such it has never developed a large cuisine. One delicious concoction is Bhel Puri, Bombay's favourite kiosk food, served cold. The original fishing tribes, the Kholis, however, had a couple of delicacies up their sleeve; Bombay Duck (page 88) and Bangda (fish head) curry.

Parsee

This is not a regional cuisine but that of a religious sect, which has evolved over the last 800 years. There are now only around 100,000 Parsees. Most live in Bombay, but there are other groups in Hyderabad and Gujarat. Traditional Parsee food shows its Persian origins (see page 20). They have no religious proscriptions on eating, so in theory they can eat pork and beef as well as lamb and shellfish and they love egg dishes. Meat mixed with vegetables and fruit is typical of Persian and Parsee food, though the latter has now incorporated the Indian spice palette and sweet and sour combinations, typified in their Patia. Jardaloo Boti is lamb cooked with dried apricots and Patrani Maachli, a coriander-coated fish dish, is a Parsee speciality. The most celebrated and popular of all Parsee dishes is Dhansak, where meat on-the-bone is incorporated with four types of lentil (polished moong, masoor, chana and toovar). Slow cooking in a heavy lidded pot amalgamates the flavours. During the cooking, a kind of ratatouille of aubergine, tomato, spinach and fresh chillies is added. Sweet comes from jaggery (palm sugar) and a slight overtone of sour from fresh lime juice. The apt derivation of the name of this dish comes from 'dhan', meaning 'wealthy' in Gujarati, and 'sak', meaning 'vegetables'. Pronounced slightly differently, Dhaan means 'rice', and this sumptuous dish is traditionally eaten as a Sunday special with brown rice. Their roasted vegetable dish, Oonbhariu, is one of the best vegetable dishes in India. Refer to the index for the 11 Parsee recipes in the book.

West coast
Goa

Goa is a tiny state on the Arabian Sea, south of Maharashtra. The food is quite different from that of the rest of India. It owes its uniqueness to 450 years of occupation by the Portuguese, though it had always depended on spices, fish and coconut whose origins extend back many centuries to its indigenous tribes and its subsequent Arab traders. Modern Goan curries are based on all these ingredients, often combined with palm

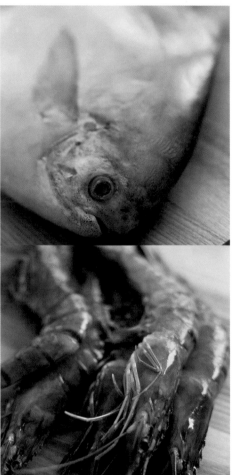

Pomfret and king prawns. Goan cuisine depends on fish – it is eaten every day

todi (feni) vinegar to create a gently unique sour taste. Goans are mostly non-vegetarian. Meat is usually confined to Sundays. Fish is mandatory at least once a day in the Goan diet. Bread-making was introduced by the Portuguese and though rice is important to Goa, bread takes precedence and is eaten with most meals. Portuguese dishes, some unspiced, are to be found on the Goan menu. Many

have evolved to be unique to Goa, with the addition of spices and coconut, yet have Portuguese names such as Vindaloo, Cafreal and Xacutti. But nothing is that simple in Goa. Many dishes can appear with two different names in Portuguese or Goan (Konkani). And even same-named dishes can be cooked in different ways by the three different Goan communities. The majority of the population is Christian (Catholic) who eat everything including pork and beef and use plenty of chillies, todi-vinegar and sugar for piquancy and sweet-and-sour tastes. There is also a significant Goan Hindu population. Hindu Goans use less heat, tamarind for souring and jaggery for sweetening. They use asafoetida, chickpeas, curry leaves, fenugreek, mustard and urid dhal. They don't eat beef, of course, and generally abstain from pork. Goa was occupied by Muslims long before the Portuguese and there is still a significant Goan Muslim population. They do not eat pork or beef, mutton (goat) being their preferred meat. Some of the more complex dishes from Kashmir and the Moghuls are to be found in the Goan Muslim home.

South-east central
Andhra Pradesh, including Hyderabad

Andhra Pradesh, formerly called Hyderabad after its major city, is the fifth largest state in India, both in area and population. In the 1930s, Hyderabad's royal ruler, the Nizam was alleged to be the richest man in the world. The state is strategically situated in south central India and forms a major link between north and south India. It has a widely diversified agricultural base with a variety of cash crops. It is the granary of the south and produces a surplus of food grain. Hyderabad has been south India's strongest Muslim enclave since the 14th century (see page 31). Today it is 40% Muslim. Hyderabad also has a Parsee population. Consequently, it is a meat-eating cuisine, but it is also one of India's hottest, as indicated by Mirchi Ka Salan (chilli curry). 'Mirchi' means chilli, 'ka' means of and Salan is a type of Urdu spicing speciality of Hyderabad and we encounter it twice more in Macchi ka Salan (fish) and Baigan ka Salan (aubergine). Biriani is also a Hyderabadi speciality. Koftas and Kebabs are popular as is Parsee Khara Soti Boti Kebab (omelette-enrobed meat chunks). Two dishes represent yoghurt's popularity, Chowgra (a yogurt-based vegetable curry) and Churri (a herby yogurt dip). Thoran (lightly spiced coconut and shredded cabbage) is called Thoora in Andhra Pradesh.

The south

South India consists of three sub-tropical and very fertile states, Karnataka, Kerala and Tamil Nadu. The main religion is Hinduism and there are many huge temple complexes all over the south, inhabited by holy men and the marvellous temple elephants used in processions and as beasts of burden. From the early days the temples have offered free food for thousands of worshippers on festivals, the most celebrated of which is Pongal, a four-day harvest festival. Rice boiled with milk and jaggery during the Pongal festival is also called Pongal and is a popular south Indian dish. There are two varieties of pongal, namely, Sarkarai Pongal (sweet pongal) and Kara Pongal (spicy pongal), also called Ven Pongal in Tamil Nadu and Huggi in Karnataka.

Since partition in 1947 the south has mostly voted communist, and its businesses are largely run by cooperatives. Unlike communism elsewhere, this has made the south, and Kerala in particular, one of India's most prosperous areas with a minimal amount of poverty.

The area was first occupied in about 1000BC by the Dravidians, who are still the largest racial group. South India's cuisine has remained virtually unmodified since that time, making it India's longest-established cuisine. When the Dravidians first arrived and cultivated the area, they encountered south India's main indigenous ingredients: ginger, coconut, curry leaves, peppercorns, turmeric and curry leaf. Many dishes use all these ingredients, such as Rasam, a hot and spicy consommé. The food is rice-based, with no wheat. Yogurt and tamarind provide two quite differing sour tastes. Because of the intense heat, thin curries are preferred because they are more easily digested than the thick-sauced versions of the north. Day to day, much of the area's population is fish-eating or vegetarian, but most will eat meat or poultry on special occasions. Some specialist groups, such as Coorgs, Nairs, Mophlas, Syrian Christians and Jews eat meat and chicken dishes on a regular basis. Food is traditionally served on banana leaves as an alternative to crockery and you will often find several courses together on one leaf. Cutlery is not used. Many dishes are common to all three south Indian states, albeit under different names, and with subtle differences in flavourings.

Karnataka

Karnataka is west of Andhra Pradesh and south and east of Goa. Its western coast is on the southern Indian Arabian Sea. The state was formerly called Mysore, after its rich and vibrant city, which until 1966 was under the rule of the Maharajas of Mysore. Two recipes come from here: Bonda Mysori (batter-coated potato balls) and Palya (lightly spiced coconut and shredded cabbage, called Thoran in Kerala). Karnataka's wealth comes from its gold mines, sandalwood and agriculture, which employs most of the population. Round-grained rice is the main crop. Other crops include bananas, citrus fruits, cashew nuts, ground nuts (mainly for oil), chickpeas and other pulses, coconut, coffee, cardamom, pepper, sugar cane, tea and tobacco. Karnataka is home to the major city of Bangalore (home to India's computer and aerospace industries). Near Bangalore is the Grover wine estate, which produces India's finest wines. Mangalore or Mangalapuram is on the Arabian Sea in south Karnataka. It was always a fishing and ship-building centre and now it is also one of India's major ports. Malayalam cuisine is largely fish-based and distinctive. As a language Malalayam did not develop in its own right until the 13th century AD. Prior to that the language had been Tamil.

The Konkan Coast or Karavali

The Konkan, also called the Konkan Coast or Karavali, is the name given to a 800-mile stretch of rugged and beautiful coastline from Mumbai through Goa to Mangalore in the south of Karnataka. Konkan is also one of six divisions of the state of Maharashtra. An indigenous tribe, the Malvani, has its own cuisine called Malvani cuisine. It is fairly extensive, and has influences from Maharashtran, Goan and south Indian (Karnatakan) cuisine. Typical recipes are Paplet Saar (pomfret curry) and Chemeen Manga Karavali (prawn with mango). The southern extremity of Konkani coastal cuisine is called Kodial. Another local tribal group, the Tuluvas, call it Kudla, whilst the Bearys, the indigenous Muslims, call it Mikal.

Udipi, Karnataka

Udipi is a small Karnataka town a few miles north of Mangalore. It is known for its Brahmin temple and one item of cuisine; south India's best-known dish, Masala Dosa, pancakes made from a thin, fermenting rice flour and white lentil-flour batter.

They are eaten like chapattis, or are traditionally stuffed with mildly spiced potato. The credit for dosa invention goes to the coastal town of Udipi, though now dosa is found all over south India.

Coorg or Kodagu, Karnataka

One other region of interest is Coorg or Kodagu, a beautiful hill region between Bangalore and Mysore in south-west Karnataka, and the source of the river Kauvery. The people of Coorg are a conglomerate of tribes: Scythians first, then Moplas and now Coorgs or Kodvas. Their dress is a bit Arabic. Coffee remains a favoured drink; wild honey, oranges, sandalwood and rice are exported around India and abroad. The staple is a millet grain called ragi from which Coorgs make a porridge or fried cakes. Their cuisine is robust and primarily non-vegetarian. Every meal must have at least one mandatory dish of meat. Chicken and mutton are popular and there is no proscription on pork. It could be a succulent roast or a stew such as Pandi – hot, sour and spicy wild boar or pork curry, or Koli Nallamalu – succulent chicken in a dark pepper sauce, which is made dark and sour by the use of Kachiyapulli, Coorg vinegar. Coorgs love to hunt and fish and are known to be partial to partridge. But their luxuriously rich mutton pilaf dates back to Tippu Sultan's occupation of Coorg. Kadumbuttu is rice dumpling; Nool Puttu is rice noodles; Votti is rice-flour flat bread, Bemla is bamboo shoot curry.

Ootakamund, Karnataka

One of the delights of the British Raj was escaping from the Indian summer to their beloved hill stations high in the mountains. They built several all over India. Ootakamund (snooty Ooty) was built in the Nigiri Hills, the blue mountains, in the state of Karnataka. There they cooled down and grew cold-weather 'English' vegetables and roses. When they came to build a botanical garden, to their surprise they found tribal inhabitants, the Badagas, living in the hills alongside. They had been in residence for

centuries, and are still there. The Badagas grow bamboo shoots, an ingredient not usually found in India, but which thrive in the Nigiri monsoon. One traditional dish is Porial Bagada Ottakuddi (shredded bamboo shoot). This is traditionally served with what the Badagas delightfully call Koo (plain basmati rice). Their sweet tooth is exemplified in Pothittu (pancakes with a sweet sauce).

Kerala

Kerala is a relatively small state located in south-western India. It has a long seaboard called the Malabar Coast. Kerala is one of India's most beautiful states and is popular with tourists. The important cities are Cochin, the port the Chinese

Chinese fishing nets in Cochin – a legacy of China's trading history with the port

were trading with by 100BC, and Calicut, where the Portuguese first landed in India. Kerala has a tropical, humid climate and is India's largest rice producer. Other vital crops include pepper, ginger, turmeric, cardamom, cinnamon, coconut, bamboo, nutmeg and cashew. Non-food crops and production includes coconut products (coir) and rubber products, much of which is exported. We normally think of Kerala as a vegetarian state. In fact there have been passionate non-vegetarians. They are, in order of arrival: Jews, Christians and Muslims, each with a distinctive cooking style.

Cochin Jewish

A group of Jews first arrived in the Konkan area after 200BC following Greek persecution, and a second group arrived in the Goa area after 70AD following the Roman destruction of their Jerusalem temple. They fled again to south India's Cochin in the 1560s, following Muslim then Portuguese persecution. Their Kosher cuisine was barely Indianized, in that it used few spices, but one item of interest is the Filowri (split pea rissoles), a variation of Egypt's felafel.

Syrian Christian

The first Christian St Thomas the Apostle is said to have landed in Kerala in 52AD to found the 'Syrian' Church at Muziris (Cranganore). His language was Syriac Aramaic, his converts known as Syrian Christians. To this day they eat spicy offal, chicken, duck, fish, shellfish, beef and wild boar. Erachi Olathiathu (beef dry-fried with a paste of coconut and spices) is masterful. As is Vevichathu Surmai (Keralan soured fish curry) which is red in colour and soured with chilli and kodam puli, a small, sour fruit about the size of a small plum, and very dark purple in colour. The rind, skin and flesh is dried by wood-smoking. It is reconstituted by soaking in water for an hour, after which it can be chopped or ground to obtain a virtually black, sour-tasting agent. The words 'kodam puli' are Malayalam (language of south India) for 'fish' (kodam) and 'tamarind' (puli). However it is neither, but it gives us the clues that it is sour and used with fish. It is most popularly found in Keralan cooking and especially their fish dishes.

Mopillah, Moplahs (Keralan Islamic cuisine)

The Mopillaha or Moplahs are descendants of an isolated Muslim tribe that arrived by sea in Kerala in the eighth century AD. The cuisine is also known as Keralan Islamic cuisine. A typical recipe is Jhinga Mopla Biriani (king prawn rice).

Nair cuisine

On the subject of bizarre diets, writings from much later (1500AD) tell that the Keralan Nair tribes ate mice as a delicacy!

Tamil Nadu

Tamil Nadu, India's southernmost state, is the second most industrialized state and contains the state capital Madras, now called Chennai, India's fourth largest city. Also known for its car manufacturing, as well as Kanchipuran silk saris, arguably the world's best, Chennai is the home of Marina Beach, the second longest beach in the world. Tamils enjoy very hot and spicy food and the Raj British capitalized on this by creating a hot masala mix which they called hot Madras curry powder, something not used in India. A century later a hot dish at the UK curry restaurant was called Madras curry, a dish unknown in Madras. India's southernmost town, Kanyakumari, lies eight degrees north of the equator at the meeting point of three seas: the Arabian Sea, the Bay of Bengal and the Indian Ocean. Elsewhere in the state, the great temple complex in Madurai is essential visiting for all Hindus.

Islands

Two main groups of islands belong to India; the Lakshadweep Islands off the Malabar Coast, and the Andaman and Nicobar Islands in the Bay of Bengal. Negroid descendants of the first arrivals into India of 60,000 years ago are found among contemporary tribes in the Andaman Islands, speaking their original language, although the main population is Hindu or Muslim. Fish is their main diet coupled with vegetables. The only representative recipe in this book is Fihunu Mas Lebai (grilled garlic red mullet, see page 136).

2 the Indian kitchen

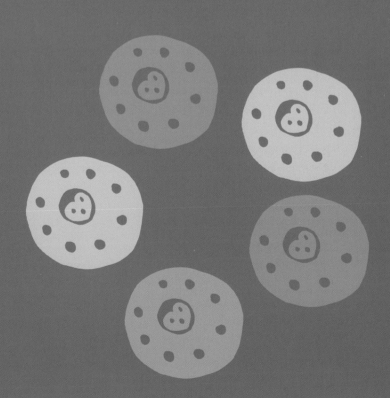

Tools and equipment

This chapter enables you to tackle any of the recipes in this book by ensuring that you have the right equipment to hand, and by taking you through a number of techniques and ingredients important to Indian cooking.

Most of India's population live in villages, hamlets or tribes. Most work the land and are just self-sufficient. They usually cook in the open air on fires and their meals are simple; often being just rice or bread with vegetables or lentils. Those near rivers or coasts eat fish, whilst others hunt and eat wildlife. Most of India's villagers eat meat, and many possess a few chickens or ducks, mainly for eggs. Goats and cattle are mainly kept for milking and are used as beasts of burden. Just occasionally, for a special occasion, the birds and animals are eaten.

We have no more in common with this lifestyle than do India's 100 million middle-class, whose homes contain the things we take for granted, but which are unknown to the villagers – electricity, running water and gadgets such as fridges, microwaves and cookers, and the luxury of servants. But not too many generations ago, our ancestors were using virtually the same techniques as Indian villagers. However, the food from both ends of society is indistinguishable. Recipes are recipes however they are cooked.

We may not have the benefit of a servant, so we must rely on our time-saving equipment. Most domestic cooks will already possess a selection of kitchen equipment, but the following is a comprehensive list of the items you will need to cook the recipes in this book.

Basic equipment

You will need a stove top (any type), a grill with tray and rack, and an oven and baking trays. Chopping boards, a rolling pin, mixing bowls in various sizes and sieves (at least one large and one small) are all necessary.

Knives

Knife prices vary very considerably. Good knives cost more and are comfortable and heavy. The blade should be thick on top and run visibly right through the handle, which should fit smoothly and snugly to the blade. The blade should be made of high-grade stainless steel which should not rust and it should be capable of being honed to provide a razor-sharp edge. A knife such as this will last for years serving you safely and well.

Cooking spoons

Plastic ones eventually discolour and melt. Wood is fine (especially for non-stick pans) but if it cracks, discard it and buy a new one – it is a breeding place for bacteria and no matter how much you scrub or what you scrub it with, it will never be clean. Ordinary tablespoons are too short for me. I like to use long-handled stainless-steel catering spoons for cooking. Despite costing more, they last indefinitely. Slotted spoons and tongs are also useful.

Casserole dishes

Best of all are the really heavy, expensive cast-iron cooking dishes, such as Le Creuset. Because they hold and transfer heat so well, your cooking results both on the stove and in the oven are greatly improved, and the chances of burning and sticking are much reduced. Treat the dishes with care and they will literally last a lifetime, enhancing your kitchen considerably, and thus making them an effective investment despite the initial heavy outlay. You need at least one casserole pot with lid at 2.25–2.8 litres (4–5 pint) capacity. Alternatively, you can use an electric slow-cooker.

Lidded saucepans

Again, the better the quality the fewer problems you will have. Stainless steel or chromium pans with copper bases are the best. They do cost more, but they look and cook better and last longer. Whether you use non-stick coated pans is a personal choice.

The coating tends to wear out rather rapidly whatever the manufacturer says. Have at least one lidded saucepan in the following sizes: 3.5 litre (6 pint), 2.25 litre (4 pint) and 1.3 litre (2¼ pint).

Wok, karahi and tava

The wok originated in China thousands of years ago as a circular, round-bottomed, all-purpose cooking vessel, made originally from heavy cast iron with a long single wooden handle. It evolved in India into a slightly deeper, more rounded pan with two handles and became the main cooking vessel, used for boiling, steaming, simmering, stir-frying and deep-frying. Known all over India as the karahi (or kari, korai, kadai or kodoi), today they are pressed from chromium-vanadium steel, making them thin but sturdy. The round bottom has been flattened to make the pan stable for the modern stovetop.

You can use either for Indian or Chinese cooking, and they are relatively inexpensive. I personally prefer woks, because I prefer the handle shape. Sizes range from over 1 m (3 ft) in diameter to just 8 cm (3 in). The 20 cm (8 in) diameter wok is ideal for roasting spices and for small portion items, whilst the large 40 cm (16 in) wok is ideal for rice or noodle dishes. A medium-sized wok 30 cm (12 in) in diameter is my all-purpose work-horse for stir-fries and general cooking. As to cleaning I prefer to scrub them thoroughly with wire wool after use (which tends to lose the blackened patina a bit, but is better in hygiene terms). Rust is a problem which is very easily overcome by wiping the pan dry with kitchen paper as soon as you've washed it, then placing it empty on your stove at high heat for a minute or two until it starts to 'blue'. Eventually it will go black. Please note a new wok or karahi is coated with machine-oil and must be thoroughly scrubbed and blackened before use.

Another useful piece of cooking equipment is the Indian tava, a large 25 cm (10 in), heavy, carbon-steel, almost-flat frying pan in which you can cook omelettes, pancakes and flat breads. Again the heavier the better. A tava is not mandatory (a frying pan will suffice) but it does all those jobs efficiently and is inexpensive.

Electric tools

Grinding spices using a mortar and pestle is hard, slow work, though it can be satisfying and useful if you just need to grind a few spices. For most dry-spice grinding, I recommend an electric coffee grinder or an electric spice mill attachment, which will achieve a good result. To create purées or the smooth texture needed in certain sauces, you can use a sieve. An electric blender does the same job in infinitely less time. A food processor is also useful for many grinding jobs, such as bulk garlic or ginger, and you will get the best kebab texture when using the food processor. As for mincing meat, it is always better to mince your own (because you know what went into it) using a mincing tool. Cheap, hand-operated mincers are perfectly acceptable, as are electric attachments, if you have them.

Deep-frying

Deep-frying is potentially dangerous. There are a number of rules to observe. It is imperative that you remain at the pan until the heat source is switched off. Use vegetable oil and never fill your deep-fry pan beyond one-third of its height with oil. Equally don't let the oil get too low either – the food being fried must be able to float.

Keep your oil as clean as you can. Breadcrumbs and flour are destructive to oil because the small particles burn easily. After every use, strain your oil while warm, though not hot, through kitchen paper in a strainer. You can reuse the oil several times.

During deep-frying the inherent water in the item you are frying is removed. At the correct oil temperature (190°C/375°F) the item's water content evaporates at exactly the right speed, preventing the oil from saturating the item. The outside seals, the deep-fried item floats and the oil stays outside. If temperature is too low, the food will absorb the oil, sink and be forever stodgy. Too hot and the surface will burn without cooking right through. If the oil gets too hot, it will begin to smoke and go darker and in the worst case scenario it can catch fire.

Thermostatically controlled, electric-powered units can be expensive. Unfortunately the thermostats are often inaccurate, and some do not reach 190°C (375°F). I now use a 3.5 litre (6 pint) stainless-steel lidded saucepan for deep-frying.

To test the oil temperature, carefully add a tiny piece of the food you are frying. When the oil temperature is correct it will sizzle and almost immediately it will rise to the surface and sizzle until cooked. If you are cooking very sticky batter-coated or wet subjects, there will be much less washing up if you remove the basket and use instead a slotted spoon and/or tongs.

Remove the fried item, shake off as much oil as you can and place it on kitchen paper to drain. Leave for a few minutes to crisp up and dry off. If deep-fried properly it will not be greasy. Finally, it is important to keep the oil temperature as constant as possible. Consequently the deep-fryer should not be overloaded, nor loaded all at once. Place the items in one at a time, allowing a few seconds between each. The wetter the item, the less you should load in. If possible, remove the items in the order that they went it. And remember to turn off the heat source when you finish.

Bottles and jars

Keep any empty sauce bottles and jam jars (with lids) for your own homemade chutneys and pickles.

Coriander leaf

Use a dishwasher if you have one or the hottest water you can get, then let them drain and dry without wiping them. When dry place them into the oven at 120°C (250°F) to sterilize them.

Tip Save money by using an oven that is switched off and cooling down after having cooked something.

Herbs and Spices

This section provides a glossary of the whole and ground spices and few herbs used in Indian food.

Herbs

Herbs are fresh aromatic leaves. Indian cooking really only uses just two: coriander and mint.

Coriander leaf

Dhania

Coriander, India's most widely used herb, is a member of the umbelliferae family. It was native to Greece, but now grows worldwide, as a herbaceous annual plant. Its leaves are mid-green and flat with jagged edges. Its distinctive, musky, candle-wax odour bears no resemblance to the coriander seed (see page 49) and is an acquired taste. The leaves are used whole, chopped or ground. Soft stalks can also be used, but thicker stalks should be discarded.

Mint

Podina

Mint grows as a herbaceous perennial, its bushy shrub growing up to 1 m (3 ft) in height. The best variety for spicy cooking is spearmint, whose distinctive flavour comes from its volatile oil. Fresh mint is used in a number of Indian recipes.

Whole spices

Spices are dried seeds, berries, pods, capsules, bark, leaves, flower buds, petals, stigmas or stamens. One spice (asafoetida), is produced from the gum of a particular tree. After harvesting, a spice is dried in the sun or artificially to preserve it. This encapsulates its essential or volatile oils for months or even years, giving each spice a unique attribute which can be piquant, aromatic, pungent, bitter or sweet. These oils are released by frying, roasting or boiling the spice. Only at these surprisingly high temperatures are the oils 'released' and the result is flavoured food. No nation uses more spices than India and there are many different ones available. Some Indian dishes need just one or two spices to acquire their distinctive flavour, whilst others need a greater number. No one spice is more important than another, though some are used in nearly every recipe whilst others are required just occasionally.

Bay leaf

Tej patta

Bay, or laurel, leaf grows on an evergreen tree or bush, found worldwide. The familiar leaf is pointed and oval in shape, and grows to an average 7 cm (2½ in) in length. It can be used fresh or dried. Fresh, it is glossy, smooth, quite fleshy, and dark green in colour, and has a more powerful flavour than dried, with a slightly more bitter undertone. Dried, it is paler, and quite brittle. Bay is used whole in aromatic Indian dishes, such as kormas and birianis.

Cardamom

Elaichi

Cardamom grows in south India, Sri Lanka, Thailand and Guatemala. Cardamoms grow on a herbaceous perennial plant, related to the ginger family, whose pod contains slightly sticky black seeds, their familiar flavour coming from the cineol in its oils. There are two main cardamom species, both of which can be used whole or ground.

Brown cardamom, also called black, bara elaichi, has a rather hairy, husky, dark brown casing about 2.5 cm (1 in) long. Used in garam masala, kormas and pullaos, they are strong and astringent, and aromatic.

Green cardamom, known as the 'Queen of Spice', is one of the most elegant, aromatic and expensive spices, and earns India considerable export revenue. Natural white and green cardamoms, chota elaichi, have smooth, ribbed, white or pale green outer casings, about 1 cm (½ in) long and are of the same species which is different from the brown. Their flavour is rather more delicate than the brown. The greener the cardamom, the fresher it is, though use of food dyes is not unknown. They are used whole or ground, with or without casing, in many savoury and sweet recipes.

Cassia/cinnamon

Dalchini

Cassia and cinnamon are both the corky, outer bark of specific trees, related to each other and sharing a similar sweet fragrance. There is

Brown cardamon, cassia bark and star anise

some confusion between the two, compounded by certain spice-packers who insist on labelling cassia bark as 'cinnamon'. Cassia originated in Burma, and is now also widely grown in the tropical forests of Indonesia and south China, giving rise to its alternative name, Chinese cinnamon (dalchini). Its tree is a large evergreen, the leaves of which are also used as a spice in the manner of bay leaves. Branches are cut down, their bark is peeled off, and formed into reddish-brown quills about 1 m (3 ft) long. Once dried, these are fragile, and by the time cassia is packed it is usually in chips, averaging 5 cm (2 in) in length. Cassia's essential oil contains cinnamic aldehyde, giving it a sweet, musky flavour. Cassia bark is usually much less fragrant, coarser, thicker and tougher than cinnamon, and it stands up to more robust cooking. It is also cheaper. It is used as an aromatic flavouring in subtle meat and poultry dishes, and as a major flavouring in pullao rice and garam masala. Although widely used in cooking, the bark cannot be eaten.

Cinnamom is native to Sri Lanka, and though it now also grows in the Seychelles, Brazil, the West Indies and Indonesia, Sri Lankan is still regarded as best. Cinnamon bark is a parchment-thin, tightly-rolled, pale brown quill of around 1 cm (^{1}/$_2$ in) in diameter, by 10–12 cm (4–6 in) long, making it more fragile than cassia, in that it can break up in robust cooking. Little pieces of cinnamon are inedible and can give an unpleasant, splintering mouth-feel. These quills are more aromatic than cassia, and are used to infuse drinks such as Cha (Indian tea) and Punch (mulled wine, see page 252). Ground cinnamon is used in some dishes, its sweetish aromatic flavour adding a haunting quality to food.

Chillies

Mirch

Chilli is the fleshy pod of shrub-like bushes of the capsicum family. There are five chilli species, and thousands of varieties. When many people think of Indian food, it is 'heat' which springs first into their minds, with chilli being the heat-giver. Yet chilli is a relative newcomer to Indian cooking. It was 'discovered' by accident in the Americas, by explorers who were seeking the source of pepper. Indeed it was they who gave the chilli and allspice their confusing identical name of 'pepper' (or 'pimiento' in Spanish). Chilli pepper soon caught on and it was taken around the world to become adored, and grown by countries like India. Chillies range in 'heat' from zero to incendiary, depending on variety. 'Heat' in this context is an ambiguous word, having nothing to do with temperature. 'Piquancy' would better describe the burning sensation in the mouth, which is caused by the alkaloid capsaicin, present to a greater or lesser degree in the flesh and the seeds of all chillies. Capsaicin is related to caffeine, nicotine and morphine, which explains why chilli is the world's most popular spice; it is mildly addictive. Novices to chilli find this substance painful to taste, but the body compensates by releasing pain-killers called endorphins, and this association of pleasure with chilli

Chillies and cloves

leads to a build-up of tolerance to capsaicin, hence the mild addiction. As tolerance levels build up, chilli-lovers will agree that capsaicin does not mask out other flavours – it enhances them. All chillies start life green and ripen through white, yellow or orange to red or purple. Contrary to what some people believe, a chilli which has ripened to red has the same piquancy as it did when green, though there is a variation in flavour. When a red apple ripens it is sweet because there is more fructose sugar present than when it was green. It is the same in a red chilli, which also has a rounder, sweeter taste. The other misleading advice is that chilli seeds should be removed and discarded. Unless the chilli is very pithy (and the milder the chilli, the more pithy it is) you do not need to remove the seeds.

Clove

Lavang

Clove grows on a smallish tropical evergreen tree, related to the myrtle family, which thrives near the sea, and is the unopened bud of the tree's flower. It is bright green at first, and must be picked just as it turns pink. The flower, if allowed to bloom, is dark pink, about 1 cm ($^{1}/_{2}$ in) in diameter. Dried clove is dark red-brown, bulbous at one end (this is the bud, and is where the flavour is, so avoid 'headless' cloves), with a tapering stalk, about 1 cm ($^{1}/_{2}$ in) in length. Clove is Britain's most familiar spice, having been used continuously since the Romans brought it here. They thought a clove resembled a nail, 'clavus' being the Latin for 'clout' or 'nail'. We still use clove to ease toothache because of its pain-killing essential oil, eugenol. Clove is the world's second most important spice, earning India alone some £20 million a year. It takes some 8,000 to 10,000 cloves to make up 1 kg (2$^{1}/_{2}$ lb).

Coriander seeds

Dhania

Coriander is a member of the umbelliferae family and the seed is India's most important spice in

Coriander seeds and cumin seeds

terms of volume (but not value). The country exports 80,000 tons a year, and uses ten times that amount at home. Dried coriander seed imparts a sweetish flavour, with a hint of orange. There are many coriander species, giving minor variations to the appearance of the seed. The seeds are used whole or ground, forming the largest single ingredient in most spice mixtures, including garam masala, and are delicious roasted – try them as a garnish. See also coriander leaf, page 46.

Cumin

Jeera

Cumin grows on a smallish annual herb of the umbelliferae family. Its thin seeds are about 5 mm ($^{1}/_{4}$ in) long. They are grey-brown to yellowy-green in colour, and have nine stripy longitudinal ridges and small stalks. Its oil, cuminaldehyde, gives it a distinctive, savoury taste with a slightly bitter overtone. Cumin, after its Latin name 'cuminum', is an ancient spice, native to Syria and Egypt, and found, intact, whole, and apparently still edible, in the tombs of the Pharaohs, having been placed there some 4,500 years ago. Cumin is mentioned in the Old Testament, and was so important to the Romans that it substituted for salt as a seasoning, causing it to be very expensive. It also became synonymous with excess and greed, to the extent that the glutton Emperor Marcus Aurelius, was nicknamed 'cuminus'. It still predominates in Middle Eastern cooking, and has found a new role in the USA in Tex-Mex Chilli-con-Carne. Cumin has always played a major role in India, its use in volume being second only to coriander. Ground, it is a major component in curry powder. Whole cumin seeds benefit greatly in taste from being 'roasted'.

Curry Leaf

Curry leaf is native to south-west Asia. Its tree grows to about 6 m (25 ft) in height and 1 m (3 ft) in diameter. It is especially prevalent in the foothills of the Himalayas, and south India. The tree is greatly adored as a garden orna-mental, when its size is much smaller. The young curry leaf is a small pale green, delicate thing, which grows up to 4 cm (1½in) in length. The leaves are widely used whole in southern Indian cooking, and

Curry leaves

impart a delicious flavour to dishes such as Fish Moilee, Rasam, Sambar and Masala Dosa. Despite its name, the leaf has a lemony fragrance, and no hint of 'curry'. This is because it is related to the lemon family. Ground curry leaf is used in many commercial curry powder blends. In addition, it is used as a tonic for stomach and kidney disorders. Fresh curry leaves are airfreighted into the West, but can be hard to locate. Dried ones are readily available from Asian stores and make passable substitutes. If you enjoy south Indian food, they are a 'must-have' spice.

Fennel

Saunf, sunf or soonf

Fennel, a European native, is a hardy perennial of the ubiquitous umbelliferae family, which grows to about 2 m (6 ft) in height. Its leaf and its bulb are relished in Europe, though not in India. Its small pale greenish-yellow stripy seed, slightly plumper and greener than cumin, grows to around 5 mm (¼ in) in length. It is quite sweet and aromatic. It is frequently confused in India with its near relative, the smaller aniseed, whose name, saunf, it shares. Fennel seed's similar, though milder, flavour comes about because it shares with aniseed and with star anise its very distinctive essential oil, anet-hole. Fennel contains 70% (compared with 90% in aniseed), with a smaller amount of fenchone. This combination gives it a sweet and aromatic flavour, making it ideal for subtle dishes, garam masala and paan mixtures. It is unique in that it is the only spice to be common to the five-spice mixtures of both India (panch phoran) and China. Grown all over north India, the variety from Lucknow is the best quality. It is used medicinally as gripe water, and for eyesight, obesity and chest problems.

Fenugreek leaves

Methi

Fenugreek has two forms used in Indian cookery, the seed and the leaf. The leaf grows, grey-green in colour, on a clover-like annual herb. Pronounced 'maytee' in Hindi, fenugreek leaf derives from the Latin 'foenum', dried grass or hay ('Greek hay'), indeed the leaf is still used as cattle fodder. The fresh leaf is popular in north Indian and Punjabi cookery, and in its dried form it keeps like any other spice. A few notes of caution: after cropping, the leaves are dried in the sun on flat roofs. Consequently, it is a good idea to pick through them to remove grit and small stones. Unfortunately, you will also always find a lot of small, tough stalks. These too should be discarded. Whilst doing this, you will notice how strongly the spice smells. It is a good idea to double pack it, in an airtight container, within another airtight container. Use small amounts only. The leaf is rich in carotene, vitamin A, ascorbic acid, calcium and iron.

As well as the leaves, the fenugreek plant yields bean-like pods, 10–15 cm (4–6 in) long, which contain 10 to 20 miniature, hard, yellow ochre-brown, nugget-like, grooved seeds about 3 mm ($^1/_8$ in) long. Though seeming to smell of curry, the seed is quite bitter, its main oil being coumarin. India produces over 20,000 tons of fenugreek seed a year, and it is in her top ten exported spices, the seed being a minor but important ingredient in curry powder, and one of the panch phoran five-spices. Light roasting gives the seed an interesting depth, and another way of using it is to soak it overnight. Incidentally, the fenugreek seed can also be sprouted, like mung beans, for small beansprouts. In Java fenugreek is used to counter baldness. It lowers blood pressure, but it contains steroids. This may explain why it was allegedly used by harem women to enlarge their chests! At the same time,

fenugreek was believed to be a good contraceptive, which two facts may explain why India has a burgeoning population.

Lovage
Ajwain or ajowan

Lovage is an annual, herbaceous plant, which grows up to 60 cm (2 ft) high, with feathery leaves and pretty vermilion flowers. It is a member of the prolific umbelliferae family, which also includes aniseed, caraway, celery, coriander, cumin, dill and fennel. This gives all of them a characteristic taste, which of course is a result of having thymol in varying quantities as a component of their volatile oil. But once again, this is a spice with a confusing nomenclature. In this case ajwain is called 'carom' or, more commonly, 'lovage', but it is not European lovage. Ajwain is indigenous to Egypt, Afghanistan and north India. Its seed is smaller than its European counterpart, and is a tiny greyish sphere about 1$^1/_2$–2 mm in diameter, with distinctive stripes. Its taste is a little bitter, with a slightly musky but quite distinctively intense flavour of thyme, which is an acquired taste.

Mace and nutmeg
Javitri and jaifal

Mace is unique, because it grows inseparably with nutmeg. Their tree is a tall, tropical evergreen, which originally grew only in the tiny Indonesian island of Ambon, but is now also found in Sri Lanka, south India and Grenada, in the West Indies.

Mace, nutmeg and mustard seeds

Mace forms a brittle, tendril-like net which surrounds a shell which itself houses the inner seed, the nutmeg. This assembly is enclosed inside a pithy, inedible, bright green case. When the green case is first opened, the mace is a delightful bright crimson or amber, which contrasts with the shiny red-brown nutmeg shell. When cropped, mace is pliable and easy to separate from its nutmeg, and flatten, before drying it in the sun. As it dries, the nutmeg goes rather greyer in colour and the mace often loses its red colour. Mace is very aromatic and oily, its volatile oil the aromatic eugenol. Its use in Indian cooking is minimal. Its subtle flavour goes well with lighter fish, vegetable and sweet dishes and it is an ingredient of garam masala. Nutmeg's eugenol is more concentrated than mace, and it is excellent freshly grated over Indian desserts.

Mustard seed

Rai or kalee sarson

Mustard is one of the world's oldest cultivated spices. Its branched annual plant is a member of the cabbage family. There are three varieties of mustard seed, brown from India, with spherical seeds around 1 mm diameter, white, which is in fact yellow ochre in colour, and black, both around 2 mm in diameter and both native to the Mediterranean. Both white and black seeds are used to manufacture mustard and cress and the familiar bright yellow powder or paste, although black is cropped less these days. The seeds are de-husked then milled. If you taste dry mustard powder, you find that it is not at first hot; its heat develops when cold water is added. This causes a chemical reaction when its components, including its volatile oil, isothiocyanate, react and develop a pungent heat.

Pepper

The brown Indian mustard seed, when tasted raw, is unappealing and bitter. When cooked, however, it becomes sweet and appetizing, and is not as hot as you might expect. It is immensely popular in Bengal, where it is one of the five spices in panch phoran, and in southern India where it appears in many recipes roasted, fried or as a garnish.

Pepper

Kala mirch

India proudly calls pepper her 'King of Spice'. Being indigenous to India, it was for thousands of years (and still is) a important export revenue-earner.

The Romans brought pepper to Britain, where it was used in lieu of money. In the thirteenth century you could buy a sheep for a handful of pepper! Foreign ships entering London paid a levy of pepper, and it paid debts, such as (peppercorn) rent. Until chilli was discovered in the sixteenth century, pepper was the main heat-giving agent in cooking, its heat coming from the alkaloid piperine. After chilli, it remains the world's most popular spice. Peppercorn grows on a climbing vine, which thrives in monsoon forests. The vine flowers, then it produces berries, called spikes, in long clusters. Green peppercorns are immature when picked, and spikes are occasionally available in the UK. To obtain black peppercorns, the spikes are picked when they start changing colour to yellow. They are then sun-dried, and quickly become black and shrivelled. To harvest white pepper, the spikes are left on the vine until they turn red. The outer red skin is removed by soaking it off, revealing an inner white berry, which is then dried. Pink pepper is obtained in the same way, from a specific variety of vine, and it is immediately air-dried, to prevent it turning white. The red peppercorn is not true pepper. It is from a South American shrub, whose reddy-brown berry is aromatic, and a little bitter, but not hot.

Saffron

Zafran

Saffron is native to Greece. The saffron crocus is a different species from the springtime, purple-leaved, flowering, English garden plant. The edible part is the stigma (a kind of stamen) a long, thin, golden stalk within the flower. In the 12th century it was grown in and around

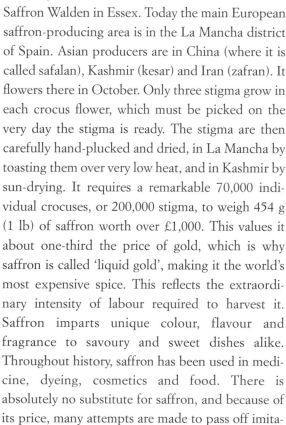

Saffron

Saffron Walden in Essex. Today the main European saffron-producing area is in the La Mancha district of Spain. Asian producers are in China (where it is called safalan), Kashmir (kesar) and Iran (zafran). It flowers there in October. Only three stigma grow in each crocus flower, which must be picked on the very day the stigma is ready. The stigma are then carefully hand-plucked and dried, in La Mancha by toasting them over very low heat, and in Kashmir by sun-drying. It requires a remarkable 70,000 individual crocuses, or 200,000 stigma, to weigh 454 g (1 lb) of saffron worth over £1,000. This values it about one-third the price of gold, which is why saffron is called 'liquid gold', making it the world's most expensive spice. This reflects the extraordinary intensity of labour required to harvest it. Saffron imparts unique colour, flavour and fragrance to savoury and sweet dishes alike. Throughout history, saffron has been used in medicine, dyeing, cosmetics and food. There is absolutely no substitute for saffron, and because of its price, many attempts are made to pass off imitation saffron. The caveat is buy a reputable brand, and remember, there is no such thing as 'cheap' saffron. Beware the tasteless, cheap, similar-coloured, but feathery safflower (bastard saffron) more often than not offered as saffron to gullible tourists in such places as Turkey. And do not substitute turmeric, even when it is called Indian saffron, such as in France and Sri Lanka.

Sesame seed

Til

Sesame is a tropical, herbaceous, annual plant growing up to 2 m (6 ft) in height, native to India and China, and elsewhere. Its capsules contain a large amount of tiny, buff, disc-shaped seeds, which grow to around 3 mm (^{1}/$_8$ in) in diameter. After polishing, they become creamy-white in colour. Sesame is very ancient, and a further contender to being the first cultivated spice. It was used to make a flour by the ancient Egyptians. It was also a main source of oil. To this day, it is still more popular in the Middle East than elsewhere. The manufacture of sesame cooking oil remains a major industry, and is a role which suits the seed well, since it is already very oily, with 60% of its content made up of oleic and linoleic volatile oils. Though sesame is a minor spice in Indian cooking, it is an important export crop there. It has a somewhat neutral, nutty taste and it is used to texture delicate cooking, and in Indian bread and confectionery. It is also used as a garnish. As with many spices, sesame improves greatly with a little 'roasting'. As a cooking oil, the nutty flavour of sesame is delightful, but wasted in anything other than subtle dishes.

Star anise

Anasphal

Star anise grows on a small, evergreen tree of the magnolia family, native to China, the Philippines and Indo-China. It flowers with single, yellow-green petals, followed by the seed, which develops into a green star, the average size of which is around 2.5 cm (1 in) in diameter. It has eight regularly-spaced arms (star points) radiating from the centre. When cropped, the still-closed

Star anise

star is dried, after which it becomes red-brown in colour. At this stage, some of the arms may slightly open, revealing one gleaming, pale brown seed. A whole specimen of star anise is arguably the prettiest spice on earth, but it is fragile, and the arms can easily break off in the packaging.

Although it has no relationship at all to aniseed, star anise gets its name from the fact that it smells and tastes of aniseed, because has the same volatile oil, anethole, as aniseed. Star anise has been used since ancient times in Japanese cooking, and as one of the spices in Chinese five-spice. Yet despite the fact that clove, nutmeg and mace were voluminously traded from China, star anise has only recently entered the modern Indian chef's spice repertoire.

Wild onion seed or nigella

Kalonji

Wild onion seed or nigella is a native of Asia and north India. It is a member of the ranunculus family, growing as a herbaceous annual, up to 60 cm (2 ft) high, also known as love-in-a-mist, with pale blue flowers. Its seed, a matt-coal-black, irregular-shaped, pentagonal nugget, is about 1.5–3 mm (¹/₈ in) in size. Nigella has a distinctive, slightly bitter, intensely aromatic, delicious, vaguely

peppery taste. It is used whole in certain Indian regional recipes, especially in the Bengal area. It is one of the five spices in panch phoran, and pressed into naan bread dough, it not only looks good, it tastes great.

Zeera black cumin seed

Jeera, kala zeera or shahi jeera

Black cumin is a herbaceous plant of the umbelliferae family, which grows up to 45 cm (18 in) in height. It yields dark brown seeds with stripy, longitudinal, charcoal-coloured ribs, ending in a short, curved tail. The seeds closely resemble caraway, at about the same 3 mm (¹/₈ in) length, though zeera seeds are darker and narrower. White cumin, on the other hand, is much paler, fatter and longer and its flavour is much less subtle and more savoury than zeera black cumin, which has an aromatic, astringent flavour, with a hint of liquorice. Its flavour comes from its oils which contain limone and cyonene. Its use is limited, but it is worth having in stock, for its great effect in such dishes as pullao rice and certain vegetable dishes.

Ground spices

So far we have only looked at whole spices. Ground spices are used in certain Indian cooking. Some spice mixes, such as garam masala (see page 60), are best ground freshly at home. Others are too difficult to grind at home – chilli because it gets in the eyes and dried ginger and turmeric because when dried, they are too hard. Some ground spices are used frequently – others are used only occasionally. Only those spices which do not appear under Whole Spices above have descriptions. For example, ground chilli, coriander, cumin and black pepper are also used extensively in Indian cooking. Other ground spices include bay, cardamom, cinnamon, clove, fenugreek, mustard and nutmeg (see Whole spices). The frequency note refers to amount of usage in the recipes in this book.

Frequently used ground spices

Paprika

Paprika is the Hungarian name for pepper. Chillies were first introduced there by Ottoman Turks in the sixteenth century. Over the centuries, a type of pepper was cultivated, especially in Hungary's Szeged and Kalocsa districts. At first paprika was deep red in colour and very pungent. Over the years the pungency has been bred out of Hungarian paprika, so what we now expect is a tasty deep-red powder used for flavouring and colouring purposes, but not for heat. However, what we actually get may be wide of the mark: paprika may be mild or it may be hot. It can range in colour from rust to crimson, and it may have unspecified additions. The worst paprika will even be bitter. The reason is that, being a major crop, numerous other countries have become producers. Spain's paprika, called pimiento para pimento is made from a different pepper to Hungary's, but ranks as second only to Hungary's in flavour and quality. As with everything else, expect to pay the most for the best, but be sure it is the best you're paying for. Once you've found your favourite brand the best thing is to stick with it.

Turmeric

Huldi

Turmeric, like ginger, is a rhizome which grows underground and is native to south India. There are several varieties. It can be used fresh in certain curries and for pickles and when halved its gorgeous vivid orange-yellow is a clue that turmeric is used to give curry its distinctive golden colour. To achieve the familiar powder, fresh turmeric is sun-dried until it is rock hard, then it is factory-ground.

Infrequently used ground spices

Asafoetida

Hing

Asafoetida is extracted from the carrot-shaped rhizome of a giant perennial plant of the fennel family, called ferula, native to Kashmir. When the ferula's rhizome is between 12–15 cm (5–6 in) in diameter, it is mature enough to yield a milky-white sap when cut. Up to a kilo of sap slowly oozes out, over the period of a few days, and solidifies into a brown resin-like substance. This is factory-ground into a grey-brown or bright greeny-lemon powder (depending on species).

The Persian word 'aza', 'resin', and the Latin word 'foetidus', 'stinking', indicate that asafoetida has an obnoxious, disagreeable odour, giving rise to its other names – 'devil's dung' and 'stinking gum'. This is due to the presence of sulphur in its composition. It was so highly prized by the Romans that culinary writer Apicius advised great thrift in its use, and care in its storage. Today, because of its smell, it is a good precaution to store it in its factory packaging, inside a second airtight container.

Its use is confined to Iranian and Indian cooking, where it is particularly specified in fish and lentil dishes. Fortunately, its unpleasant odour disappears once cooked, to give a further distinctive and pleasant fragrance and sweetish taste. Used in small quantities, it is supposed to aid digestion by combating flatulence.

Mango, dried

Am chur or kachcha am

This grey, powdered spice is made by grinding sour, unripened, pitted, sun-dried mangoes. The resultant spice is exceedingly sour, but very distinctive. It is mostly used in chaats (snacks) and some vegetable dishes.

Storing herbs and spices

Fresh mint and coriander leaves have a short life. Spices should be stored in airtight containers in a dark place. Daylight quickly fades taste and colour. Whole spices should be used within twelve months of opening and ground spices four months.

Essential ingredients

Nuts

Nuts are used extensively in Indian cooking, and can be used to thicken sauces, add subtle flavour or toasted and used as a garnish.

Almonds

Badam

Almonds are widely used in northern Indian and Pakistani sauces. They are used whole unpeeled or peeled (blanched) and raw or fried in certain rich curries. They make a great garnish as do almond flakes, which can be raw or toasted. Ground almonds are used to thicken and flavour sauces.

Cashew nuts

Kaju

Whereas almonds are used in north India, cashews perform the same role in the south. They are used peeled (blanched) and raw or fried in certain curries. They make a great garnish as do almonds. Being soft, they make a good paste by grinding them down with water, and are used to thicken certain sauces.

Peanuts

Peanuts are used to a lesser extent in Indian cooking.

Pistachio nuts

Certain Indian recipes require pistachio nuts. Always use fresh, unsalted, shelled pistachio nuts, easily identified by their green colour.

Fruit

There are certain fruits that form an essential part of Indian cooking.

Citrus Fruit

Nimbu

Lemons originated in the Bay of Bengal, and were taken to the Arabian Mediterranean in the 1300s for cultivation and trade. Limes originated slightly further east, probably in Thailand and the East Indies. There is a marked variation in the flavour of lime and lemon. In fact though, lemons are rarely found in India, but since we have access to both, feel free to use either or both.

Coconuts

Narial

Despite its name, coconut is not a nut; it is in fact a drupe, or a fruit with a hard stone. Coconut probably originated in Papua New Guinea millennia ago and now thrives world-wide in tropical coastal zones, requiring a balance of humidity, water, sea salt and sea air. Given these conditions, coconut grows wild and is very prolific. The tree, a species of palm tree, averages 24 m (80 ft) high and annually yields a number of coconuts, each weighing over 5 kg (11 lb). When ripe enough, they drop to the ground, in such profusion that no one has to pay for them, they simply pick them up off the ground and use them. The coconut itself is enclosed by a green, thick, smooth circular casing. One early explorer, John of Monte Corvina, said in 1292AD, *'they are as big as melons and as green as gourds'*. After harvesting, each green case is de-husked with a cleaver, revealing a pallid item, which when sun-dried becomes the familiar brown hairy coconut, with three small depressions, or 'eyes'. In terms of usefulness, coconut is to India what soy bean is to China, except that coconut is even more diverse in that every part of the plant is used.

Once opened (halved) the coconut creates an array of coconut products widely used in south

Indian cooking. First, there is the liquid (coconut water) which should be present in all coconuts, and is a pleasant street-side drink. This is not coconut milk. This is pressed from the coconut flesh which is first scraped out as chippings. It is mixed with water and pressed and strained to create coconut cream or milk. Coconut cream is the first straining and is thick, creamy and rich. Coconut milk is the second and third pressing, using new water each time, but the same flesh. The second pressing resembles milk, the third, cloudy water. All three are available as canned or tetrapack products. Each pressing has a lower fat content and costs less than the one before it. Freshly grated flesh is freeze-dried and finely ground to create coconut milk powder, which when reconstituted with water creates rich coconut milk. It is convenient in this form, because it can be stored in a jar like a spice, for use bit by bit. So too can desiccated coconut. Here the chippings are sun-dried, then finely grated. Desiccated can be used by adding it dry to your cooking, or by simmering it in water and straining it to create a rather weak coconut milk. Coconut oil is extracted by a distillation process, and used for certain south Indian cooking. It is white when solid, and transparent when hot. The oil is also mixed with freshly ground flesh to make blocks of creamed coconut, and though this product is never used in Indian cooking, it has a large export market to the West only. Even coconut flowers are edible.

There are yet more uses. The thin brown coconut shell, the testa, is used as a cup, serving

Coconut

vessel, ladle or spoon, whilst its husk or hairs, the tough fibres or exocarp, becomes coir, or coconut matting, the well-known component used in door mats, ropes and fishing nets. The living tree can be tapped to yield a sap which is processed to make palm sugar or an alcoholic beverage called todi or feni. The tree is also an important source of timber and its leaves are used as disposable food plates, for basket-weaving and roofing material. Anything left over is burnt as fuel.

There is a down-side, however. Coconut, whilst being profoundly useful, will have a lethal effect on anyone unfortunate enough to be under a drop; hundreds of people are killed or seriously injured each year after being hit by a falling coconut.

Tamarind

Imli

Tamarind, also known as the Indian date, is a major souring agent, particularly in southern Indian cooking. The tamarind tree bears pods of about 15–20 cm (6–8 in) long which become dark brown when ripe. These pods contain seeds and pulp, which are preserved indefinitely by compression into a rectangular block, weighing 300 g (10 oz). See page 62.

Oils

Ghee (see page 61) is commonly used in the cooking of the northern subcontinent. It is popular for its flavour and its high burning temperature, which enables the initial cooking of spices, garlic etc, to be done without burning. Vegetable oil (usually made from rape seed), corn oil (from maize) or groundnut oil (from peanut) are acceptable and less saturated than ghee, and are neutral in flavour. Polyunsaturated oils (such as soya and sunflower oil) are also acceptable, although their burning temperature is much lower and they cost more. Specialist oils used in different regions of the subcontinent include sesame oil, coconut oil used in the south and pure mustard oil (used particularly in the north-east). Strongly flavoured oils, such as olive oil and walnut oil, etc, are not used in Indian cooking, because they impart the wrong strong flavour into the spices. Butter is rarely used because of its low burning temperature.

Salt
Namak, kala namak or saindhar

Salt is the most important taste additive, or seasoning, in the world, as well as the most ancient. It is an inorganic mineral, whose taste comes from sodium chloride, and it is essential to life. References to salt appear throughout history. For example, it was so important to the Romans that they part-paid their troops and officials with salt, hence the word 'salary'. Unique to India is black salt (kala namak) from the Ganges district of central India. Ground, this salt is a pretty pink colour. Other mines give grey, or even blue salt. It has an acquired, distinctive taste, essential to certain recipes.

The Indian trinity – garlic, ginger and onion

Whereas spices give individual Indian dishes their unique flavours, it is the use of garlic, ginger and onion which largely creates the texture of many of the sauces. Many dishes use all three, some use just one or two, but very few dishes use none.

Garlic
Lasan

Garlic has an history unparalleled by any other ingredient. It probably originated in Turkestan and Siberia. The ancient Egyptians valued it highly, believing that a bulb of garlic represented the cosmos, and each clove parts of the solar system. It was fundamental to their diets, and it is recorded that 7 kg (15 lb) of garlic would buy one slave. Indeed an inscription on the great pyramid of Cheops states that the builders (none of whom were slaves) were supplied garlic and radishes daily for health. History's first recorded industrial dispute took place 3,000 years before Christ, when these builders mustered up the courage to go on strike because their garlic ration was cut. Garlic was found in Tutankhamun's tomb and it also had a large role to play in warding off the evil eye.

The Babylonians of 3000BC considered garlic to be miraculous especially medicinally, as did the Greeks. In 460BC Hippocrates extolled its virtues, as did Aristotle eighty years later, and Aristophanes believed it enhanced virility. The Phoenicians carried garlic in their Mediterranean trading ships and Hebrew Talmudic Kosher rules prescribe when and where garlic may be used. Mohammed respected garlic; amongst other things he recommended its use to counteract the stings and bites of venomous snakes. Yet he warned that it could have powerful aphrodisiac qualities, and had a vision of Satan in the Garden of Eden with onion on the ground at his left foot and garlic at his right. We know how the Europeans have revered garlic for centuries, but it is hard to believe that it took until the 1980s before garlic became widely available in Britain.

Garlic is indispensable to cooking Indian food. It is best to buy one or more bulbs on which are clustered a number of individual cloves. There is no short cut to discarding skin, but once done you should be left with a creamy, plump, firm clove. To use, I prefer to chop the cloves finely, but you can use a garlic crusher. Or you can also simply crush them under the flat side of a knife blade. Purée bulk garlic in an electric food processor using one part of water to four of garlic. Once puréed, put the garlic into an ice-cube tray (reserved specifically for this

Ginger

purpose) and freeze it. Once frozen, transfer it to an airtight container and use the cubes as required.

Ginger

Adrak

Ginger is a rhizome that grows to a considerable size underground. Ginger provides an important flavour in Indian cooking, though it is not used in every dish. It originated in India, and the best and juiciest ginger still grows in south India. Other ginger grows in Thailand, Malaysia, Indo-China and China itself. Externally, its beige-pink skin should have a bright sheen or lustre. When cut in half, the flesh should be moist and a creamy-lemon colour, with no trace of blue (a sign of age). Ginger can also be puréed in the food processor, and frozen as for garlic (see left).

Onion

This ancient bulb originated in central Asia, and was much used in Egypt and China alike. The onion, of which there are some 500 varieties, is related to the chive, garlic and leek. An onion consists of about 88% water and 10% carbohydrate. The 'heat' that makes onions so hard to prepare is caused by the onion's volatile oils called disulphides. The process of browning onion (see page 61) is basically the reduction of this huge water content, which means the onion can be slowly fried without becoming incinerated. The browning and slight burning is caused by the carbohydrate turning to sugar and caramelizing. The disulphides are neutralized, and the onion tastes savoury, yet sweet and delicious.

Second to spices and along with garlic, this taste is the most important ingredient in curry cooking. When cooked and puréed, it is onion that gives the base for the creamy sauce so essential to most curries. The best types for Indian cooking are the pink onion, also very decorative for fresh chutneys and garnishing, and the equally attractive white onion. The larger 'Spanish' onion, which grows all over the world, is very mild, and with an average weight of around 225 g (8 oz), is easy to peel and prepare. Onion is an excellent source of Vitamin C.

Basic preparations and recipes

This small collection of recipes appears from time to time as requirements for other individual recipes throughout the book.

FRAGRANT STOCK

Akhni

The subtler authentic Indian recipes often need water added at some stage in their cooking. Akhni, sometimes called yakhni, is an aromatic, clear all-purpose vegetable stock. It probably originated in ancient Persia, and stocks like this, with minor adjustments, are used all over India. You can freeze it in plastic containers or you can keep it in the fridge for a couple of days, but it is essential to re-boil it after this time; it will be safe for several re-boils, but use it finally in a soup or other cooking. A useful tip is to add the brine or water from tinned vegetables to your stock. You can top up with fresh or leftover ingredients as required.

Makes about 700 ml (1 1/4 pints)

10–12 green cardamoms

10–12 cloves

5 or 6 bay leaves

6–8 pieces cassia bark

2 tablespoons chopped onion

1 tablespoon ghee

750 ml (1¹/₂ pints) water

1 Simply simmer all the ingredients together for about 20 minutes, then strain the stock, discarding the solids. The stock can be frozen in small batches, in plastic containers.

GARAM MASALA

'Garam' means hot or warming, 'masala' means mixture of spices. It is a blend of spices much-loved in northern Indian cookery, which originated in Kashmir and is added towards the end of cooking in certain dishes. There are as many recipes for garam masala as there are cooks who use it. Some Kashmiri recipes use up to 20 spices. This garam masala contains nine spices. Just mix together the aromatic spices you enjoy. The 'hot' is an Ayurvedic philosophy definition, where certain ingredients 'warm' the body, while others 'cool' it. However to get the best from garam masala, the mixture must contain heat (pepper), but never chilli or turmeric. Also, to release the essential oils, heat must be applied and the spices should be roasted, cooled and ground. The whole spices are cooked by dry-frying (with no oil or liquid) or 'roasting'. They are then cooled and ground. Compare it with any factory-made garam masala of your choice. You will always make it fresh from now on, I guarantee! This Kashmiri recipe will create enough garam masala for about 15 uses. Please note the recipe is for a relatively small quantity and its accuracy may not be achieved exactly. This does not matter; it simply goes to prove how flexible garam masala is.

Makes about 125 g (5 oz) when ground

30 g (2 tablespoons) coriander seeds

25 g (1¹/₂ tablespoons) cumin seeds

20 g (1¹/₂ tablespoons) fennel seeds

15 g (1 tablespoon) black peppercorns

5 g (1 teaspoon) cloves

4 brown cardamoms

2 pieces mace (enough to cover 2 nutmegs)

15 g (¹/₂ oz) cassia bark pieces

4 bay leaves

1 Heat a wok, keeping it dry. Mix the spices together in your pan. Stir the mixture continuously as it heats up.

2 Very soon the mixture will give off steam, rather than smoke. The process is called 'roasting'. The volatile oils, or aromas, are now being released into the air. Stir for a few seconds more, then transfer the spices to a cold pan or bowl, to stop them cooking. They must not burn. If they do, your cooking will have a bitter, carbonized taste. If they burn, discard them and start again.

3 Allow the garam masala to go completely cold for two reasons. Firstly, it will go more brittle, so will grind more easily. Secondly, if the mixture is hot when you grind it in an electric grinder, the blades could overheat the spices, and burn off the very volatile oil you are striving to capture.

4 Whether you use a mortar and pestle or an electric grinder (e.g. a coffee grinder), do so in small batches. This avoids overloading the machine.

5 Grind until all the clattering noises change to a softer similar sound, then grind on until the mix is as fine as you want it, or as fine as the grinder will achieve.

6 Thoroughly mix all the ingredients together. Store it in an airtight jar in a dark, dry place. Like all ground spices, though it will last for many months, it will gradually lose fragrance until eventually it tastes of little or nothing. It is best to make garam masala freshly in batches even smaller than this example.

GHEE

Ghee is clarified butter, is very easy to make and gives a distinctive and delicious taste. When cooled and set, it will keep for several months without refrigeration.

900 g (2 lb) butter, any type

1 Place the butter blocks whole into a medium non-stick pan. Melt at a very low heat.
2 When completely melted, raise the heat to achieve a simmer. Then lower the heat a little. Ensure it does not smoke or burn, but don't stir. Leave to cook for about 1 hour. The impurities will sink to the bottom and float as a froth on the top. Carefully skim any froth off the top with a slotted spoon, but don't touch the bottom.
3 Turn off the heat and allow the ghee to cool a little. Then strain it through kitchen paper or muslin into an airtight storage jar. When it cools it solidifies, although it is quite soft. It should be a bright pale lemon colour and it smells life toffee. If it has burned it will be darker and smell different. Providing it is not too burned it can still be used.

CARAMELIZED ONIONS

Normally, one fries raw, chopped onion slowly until it browns or caramelizes, (at which point the starch and acids in the onion turn to sugar). This can take 20 minutes or more of frequent stirring. 88% of an onion is water and the first 15 minutes is reducing or removing that water content. After that the actual caramelization takes place quite fast. Here is an easier way to do it.

Makes about 400 g (14 oz)

1 kg (2.2 lb) white onion, coarsely chopped
50 ml (2 fl oz) vegetable oil

1 Pre-heat the oven to 190°C/375°F/Gas 5.
2 Spread the onions out evenly in oven trays, to a depth of about 2.5 cm (1 in) and coat them with the vegetable oil. Place in the oven.
3 Bake them for about 35–40 minutes, stirring once midway. The outer edges will be almost burnt but this is good and is called 'tarka' (see page 208).
4 Separate the darker onions from the paler ones. Any leftover onions can be frozen once cool.

BROWN/WHITE ONION PASTE

Onion paste is often used to thicken and flavour sauces. For a white onion paste, fry or bake the onions for just 25 minutes before puréeing.

Makes about 400 g (14 oz) when puréed

1 kg (2.2 lb) white onion, coarsely chopped
50 ml (2 fl oz) vegetable oil

1 Fry or bake the onions until they caramelize (see Caramelized onions above).
2 Blend the onions and their oil down to a purée using a little water as needed.

ONION MASALA SAUCE

This sauce is a modern creation not used in the traditional home, but it is immensely useful to have up your sleeve in the freezer. It has the consistency of a puréed vegetable soup and a really pleasant taste. Make up a large batch and freeze in different size containers once cooled. Your average usage will 250 ml (9 fl oz).

Makes about 500 ml (18 fl oz)

500 ml (18 fl oz) water
40 ml (3 tablespoons) vegetable oil
1 teaspoon fennel seeds
2 or 3 garlic cloves, peeled
450 g (1 lb) whole onions, peeled
1/2 carrot, coarsely chopped
1/4 green pepper chopped
1 teaspoon salt

1 Put the oil and water into a 2.25 litre (4 pint) saucepan and bring to a low boil.

2 Lower the heat and add the fennel seeds, garlic, onions, carrot and green pepper and simmer for about 45 minutes.

3 Add the salt and then mulch the mixture down using a hand blender or jug blender, until you achieve a pourable gravy-like purée. It is a gorgeous golden colour and has the taste of a gentle soup.

PANCH PHORAN

Panch phoran is a Bengali mixture of five (panch) whole aromatic seeds, used alone in certain dishes. Simply mix together equal parts of each spice (a teaspoon of each is plenty) and store in an airtight container.

> White cumin seeds
> Fennel seeds
> Fenugreek seeds
> Black mustard seeds
> Wild onion seeds

PANEER

Paneer is the only form of cheese made in India. It is really simple to make by heating and curdling milk, and then separating the solids. It is used in curries and sweetmeats (see index), either crumbled or in its denser cubed form. It goes hard and rubbery if kept overnight so it should always be freshly made.

Makes about 225 g (8 oz)

2 litres (3 1/2 pints) full cream milk
freshly squeezed juice of 1 or 2 lemons

1 Bring the milk just up to boiling point, making sure it doesn't boil over.

2 Remove from the heat, and add lemon juice until the milk starts to separate. Stir to assist separation.

3 Using a clean tea-towel and a large sieve, strain off the liquid (whey). Relative to the solids (curds), there is always a lot of whey, and whilst you can use some for stock or soup, you will probably discard most of it.

4 Fold the tea-towel over the curds, and form them into a flat disc which must now be compressed. The easiest way to do this is to put a large saucepan filled with water on top of it, and put it, with a weight on its lid, on top of the disk, which itself is on the drainer.

5 For crumbled paneer, remove the weight after 15 to 20 minutes and crumble the paneer with your fingers. For cubes, leave the weight in place for at least an hour, maybe two, then the disc can be cut into cubes or chip (french-fry) shapes.

TAMARIND PURÉE

300 g (11 oz) block compressed tamarind
about 700 ml (24 fl oz) water

To use the tamarind block, soak it overnight in twice its volume of hot water. The next day pulp it well with the back of a spoon, then strain through a metal sieve, discarding the husks. The brown liquid should be quite thick, and there will be plenty of it. Freeze any spare.

Alternatively for a small portion cut off about an eighth of the block – a piece about 4 cm (1 1/2 in). Soak this in about 3 1/2 fl oz (100 ml) water for half an hour or more. Pulp and strain as above. More labour-intensive but better results can be achieved by boiling the block in plenty of water and then sieving it whilst hot. Remove the pulp and then boil again in fresh water and sieve as before. Repeat this process twice more.

Lemon or vinegar, which can be used as substitutes, will give completely different flavours.

3 recipes of India

Useful Information

Weights and measures

Most of the world uses the metric system to weigh and measure. This book puts metric first, followed by imperial because the US uses it (with slight modifications which need not concern us). The American system is called US Customary, Standard or English Units. Perversely since 1995 British law has required food and drink weights to be sold metrically (though not measures). But old habits die hard. Her young population think metric, whilst the rest of us hanker after the ancient imperial system. Local publicans and greengrocers have even been fined for selling pints of beer and pounds of apples.

The US will probably never go metric, preferring its spoonfuls and standard 8 fl oz cupfuls as measures. However, I have avoided cupfuls because solid weights vary considerably, according to their densities. For example, a US cupful of white granulated sugar is 200 g, brown sugar is 220 g, whereas shredded cheese is 115 g. The system is none-the-less great for visualising a quantity, and if you prefer this method, weigh ingredients and make a reference list.

My metric and imperial conversions use the standard UK system. Unless otherwise stated, my recipes work even if you use a mixture of systems. All spoon measures are level. Where spoon measures are used they require the same pragmatic approach about accuracy, as do oven temperatures, which are clearly stated in the relevant recipes.

Ovens rarely deliver their stated temperature. None of my oven recipes will ruin by being cooked a few degrees higher or lower, or several minutes longer or shorter. Inspection from time to time is your safest bet.

Finally, appetites vary. Portion sizes given with each recipe, are for average appetites.

Allergies

Food allergies should be taken very seriously. According to www.food.gov.uk, 40% of UK population have food allergies. This is remarkable. The reason is in debate, and the condition is on the increase.

Many people do not realise they have an allergy. The sufferer's nose may run soon after the offending item is eaten; if there are no further symptoms, the matter is easily overlooked. For those with a greater allergic reaction, symptoms include severe congestion, stomach cramps, diahorea or constipation. Sufferers should consult a doctor. Because the ultimate symptom is death.

Greatest risk is at the restaurant. 90% of staff know nothing about allergies, and their inept advice causes the death of at least one person each week in Britain, usually as a result of anaphylaxia, the nut allergy. Symptoms are a rapid swelling of the airways, which can can lead to suffocation.

It is the duty of all cooks to know which foods cause allergies. Traces as little as ten parts per million of peanut, tree nuts, lactose, gluten, fish, shellfish, soya bean, celery, celeriac, mustard, sesame seed, food colouring and sulphites are sufficient. Such ingredients can be avoided if there are suffers within the immediate family.

But if you intend to cook for guests, and you do not know them that well, do not be afraid to ask them if there is anything they are allergic to before planning the menu. When cooking day arrives, scrub hands, utensils, serving dishes and work surfaces thoroughly before commencing (you should do this in any case). Avoid using any offending ingredients. If this is not possible, prepare and cook them last, and keep the dishes they are in separate. Take great care not to cross-contaminate at any stage, particularly with a serving spoon. And tell your guests exactly what each dish contains.

1 | starters, snacks, soups & salads

Charu
SPICY TAMARIND COOLER

Orissa, east India

Recipes from east India are relatively scarce. This summer cooler typifies the tart tastes enjoyed in the region, countered here by the crunch of the raw onion.

Serves 4

900 ml (1½ pints) water
2 tablespoons tamarind purée (see page 62)
50 g (2 oz) onions, finely chopped
1 teaspoon mango powder
salt, to taste
ice cubes, to serve

1 Simply mix all the ingredients together and serve at once with ice cubes.

Jal Jeera
CUMIN WATER

Gujarat, west India

This savoury consommé is delicately spiced with salt and cumin. Serve it cold.

Serves 4

600 ml (20 fl oz) water
1 teaspoon salt
2 teaspoons ground cumin
¼–1 teaspoon chilli powder (optional)
Worcestershire sauce, to taste
crushed ice, to serve

1 Mix together all the ingredients, except the ice. Pour into a jug and refrigerate until required.
2 Stir well and add the crushed ice just before serving.

Kanne
PEPPER SOUP

Coorg, Karnataka, southern India

Here, chicken is simmered with garlic, onion and black pepper, and then removed to produce a consommé.

Serves 4

2 skinned chicken drumsticks, about 200 g
    (7 oz) each
½–1 teaspoon ground black pepper
2 or 3 cloves garlic, quartered
225 g (8 oz) onion, coarsely chopped
900 ml (1½ pints) water
salt, to taste
fresh coriander leaves, to garnish

1 Place all the ingredients in a saucepan and simmer for 30–40 minutes. Skim off any scum that accumulates from time to time.
2 Strain off the liquid, discarding the solids. Season with salt, garnish with coriander leaves and serve hot.

Kadhi Shorba
CURRY SOUP

Gujarat, west India

Made from spices, gram flour and yogurt, this creamy, mild golden-coloured soup has a slightly sweet and sour taste.

Serves 4

1 heaped tablespoon gram flour (besan)
2 green chillies, finely chopped
400 ml (14 fl oz) water
2 tablespoons sunflower or soya oil
375 g (13 oz) natural yogurt
10–12 fresh or dried curry leaves (optional)

1 teaspoon white granulated sugar (optional)
1 tablespoon finely chopped fresh coriander
salt, to taste

Masala

1 teaspoon cumin seeds
1 teaspoon turmeric
1/2 teaspoon asafoetida

1 Mix the gram flour, chillies, masala and a little of the measured water in a bowl to make a pourable paste.
2 Heat the oil in a pan, add the chilli paste and stir-fry. It will quickly start to thicken, so be prepared to drizzle in more of the water. Keep stirring until it won't thicken any further.
3 Put the yogurt and curry leaves, if using, in a 2.75 litre (5 pint) saucepan. Stir in the remaining water, using a fork or whisk.
4 Bring to a simmer, regularly whisking, but do not allow to boil.
5 Whisk in the chilli paste. Continue the rolling simmer for about 15 minutes, whisking from time to time. Add more water if it becomes too thick.
6 Add the sugar, if using, fresh coriander and salt and serve the soup hot.

Milagu-Tannir
PEPPER WATER
Tamil Nadu, south India

The English translation 'pepper water' gives the clue that this is a fiery hot soup. Pepper was India's original, indigenous ancient heat-giver (see page 52) and this recipe dates as far back as 1000BC. Chilli arrived in India only 500 years ago but it, too, plays a part in this recipe. During the British Raj milagu-tannir evolved into a thick meat-based soup called mulligatawny (see page 20). This is the original Tamil recipe.

Serves 4

1 litre (13/4 pints) water
2 tablespoons vegetable oil
2 or 3 cloves garlic, finely chopped
100 g (4 oz) finely chopped onion
1–4 fresh red chillies, shredded
1 tablespoon uncooked basmati rice (see rice note page 206)
1 tablespoon split and polished red lentils (masoor dhal)
1 tablespoon tamarind purée (see page 62)
2 tablespoons chopped fresh coriander leaves
10–12 fresh or dried curry leaves (optional)
salt, to taste

Masala

1/2 teaspoon turmeric
1/4–1 teaspoon chilli powder
1 teaspoon ground coriander

1 Bring the water to a simmer in a 3 litre (51/4 pint) saucepan.
2 Heat the oil in a karahi or wok and stir-fry the masala for 30 seconds. Add the garlic, onion and fresh chilli, and stir-fry for a further 3–4 minutes.
3 Add the contents of the karahi or wok, together with the rice and the lentils to the simmering water, stirring at first to ensure that nothing sticks to the bottom of the pan.
4 Simmer for 10 minutes, then add the tamarind and the coriander leaves.
5 Give the soup a final 3–4 minutes simmering, then season with salt. Serve hot or cold.

Shorba Nawabi
LEEK, POTATO & CASHEW SOUP
Lucknow, northern India

This soup predates vichyssoise by centuries, but is a similar thick purée. Its richness is typical of the food enjoyed by the Oudhs and Nawabs of Lucknow (see page 35). Serve cold or hot.

Serves 4

600 ml (20 fl oz) boiling water
200 g (7 oz) leek, coarsely chopped
200 g (7 oz) potatoes, peeled and chopped
1/2 teaspoon fenugreek seeds, roasted and ground
2 cloves garlic, whole
50 g (2 oz) onion, peeled and quartered
25 g (1 oz) unsalted butter
50 g (2 oz) cashew nuts, fried (see page 87)
1 fresh red chilli, shredded (optional)
1 teaspoon mustard seeds, roasted
1/2 teaspoon black peppercorns, crushed
salt, to taste
milk, to taste

Garnish
finely chopped fresh coriander leaves
thick pourable cream

1 Put the boiling water in a 2.75 litre (5 pint) saucepan. Add the leek, potatoes, fenugreek seeds, garlic, onion and butter and leave to simmer for 30–45 minutes.
2 Add the cashews then, using a hand or jug blender, 'pulse' the mixture to a pourable, gravy-like purée.
3 Stir in the chilli, if using, mustard seeds and peppercorns and season with salt. Add a little milk if you prefer a thinner soup.
4 Serve the soup hot, garnished with coriander and a curl of cream.

Rasam
GOURD SOUP
Southern India

This hot and spicy consommé contains lentils, gourds and tomato.

Serves 4

900 ml (1½ pints) water or stock
1 tablespoon tamarind purée (see page 62)
1 tablespoon split and polished red lentils (masoor dhal)
1 teaspoon chopped dried red chillies
2 tablespoons vegetable oil
1 teaspoon mustard seeds
1 teaspoon sesame seeds
1/2 teaspoon turmeric
4 or 5 cloves garlic, sliced
1–3 fresh red chillies, chopped (optional)
225 g (8 oz) onion, thinly sliced
10–12 fresh or dried curry leaves (optional)
200 g (7 oz) gourd (such as squash or marrow) flesh, cut into bite-sized cubes
1–2 tomatoes, quartered
2 tablespoons chopped fresh coriander leaves
salt, to taste

1 Simmer the water, tamarind, lentils and dried chillies in a 2.25 litre (4 pint) saucepan for about 15 minutes.
2 Heat the oil in another pan. Add the seeds and fry for 10 seconds. Add the turmeric, garlic, fresh chillies, if using, and onion and stir-fry for about 3 minutes. Add this to the soup and simmer for another 5 minutes.
3 If liked, strain the soup at this stage, discarding the solids, then return the soup to the saucepan.
4 Add the curry leaves, if using, gourds, tomato, coriander leaves and salt. Simmer for 5–10 minutes more then serve hot.

Leek, potato & cashew soup

Dhal Doyi Jhol
SOUR LENTIL & YOGURT SOUP
Bengal, north-east India

This sour tasting, nutritious Bengali dish could be served with plain rice, to provide a satisfying main course meal. Here it is offered as a soup.

Serves 4

1 litre (1³/4 pints) water
100 g (4 oz) split and polished red lentils (masoor dhal), rinsed and drained
4 tablespoons natural yogurt
2 tablespoons tamarind purée (see page 62)
3 tablespoons sunflower oil
3 or 4 cloves garlic, finely chopped
100 g (4 oz) caramelized onions (see page 61)
2 or 3 tomatoes, chopped
2 or 3 green cayenne chillies, chopped
   lengthwise
several fresh coriander leaves, chopped
white granulated sugar, to taste (optional)
salt, to taste

Masala
¹/2 teaspoon turmeric
1 teaspoon panch phoran (see page 62)
2 or 3 bay leaves
1–2 teaspoons chopped dried red chillies

1 Bring the water to a simmer in a 4 pint (2.25 litre) saucepan then add the lentils, yogurt and tamarind. When simmering, stir thoroughly once to prevent the lentils sticking to the bottom of the pan.
2 Meanwhile, heat the oil in a karahi or wok. Stir-fry the masala for 30 seconds, add the garlic and stir-fry for 30 seconds more. Then add the onion tarka, tomatoes and green chillies and stir-fry for about 2 minutes.
3 Add the fried items to the pan of lentils at any time.

4 The soup will need around 45 minutes to simmer. Just before serving, add the coriander and sugar, if using, and season with salt.

Dahi Batata Pava
CRISP, CHEWY STREET FOOD
Mumbai, western India

Little known outside Mumbai (Bombay), this is one of a small family of favourite kiosk foods. To make it you need sev (crisp squiggles) and mamra (savoury crisp puffed rice), both available in packets from Asian stores. These are mixed with potato (batata) and yogurt (dahi) and laced with chilli-hot and sour sauces.

Serves 4

50 g (2 oz) sev
50 g (2 oz) puffed rice (mamra)
2 large potatoes, boiled and chopped into 8 mm
   (³/8 inch) cubes
3 tablespoons finely chopped onion
2 green chillies, finely chopped
2 tablespoons finely chopped fresh coriander
   leaves
1–2 teaspoons garam masala (see page 62)
200 g (7 oz) natural yogurt, to serve
salt, to taste

Sweet & Sour Brown Tamarind Chutney (Imli)
100 g (4 oz) tamarind purée (see page 62)
50 g (2 oz) dates, pitted
50 g (2 oz) brown sugar
¹/2 onion, chopped
1 teaspoon garam masala (see page 60)
chilli powder, to taste
black salt (kala namak) or white sea salt, to
   taste (see page 58)

Hot Green Chutney
100 g (4 oz) fresh coriander leaves and soft
    stalks
25 g (1 oz) green chillies, chopped
100 g (4 oz) chopped onion
1 teaspoon salt

1 Start by making the two chutneys first. For each
chutney, grind the ingredients in a blender or food
processor, adding just enough water to make a
smooth purée.

2 Mix together all the ingredients for the main
recipe, except the yogurt, and divide between four
serving bowls. Drizzle with the yogurt, brown and
green chutneys. Serve immediately.

Kosumbri
BEAN & CHICKPEA SALAD
Southern India

Nutritionally excellent, containing protein and
carbohydrates, this dish is a meal in itself.

Serves 4

100 g (4 oz) dried black-eyed beans
100 g (4 oz) dried red kidney beans
100 g (4 oz) dried chickpeas
2 tablespoons sesame oil
2–4 cloves garlic, finely chopped
2.5 cm (1 inch) piece of fresh root ginger,
    shredded
100 g (4 oz) finely chopped onion
2 green chillies, finely chopped
1 teacupful fresh coriander leaves, chopped
salt, to taste
fresh lime juice, to serve

Masala 1
2 teaspoons mustard seeds
1$\frac{1}{2}$ teaspoons cumin seeds
$\frac{1}{2}$ teaspoon wild onion seeds

Masala 2
1 teaspoon ground coriander
1 teaspoon garam masala (see page 60)
$\frac{1}{2}$ teaspoon turmeric
$\frac{1}{2}$ teaspoon mango powder

1 Soak the beans and chickpeas separately
overnight in plenty of water.

2 Next day, drain and rinse them well several times
in cold water. Boil the beans and chickpeas in
different saucepans of water until tender – between
30 and 45 minutes. When cooked, rinse in cold
water, drain and combine.

3 Heat the oil in a karahi or wok, add Masala 1 and
stir-fry for 30 seconds. Add Masala 2 and stir-fry for
a further 30 seconds, then add the garlic, ginger,
onion and chillies and stir-fry for about 5 minutes
more, adding a little water if needed to keep the
mixture loose.

4 Then add the beans and chickpeas and half the
fresh coriander. Mix well, remove from the heat and
season with salt.

5 When cooled, transfer to a bowl and refrigerate
for between 1 and 4 hours.

6 Serve the salad garnished with the remaining
coriander and a squeeze of lime juice.

COOK'S TIP You could used tinned beans and
chickpeas if you prefer, although the salad will not
taste quite as good. Drain the liquid from each tin and
rinse the beans and chickpeas in cold water. Omit
steps 1–2 above then proceed with the recipe.

Dakshini Salat

RICE, LENTIL & COCONUT SALAD

Tamil Nadu, south India

Dakshin means 'vegetarian' in Tamil, and this salad is composed of spiced cold rice, lentils and coconut, with a spicy dressing and a garnish of tomato and coriander leaves. The lentil in question is cooked chana dhal snack (gram).

Serves 4

90 g (3½ oz) cooked cold plain rice
90 g (3½ oz) fresh coconut flesh, cut into julienne strips
2 cloves garlic, chopped
50 g (2 oz) packet cooked chana dhal snack (gram)
50 g (2 oz) peanuts, pan-roasted (see page 86) and coarsely crushed
90 g (3½ oz) dark salad leaves, such as rocket, lamb's lettuce, baby spinach, chopped

Masala

20 g (¾ oz) coriander seeds
½ teaspoon cumin seeds
1 teaspoon black/brown mustard seeds

Salad Dressing

150 ml (5 fl oz) bottled rice vinegar
25 ml (1 fl oz) extra virgin olive oil
2 teaspoons fennel seeds, roasted and ground
1 teaspoon salt
½ teaspoon chilli powder
½ teaspoon turmeric

Garnish

6 baby plum tomatoes, sliced into thin rounds
2 tablespoons whole fresh coriander

Rice, lentil & coconut salad

1 Heat the masala in a dry karahi or wok for about 30 seconds, then allow to cool.
2 Mix the masala and salad ingredients together in a salad bowl.
3 Mix the dressing ingredients together in a screw-top jar. Shake well. (This dressing improves as it matures, and will keep indefinitely.)
4 When ready to serve the salad, shake the dressing in the jar one more time, then add it to the salad to your taste. Garnish and serve cold.

Pasanda Kebab

SPICY GRILLED ESCALOPES

Moghul origin, northern India

Here, lamb, beef or veal is beaten to escalopes, spread with a spicy paste, crumbed and fried. In Moghul days, the pasanda had to be very thinly beaten and cooked until tender, because their royal highness' teeth were so rotten!

Serves 4

2 eggs, beaten
several tablespoons dried breadcrumbs
4 x 150 g (5 oz) lamb, beef or veal escalopes
4 tablespoons vegetable oil
1 lemon, quartered

Masala

6 cloves garlic, finely chopped or puréed
1 tablespoon finely chopped fresh mint
1 teaspoon garam masala (see page 60)
1 teaspoon chilli powder
½ teaspoon turmeric
salt, to taste

1 Mix the beaten eggs with the masala and pour into a large shallow bowl. Tip the breadcrumbs into another large shallow bowl.
2 Dip the escalopes into the egg mixture, then dab them in the breadcrumbs to cover completely.

3 Heat the oil in a frying pan and fry the escalopes for 3–4 minutes each side. Serve with a squeeze of lemon juice on a bed of plain rice or, for a modern Indian touch, on a bed of buttered spaghetti.

Khara Soti Boti Kebab

OMELETTE-WRAPPED MEAT CHUNKS

Parsee origin

Parsees (see page 20) adore eggs and slightly sweet tastes, and this combination of meat kebabs and omelette makes a glorious snack or starter. You will need 8 skewers.

Serves 4

32 cubes of lean lamb, about 3 cm
   (1¼ inches) square
4–5 tablespoons ghee (see page 61)
2–4 cloves garlic, finely chopped
2.5 cm (1 inch) piece of fresh root ginger,
   shredded
100 g (4 oz) onion, very finely chopped
4 eggs
1 or 2 green chillies, finely chopped (optional)
   fresh coriander leaves, to garnish

Marinade
175 ml (6 fl oz) milk
1–3 teaspoons brown sugar
1 tablespoon soy sauce
2 cloves garlic, crushed
1 teaspoon garam masala (see page 60)
½–1½ teaspoons chilli powder
1 teaspoon salt

Masala
¼ teaspoon ground cumin
½ teaspoon turmeric
½ teaspoon chilli powder
1 teaspoon ground coriander

1 Mix the marinade ingredients together in a non-aluminium bowl (see cook's tip below). Immerse the cubes of meat and refrigerate for 24–60 hours.
2 Once marinated, heat 2 tablespoons of the ghee in a karahi or wok, add the masala and stir-fry for 30 seconds. Add the garlic and ginger and stir-fry for 30 seconds more.
3 Add the onion and the meat, together with its marinade, and stir-fry over a low heat for 5 minutes.
4 Transfer the contents of the pan to a 2.25–2.75 litre (4–5 pint) lidded casserole dish. Cover and place in a preheated oven, 190°C/375°F/Gas 5. After 20 minutes, stir and taste. Add a little water if needed and return the casserole dish to the oven.
5 After a further 20 minutes, taste the meat – it should be tender but not soft enough to break up. If it is still a bit tough, give it more oven time.
6 Leave the meat until cool enough to handle, then thread 4 pieces of meat onto each skewer, leaving gaps between each piece.
7 Transfer any spare cooked marinade sauce to a saucepan and keep warm.
8 Break the eggs into a bowl, add the chopped chilli, if using, and beat with a whisk.
9 Heat a teaspoon of the remaining ghee in a non-stick frying pan or tava. When hot, pour in one-eighth of the egg mixture and swirl around to coat the base of the pan, as though making a thin omelette. Before it starts to set, place a skewer of warm lamb pieces into the centre of the omelette and fold over the top and bottom edges of the omelette to enclose the kebab. The egg will stick to the kebab as it cooks and sets.
10 Keep the kebab warm while you repeat the process with the remaining kebabs and egg.
11 When all the kebabs are wrapped in omelette, pour over any remaining sauce. Garnish with coriander leaves and serve as a starter on top of a salad, or as part of a main course on a bed of rice.

Omelette-wrapped meat chunks

COOK'S TIP For marinating always use a ceramic, enamel, glass, plastic, stainless steel or non-stick bowl or pot. Do not use an aluminium bowl because the acids in the ingredients will react with the aluminium. The purpose of marinating is to tenderize meat or chicken, and to impart flavour, so the longer it can be left the better. Providing your meat or poultry is from a top-quality supplier, and is fresh, or has been frozen only once, it can marinate for as long as 60 hours, covered in the fridge. Alternatively, items can also be frozen as soon as they are marinated.

Murgh Malai Tikka
CREAMY CHICKEN PIECES
Modern chef's recipe

Pieces (tikka) of chicken (murgh) are marinated in yogurt, cream (malai), cream cheese and light spices, then baked to succulence in this modern Indian chef's method. Probably the first exponent of this method was Arvin Saraswat, chef director of cuisine, Taj Group Delhi.

Serves 4

24 x 3 cm (1¼ inch) cubes skinned chicken breast

Malai Tikka Marinade
50 g (2 oz) natural yogurt
50 ml (2 fl oz) single cream
1 tablespoon cream cheese
2 or 3 cloves garlic, finely chopped or puréed
1 teaspoon bottled mint sauce
1 teaspoon garam masala (see page 60)
2 tablespoons finely chopped fresh coriander leaves
½ teaspoon salt (omit at this stage if going on to make butter chicken (see page 96).

Creamy chicken pieces

1 Mix the marinade ingredients together in a non-aluminium bowl. Immerse the pieces of chicken in the marinade, cover and refrigerate for up to 36 hours.
2 To cook, the chicken can be grilled, barbecued or oven-baked for 12 minutes at 190°C/375°F/Gas 5. Ensure that the pieces are in one layer in the oven tray.
3 Cut through one piece to ensure that it is fully cooked – it should be white right through with no hint of pink. If not, cook for a while longer. (Use any leftover cooked marinade in subsequent cooking.)

Galouti Kebab
VELVETY SMOOTH MINCED MEAT RISSOLES
Moghul origin, northern India

Galouti in this Moghul dish literally means a ball made from finely ground meat. Here the meat is spiced and shaped into discs like hockey pucks then fried.

Makes 16

450 g (1 lb) lean lamb leg or beef rump, cut into 5 cm (2 inch) cubes
2 or 3 cloves garlic, quartered
2.5 cm (1 inch) piece of fresh root ginger, chopped
2 green chillies, chopped
1 tablespoon fresh coriander leaves
1 teaspoon chopped fresh mint
50 g (2 oz) gram flour (besan)
4 tablespoons vegetable oil
salt, to taste

Masala
1 teaspoon chilli powder
1 teaspoon green cardamom seeds, ground
½ teaspoon ground mace

1 Grind all the ingredients except the oil in a blender or food processor. This may have to be done in 2 batches.

2 Remove and mix thoroughly by hand, picking out all unwanted meat matter as you go.

3 Re-run the mixture in the food processor. Keep doing this until you have a mixture as soft as paté.

4 Divide the mixture in half, then half again, and repeat until you have 16 equal-sized amounts. Shape them into small disc shapes.

5 Heat the oil in a frying pan or tava. Fry the kebabs for 3–4 minutes each side, then serve.

Kakrar Chop
CRAB & CHILLI RISSOLES
Modern chef's recipe

Fresh white and brown crab meat, spiked with green chilli, is shaped into rounds like fishcakes. These are then breadcrumbed, shallow-fried and served with Chuk (beetroot and cucumber chutney, see page 230). This recipe is inspired by one of Britain's foremost Indian chefs, Udit Sarkhell.

Serves 4

1 tablespoon vegetable oil, plus extra for frying
2 tablespoons desiccated coconut
2 teaspoons tamarind purée (see page 62)
200 g (7 oz) finely chopped onion
350 g (12 oz) fresh white crab meat
150 g (5 oz) fresh brown crab meat
1 tablespoon tomato purée
2 or 3 green chillies, chopped
salt, to taste
1 tablespoon chopped fresh coriander leaves, to garnish

Masala

10–12 fresh or dried curry leaves (optional)
2 teaspoons ground coriander
1 teaspoon turmeric
1/2 teaspoon chilli powder
1/2 teaspoon black/brown mustard seeds

1 Heat the oil in a karahi or wok. Add the masala and stir-fry for 30 seconds.

2 Add the coconut and stir-fry for 1 minute then add the tamarind and onion and continue stir-frying for 5 more minutes.

3 Add the crab meat, tomato purée and green chillies and turn off the heat. Season with salt.

4 Using your hands, form the mixture into rounds about 5–6 cm (2–2 1/2 inches) in diameter.

5 Heat the oil for frying in a frying pan. Add the rissoles and fry for about 1 minute on each side until brown. Serve garnished with coriander leaves.

Hara Kebab
GREEN VEGETARIAN RISSOLES
Modern chef's recipe

Ground cashews, fresh chillies, paneer (Indian cheese) and spinach are the principal ingredients of this vegetarian green dish. This recipe comes from chef tutor M. Raman of the Maurya Sheraton Hotel, Agra.

Makes 16

150 g (5 oz) crumbled paneer (see page 62)
200 g (7 oz) spinach, cooked and well drained
300 g (11 oz) potatoes, peeled, cooked and cooled
175 g (6 oz) fresh peas, cooked or frozen peas, thawed, coarsely mashed
50 g (2 oz) cashew nuts, fried (see page 87)
2 or 3 cloves garlic, chopped
2.5 cm (1 inch) piece of fresh root ginger, chopped

Crab & Chilli Rissoles

1 tablespoon fresh coriander leaves
1 teaspoon chopped fresh mint
50 g (2 oz) gram flour (besan)
2 green chillies, chopped
1 teaspoon salt
several tablespoons dried breadcrumbs
vegetable oil for deep-frying

Masala

1 teaspoon garam masala (see page 60)
1 teaspoon cumin, ground
1 teaspoon ground coriander
1 teaspoon chilli powder
1/2 teaspoon lovage seeds

1 Grind all the ingredients except the breadcrumbs and oil in a blender or food processor. This may have to be done in 2 batches, depending on the size of your motor. If the mixture is too dry to be mouldable, add water drop by drop as too wet a mixture is a disaster for this recipe.
2 Divide the mixture in half, then half again, and repeat until you have 16 equal-sized amounts. Form into small disc shapes.
3 Heat the oil in a deep frying pan to 190°C/375°F (chip-frying temperature).
4 While it is heating up, cover each rissole in breadcrumbs.
5 Add the rissoles, a few at a time, to the oil and try to separate them at first by keeping them on the move to prevent them from sticking together. When the surface area of the pan is full, but not crowded, fry them until they stop sizzling and the moisture is cooked out. They will be an attractive golden colour.
6 Remove them from the pan using a slotted spoon. Shake off the excess oil and place them on absorbent kitchen paper until cool, then serve.

Dosa
RICE PANCAKE
Southern India

Southern India's best-known pancakes, dosa are made from a watery, fermenting rice flour and lentil flour batter. Dosa are made very thin and crisp in Karnataka (as here), and thick and small in Tamil Nadu. They can be eaten as plain pancakes or stuffed with a filling as in the next recipe.

Serves 4

200 g (7 oz) cooked, cold round rice
90 g (3 1/2 oz) split and polished black lentils
   (urid dhal)
1/2 teaspoon fenugreek seeds, ground
1/2 teaspoon salt
4 tablespoons sunflower or soya oil

1 Soak the rice and lentils separately in plenty of water for at least 12 hours. Drain, then mix them together and grind in a blender or food processor with a little warm water to make an easily pourable pancake batter.
2 Cover the batter, put it in a warm place and leave it to ferment. For this to happen, ideally the temperature should be between 28° and 42°C (82–108°F) and the place should be draught-free – the airing cupboard is ideal. Leave the batter for at least 6 hours, after which time it should occasionally bubble and have the yeasty smell associated with fermentation.
3 Mix in the fenugreek and salt.
4 Heat 1 tablespoon oil in a large frying pan, tava or flat griddle pan. Pour in one-quarter of the batter and spread it around the pan so that it becomes a thin disc. When off-white, about 30 seconds later, ease the dosa off the pan and keep warm while you make the other 3 dosa in the same way.

Masala Dosa
CURRY-FILLED RICE PANCAKES
Southern India

Dosa pancakes traditionally have the light potato curry filling given in this recipe. Dosa are usually accompanied by Rasam (gourd soup, see page 68), Sambar (spicy lentils, see page 204) and Narial (coconut chutney, see page 231).

Makes 4

2 tablespoons sunflower or soya oil

2 teaspoons mustard seeds

1 tablespoon split and polished gram lentils
  (chana dhal)

1 tablespoon whole black lentils (urid dhal)

1 teaspoon turmeric

4 cloves garlic, chopped

100 g (4 oz) onions, chopped

350 g (12 oz) potatoes, peeled, cooked and cut
  into 1 cm (1/2 inch) cubes

1–4 dried red chillies, chopped

2 tablespoons cooked cashew nuts (see
  page 87) (optional)

10–12 fresh or dried curry leaves (optional)

4 cooked dosas (see left)

salt, to taste

1 Heat the oil in a karahi or wok. Stir-fry the mustard seeds and the lentils for about 1 minute.
2 Add the turmeric, garlic and onions and stir-fry for 2–3 more minutes. Add a splash of water to keep the mixture loose.
3 Stir in the potato cubes and chillies and the nuts and curry leaves, if using. When sizzling, season with salt.
4 Spread one-quarter of the masala filling across the centre of each cooked dosa and roll the dosa over the filling. Serve hot.

Uthappam
RICE PIZZA
Southern India

Uthappam, or oothappam, are savoury pancakes of pizza thickness, native to southern India. The pancake batter is made with rice and lentils, which are soaked and ground before being left to ferment. If possible, the rice should be sambar rice, a small oval-grained variety available from Asian stores. If not available, use any round-grained rice. Traditionally, the batter contains dried red chilli, fresh root ginger and onion.

Makes 4

100 g (4 oz) round rice

50 g (2 oz) split and polished black lentils
  (urid dhal)

4 dried red chillies

2.5 cm (1 inch) piece of fresh root ginger,
  chopped

100 g (4 oz) finely chopped onion

1/2 teaspoon sugar

1/2 teaspoon salt

6 tablespoons sunflower or soya oil

Topping (optional)
1–2 cloves garlic, thinly sliced
2 tablespoons caramelized onions (see page 61)
1 small tomato, thinly sliced
2–4 green chillies, finely chopped into rings

1 Soak the rice and lentils separately in plenty of water for at least 12 hours. Drain, then mix them together and grind in a blender or food processor with a little warm water to make an easily pourable pancake batter.
2 Cover the batter, put it in a warm place and leave it to ferment. For this to happen, ideally the temperature should be between 28° and 42°C (82–108°F) and the place should be draught-free –

the airing cupboard is ideal. Leave the batter for at least 6 hours, after which time it should occasionally bubble and have the yeasty smell associated with fermentation.

3 Stir the dried chillies, ginger, onion, sugar and salt into the batter.

4 If opting for a pizza-style topping, mix the topping ingredients together.

5 Add one-quarter of the oil to a hot 15 cm (6 inch) diameter non-stick pan. Pour in one-quarter of the batter. Quickly swirl it around the pan, then spread one-quarter of the topping over the pancake.

6 Cook for about 1 minute until the pancake sets, then turn it over and cook the other side. Turn it out and make 3 more pancakes in the same way.

Aloo Chop
MASHED POTATO RISSOLES WITH A SPICY CENTRE
Throughout India

Tiny walnut-sized amounts of chickpea (kabli chana) curry or minced beef curry (keema), are enclosed in mashed potato, shaped into discs, coated in breadcrumbs and shallow-fried. Also called aloo tikki, this recipe is from the street stalls of the Kolikot (Calcutta) railway station. Although time-consuming to make, they are worth the effort and can be eaten with chutneys or, in the traditional Punjabi fashion, with Aloo Chole (potato and chickpea curry, see page 199), plain yogurt and Imli Gajar (tamarind and carrot chutney, see page 230).

Makes 8–10

450 g (1 lb) potatoes, mashed
175 g (6 oz) frozen peas, thawed
1 or 2 green chillies, finely chopped
1/2 teaspoon salt

100 g (4 oz) cold cooked potato and chickpea curry (see page 199) or 100 g (4 oz) strained minced beef curry (see page 117)
2 eggs, beaten
several tablespoons dried breadcrumbs
vegetable oil for frying

Masala
1/2 teaspoon ground coriander
1/2 teaspoon cumin seeds
1/2 teaspoon chilli powder

1 Mix together the potatoes, peas, chillies, salt and masala.

2 Using your hands, form the mixture into cup shapes of 5–6 cm (2–2 1/2 inches) in diameter. Depending on the size of your 'cups', the recipe should make 8–10 rissoles.

3 Put a little of the potato and chickpea curry or keema mixture in each 'cup' and enclose it in the potato by gently squeezing. Flatten each filled cup into a round and brush with the beaten egg, then cover in breadcrumbs.

4 Heat the oil in a frying pan. Add the rissoles and fry for about 1 minute on each side until brown. Serve hot or cold.

Bonda Mysori
BATTER-COATED POTATO BALLS
Mysore, Karnataka, southern India

Bonda literally means 'balls' and in this case balls of mashed potato are dipped in gram flour batter and deep-fried to create Mysore's 'national' dish. They are available from street kiosks for mere pennies, or served at the upmarket hotel restaurants for big dollars. Serve them with Sambar (spicy lentils, see page 204) and chutneys.

Makes 6–8

250 g (9 oz) split and polished black lentils
  (urid dhal)
250 g (9 oz) boiled potatoes
25 g (1 oz) desiccated coconut
4 green chillies, finely chopped
pinch of asafoetida
pinch of bicarbonate of soda
2 tablespoons vegetable oil
1/2 teaspoon salt
vegetable oil for deep-frying

Batter

75 g (3 oz) gram flour (besan)
1/2 teaspoon turmeric
1 teaspoon salt
1 egg

1 Grind all the ingredients, except the oil for deep-frying, together in a blender or food processor. This may have to be done in 2 batches, depending on the size of your motor.

2 If the mixture is too dry to be mouldable, add water drop by drop as too wet a mixture is a disaster for this recipe. Form the mixture into 6–8 balls.

3 Whisk the batter ingredients together in a bowl with just enough water to make it pourable.

4 Heat the oil in a deep-frying pan to 190°C/375°F (chip-frying temperature).

5 Coat the first ball with batter, then lower it into the hot oil, and after a few seconds add the next ball. Continue until the surface area of the pan is full but not crowded. This maintains the oil temperature. Fry for 8–10 minutes.

6 Remove the cooked balls from the pan using a slotted spoon. Shake off the excess oil and drain them on absorbent kitchen paper.

7 Repeat until all the balls are cooked. Serve hot.

Filowri
SPLIT PEA RISSOLES
Jewish origin, Kerala, south India

Egypt's falafel uses chickpea as its main ingredient. This version, also called philoorie, evolved from the falafel in Kerala's Cochin Jewish community centuries ago. It uses ingredients not normally associated with Indian cookery – ground split peas (chunna-ka-dhal), spring onions and caraway seeds.

Makes 10–12

500 g (1 lb 2 oz) split green peas
50 g (2 oz) spring onions, finely chopped
4 tablespoons finely chopped fresh coriander
2 teaspoons caraway seeds
2 or 3 green chillies, chopped (optional)
vegetable oil for deep-frying
salt, to taste

1 Soak the split peas in plenty of water for 8 hours or overnight. Drain and rinse.

2 Grind the split peas in a blender or food processor. This may have to be done in 2 batches, depending on the size of your motor. If the mixture is too dry to be mouldable, add water drop by drop as too wet a mixture is a disaster for this recipe.

3 Add the remaining ingredients except the oil and mix well. Form the mixture into 10–12 balls.

4 Heat the oil in a deep frying pan to 190°C/375°F (chip-frying temperature).

5 Add one filowri to the hot oil. After a few seconds add the next, and continue until the surface area of the pan is full but not crowded. This maintains the oil temperature. Fry for 8–10 minutes.

6 Remove the filowri from the pan using a slotted spoon. Shake off the excess oil and drain them on absorbent kitchen paper.

7 Repeat until all the filowri are cooked. Serve hot or cold with chutney.

Samosas
TRIANGULAR FILLED & FRIED PASTRIES
Throughout India

These deep-fried meat or vegetable pastries are enjoyed throughout India, with minor regional variations including the method of wrapping and the type of filling. For example 'singhoda' is the Gujarati name for samosa, whereas 'shingara' is the Bengali version. This recipe uses a traditional vegetable filling; for meat samosas use Keema (minced beef curry, see page 117) as the filling, having first strained off any excess liquid to ensure the filling is dry enough.

Makes 16

2 tablespoons vegetable oil, plus extra for deep-frying
450 g (1 lb) strong white plain flour, plus a little extra for pastry-making
sweet and sour brown tamarind chutney (imli, see page 70), to serve

Vegetable Filling
2 large potatoes, peeled, cooked and lightly mashed
$1/2$ cup fresh peas, cooked or frozen peas, thawed
1 teaspoon salt
1 teaspoon garam masala (see page 60)
1 teaspoon ground black pepper
$1/4$ teaspoon chilli powder
1 teaspoon ground coriander
1 teaspoon ground cumin
chopped fresh coriander
1 teaspoon dried fenugreek leaves (optional)
1–3 green chillies, finely chopped (optional)

1 Mix the ingredients for the samosa filling together in a bowl and set aside.

2 For the samosa pastry, mix together the measured oil, flour and enough water to make a dough which, when mixed, does not stick to the bowl. Leave it to stand for about 1 hour.

3 Divide the dough into 4, then shape each piece into a square. Roll out each square on a floured surface and cut each into 4 rectangles measuring 7.5 x 20 cm (3 x 8 inches). Remember, the thinner you roll the pastry, the crisper the samosas will be.

4 Take one pastry rectangle and place a teaspoon of filling at one end. Make the first diagonal fold, then the second and third. Open the pouch and top up with some more filling but do not overfill or the samosa will burst during deep-frying.

5 Brush some flour and water on the remaining flap, and seal. Trim off the excess pastry. Make the remaining samosas in the same way.

6 Heat the oil in a deep frying pan to 190°C/375°F (chip-frying temperature).

7 Add one samosa to the hot oil. After a few seconds add the next, and continue until the surface area of the pan is full but not crowded. This maintains the oil temperature. Fry for 8–10 minutes.

8 Remove the samosas from the pan using a slotted spoon. Shake off the excess oil and drain them on absorbent kitchen paper.

9 Repeat until all the samosas are cooked then serve them hot with the chutney.

COOK'S TIP Substitute ready-made sheets of spring roll or filo pastry or samosa pads (available from Asian stores) for the homemade samosa pastry, if preferred.

Triangular filled & fried pastries

Kachori
FILLED & FRIED PASTRY BALLS
Madhya Pradesh, central India

A lentil and pea filling is wrapped in a ball of pastry about the size of a ping pong ball and deep-fried. Not only is this crisp, stuffed delicacy a favourite snack in Madhya Pradesh, it is also a must at every wedding in the region.

Makes 12

250 g (9 oz) strong white plain flour
1/4 teaspoon bicarbonate of soda
1/2 teaspoon salt
5 tablespoons vegetable oil, plus extra for deep-frying
green puréed chutney (see page 229), to serve

Filling
100 g (4 oz) split and polished black lentils (urid dhal)
225 g (8 oz) fresh peas, cooked or frozen peas, thawed
2 or 3 cloves garlic, finely chopped
2.5 cm (1 inch) piece of fresh root ginger, shredded
1–4 green chillies, finely chopped
2 teaspoons ground coriander
1/2 teaspoon salt
1/2 teaspoon chilli powder
pinch of asafoetida

1 To make the dough, mix the flour, bicarbonate of soda, salt and 5 tablespoons vegetable oil together in a bowl. Gradually add just enough water (about 100 ml/3 1/2 fl oz) to make a soft dough when kneaded. Leave it to stand for 40 minutes.
2 Meanwhile, soak the lentils in plenty of water for 30 minutes then drain.
3 Grind the soaked lentils and other filling

ingredients in a blender or food processor. This may have to be done in 2 batches, depending on the size of your motor. If the mixture is too dry to be mouldable, add water drop by drop as too wet a mixture is a disaster for this recipe. Divide the mixture into 12 equal portions.
4 Divide the dough into 12 equal-sized balls. Shape each ball into a disc and place a portion of filling in the centre of each one. Fold the dough over the filling, into pouch-like shapes. Gently pull away any spare pastry then gently squeeze to make balls.
5 Heat the oil in a deep frying pan to 190°C/375°F (chip-frying temperature).
6 Add one kachori to the hot oil. After a few seconds add the next, and continue until the surface area of the pan is full but not crowded. This maintains the oil temperature. Fry for 6–8 minutes.
7 Remove the kachori from the pan using a slotted spoon. Shake off the excess oil, and drain them on absorbent kitchen paper.
8 Repeat until all the kachori are cooked then serve them hot with the chutney.

Moonfali Tava
PAN-ROASTED PEANUTS
Throughout India

Oven-roasted peanuts (also called moong phali or kalakai) are unrivaled in flavour and make a great snack served with apéritifs.

Makes 500 g (1 lb 2 oz)

500 g (1 lb 2 oz) raw, shelled, skinless peanuts
chilli powder, to taste (optional)

1 Arrange the peanuts in a single layer in one or more oven trays and bake in a preheated oven, 160°C/325°F/Gas 3, for about 15 minutes.
2 Sprinkle with chilli powder, if using, cool and eat at once. Like any nuts, they will last for several months if stored in a dry container.

Kaju
DEVILLED FRIED CASHEWS
Goa, Indian west coast

Shelled raw cashews make a good paste when ground with water, and can be used to thicken certain curry sauces. Here cashew nuts are briskly fried until golden brown to make a great garnish, as well as a delightful snack.

Makes 500 g (1 lb 2 oz)

100 ml (3½ fl oz) vegetable or corn oil
500 g (1 lb 2 oz) raw, shelled cashew nuts
salt, to taste
chilli powder, to taste

1 Heat the oil in a karahi or wok over a high heat.
2 Carefully add all the nuts. Reduce the heat to medium, stir-fry briskly and continuously until the nuts start to go golden. Keep moving them to prevent patchy burning and watch out as they will suddenly turn golden. Bear in mind, too, that they will continue to change colour for a while after you've strained them, so do under-cook rather than overcook them.
3 Strain the nuts (keep the oil for future use) and put the hot nuts into a bowl. Immediately sprinkle with salt and chilli powder.
4 Allow to cool then eat at once. Like any nuts, they will last for several months if stored in a dry container.

COOK'S TIP Raw, shelled skinless almonds can also be cooked by this method.

Pakora
DEEP-FRIED FRITTERS
Throughout India

Pakora is the Indian equivalent of Japanese tempura. Pieces of raw vegetable are coated with a batter made from spiced gram flour. Pieces of raw meat, chicken, fish, prawn and paneer (Indian cheese) can also be used. The batter lightly coats the ingredient to form a crisp outer shell when deep-fried. Pakora are similar to bhajia, meaning 'fried' and anglicized to bhaji or bhajee. Bhajia use the same batter mix but the ingredient is often shredded so that the batter mixes with the ingredient rather than coats it. Pakora are best freshly cooked and served hot.

Makes 8–10

225 g (8 oz) vegetable pieces, such as onion rings, chillies, potato slices, broccoli or cauliflower florets, whole mushrooms
vegetable oil for deep-frying

Batter
75 g (3 oz) gram flour (besan)
1 teaspoon garam masala (see page 60)
1 teaspoon ground coriander
½ teaspoon ground cumin
½ teaspoon turmeric
½ teaspoon cumin seeds
pinch of lovage seeds
2 teaspoons dried fenugreek leaves (optional)
2 tablespoons finely chopped fresh coriander
1 tablespoon chopped fresh mint (optional)
1–2 green chillies, chopped (optional)
1 tablespoon split and polished red lentils (masoor dhal)
1 teaspoon salt
1 egg
1 teaspoon lemon juice

1 Mix all the batter ingredients together in a bowl with just enough water to make a paste thick enough to drop sluggishly off a spoon. Make sure that the batter is well mixed.
2 Heat the oil in a deep frying pan to 190°C/375°F (chip-frying temperature).

3 Coat a vegetable piece in the batter mixture and place it carefully in the hot oil. Continue adding more pakora but allow a few seconds between each one so the oil can maintain its temperature. When the surface area of the pan is full but not crowded, fry the pakora for 8–10 minutes, turning over a few times.

4 Remove the pakora from the pan using a slotted spoon. Shake off the excess oil and drain them on absorbent kitchen paper. Repeat until all the pakora are cooked then serve them hot with salad garnishes, lemon wedges and chutneys.

Ghee Paneer Tikka
CHEESE CUBES FRIED IN GHEE
Throughout India

Paneer (Hindi), or chhana (Bengali), is a curd cheese staple eaten all over India (see the basic recipe, page 62). Here, cubes of paneer are enhanced by frying them in ghee.

Makes 20–24

6 tablespoons ghee (see page 61)
about 225 g (8 oz) paneer cubes (see page 62)

1 Heat the ghee to a medium heat in a non-stick frying pan or tava.
2 Nearly fill the pan with one layer of paneer. Fry for about 2 minutes, then turn the paneer pieces over and continue to fry for 2 more minutes.
3 Serve alone or use in paneer vegetable dishes.

Chilli Paneer Tikka
CHEESE CUBES FRIED IN SWEET CHILLI DIPPING SAUCE
Modern chef's recipe

There are many different dipping sauces available from Asian stores. This simple paneer dish is the invention of chef Kuldeep Singh from London, UK.

Makes 20–24

6 tablespoons sweet red chilli dipping sauce
about 225 g (8 oz) paneer cubes (see page 62)

1 Heat the dipping sauce to a medium heat in a non-stick frying pan or tava.
2 Add enough paneer to nearly fill the pan in one layer. Fry for about 2 minutes, then turn the paneer pieces over and continue to fry for 2 more minutes.
3 Spear the pieces with cocktail sticks and serve as a canapé or starter.

Bommaloe Macchli
BOMBAY DUCK
Mumbai, western India

This condiment derives from a dried fish with a curious name, one of the very few dried fish to appear in Indian cuisine. It is an eel-shaped fish, which abounds in the rivers and estuaries around Bombay, where it is known locally as Bommaloe Macchli or Machi. This was apparently too hard for the British Raj to pronounce, to whom it became known as Bombay Duck. Once caught, the fish is topped, tailed and filleted, and then hung on cane frames to dry in Bombay's fierce sun. When dried it appears in flat, hard strips which are yellowish, tough and visually unpromising, and it will keep indefinitely in a screw-top jar. It can be used in curry, or pickled. More commonly, it is eaten as a crisp, salty nibble with an apéritif, as a starter, or crumbled over curry and rice as a garnish. Some years ago, a ban was incorrectly imposed on imports of dried fish within the European Union. It took years to get the ban lifted, by which time the damage had been done and it had fallen out of fashion. This is a shame because it is a unique condiment. To cook it, deep-fry until crisp and golden. Its strong fishy smell diminishes on cooking but it is still an acquired taste. It has a resemblance to crisp bacon.

2 | poultry

Bhoona Murgh
MILD CHICKEN CURRY
Orissa, east India

Bhoona is the Hindi and Urdu term for the process of cooking a wet-ground masala or ground spice paste in hot oil to create a dryish dish, which is found all over India. In this recipe, the bhoona is enhanced with coconut and fresh coriander.

Serves 4

2 tablespoons vegetable oil
2 or 3 cloves garlic, finely chopped
150 g (5 oz) onion masala sauce (see page 61)
2 tablespoons tinned coconut milk
750 g (1¹/₂ lb) chicken breast, skinned and cut into 2 cm (³/₄ inch) cubes
2 tablespoons finely chopped fresh coriander
salt, to taste

Masala 1
1 tablespoon garam masala (see page 60)
1–2 teaspoons chilli powder
2 teaspoons ground coriander
1 teaspoon turmeric

Masala 2
4 bay leaves
2 pieces of cassia bark, each about 5 x 1 cm (2 x ¹/₂ inch)
6 cloves

1 Mix Masala 1 with a little water to form a paste. Heat the oil in a karahi or wok and stir-fry the paste for a few seconds. Add the garlic and continue to stir-fry for about 30 seconds more.
2 Then add Masala 2, the onion masala sauce and coconut milk, and stir-fry for about 1 minute more.
3 Add the chicken pieces and stir-fry for 10 minutes to make a fairly dry dish, although a little water may be needed to prevent the ingredients sticking to the pan.
4 Add the fresh coriander and stir-fry for a further 2–3 minutes. Cut through one piece of chicken to ensure that it is fully cooked – it should be white right through with no hint of pink. Season with salt and serve.

Cafreal
OVEN-COOKED MARINATED CHICKEN
Goa, Indian west coast

Portuguese Africans from Mozambique, a 16th-century staging post to and from Goa, were employed for menial tasks including cooking. They were known as 'kaffirs' and this dish, cafreal, in which on-the-bone chicken pieces are marinated and then oven-cooked, is said to have been invented by them and named after them.

Serves 4

4 large chicken legs (thigh and drumstick), skinned

Marinade
175 ml (6 fl oz) fresh lemon juice
200 ml (7 fl oz) tinned coconut milk
10–12 cloves garlic, chopped
1–3 fresh red chillies, chopped
1 tablespoon sunflower oil
1 teaspoon salt

Garnish
fried cashew nuts (kaju, see page 87)
snipped fresh chives

1 Mix the marinade ingredients together in a bowl.
2 Cut small gashes in the chicken legs using a sharp knife and work the marinade into the flesh. Put the chicken in a shallow non-aluminium bowl

(see cook's tip page 77) with all the excess marinade. Cover and refrigerate for up to 24 hours.

3 Place the chicken legs, topped by any excess marinade, in an oven tray. Cover with foil and cook in a preheated oven, 190°C/375°F/Gas 5, for 10 minutes.

4 Turn the chicken legs over, baste with the marinade, cover them with foil again and cook for 10 minutes more.

5 Using a sharp knife, cut to the bone to test that the chicken is fully cooked – the juices should run clear. Serve garnished with cashew nuts and fresh chives.

Kobiraji
CHICKEN FRIED IN EGG BATTER

Assam, north-east India

In the the foothills of India's Assam, west Bengal and the former East Bengal, now Bangladesh, a Bhuddist tribe called the Mogs can still be found. In the days of the British Raj, Mogs became household cooks, and working with their British memsahibs, they created Anglo-Indian food. This is one such recipe.

Serves 4

vegetable oil for deep-frying
500 g (1 lb 2 oz) chicken breast, skinned and
   cut into 2 cm (³/₄ inch) cubes

Sauce

3 tablespoons sunflower or soya oil
2 or 3 cloves garlic, finely chopped
300 ml (10 fl oz) brown onion paste (see
   page 61)
1–3 green chillies, finely chopped
400 ml (14 fl oz) water or fragrant stock (see
   page 59)
salt, to taste

Masala

2 tablespoons mustard powder
1 teaspoon turmeric
1 teaspoon nigella (wild onion) seeds
1 teaspoon yellow mustard seeds
¹/₄–1 teaspoon chilli powder

Batter

100 g (4 oz) gram flour (besan)
1 teaspoon turmeric
1 or 2 green chillies, finely chopped
1 teaspoon salt
1 egg

1 Start by making the sauce. Heat the oil in a karahi or wok. Stir-fry the masala for 15 seconds. Add the garlic and stir-fry for 15 seconds. Add the onion paste and fresh chillies and stir-fry for 2 more minutes.

2 Add the water or stock, little by little, and simmer to reduce the sauce to the consistency that you like.

3 Meanwhile, mix the batter ingredients together in a bowl with just enough water to make a paste thick enough to drop sluggishly off a spoon. Set aside.

4 Heat the oil for deep-frying in a deep frying pan to 190°C/375°F (chip-frying temperature).

5 Inspect the batter mixture. Make sure that it is well mixed and there is no 'powder' left. Coat one chicken piece in the batter mixture and place it carefully in the hot oil. Coat and add more chicken pieces in the same way but allow a few seconds between each addition so that the oil maintains its temperature. When the surface area of the pan is full but not crowded, fry the chicken pieces for 8–10 minutes each, turning over a few times.

6 Remove them from the pan, in the order they went in, using a slotted spoon. Shake off the excess oil and leave them to drain on absorbent kitchen paper.

7 Repeat until all the chicken pieces are cooked. Serve them hot with the sauce poured over the top.

Chachchori Morog
STIR-FRIED CHICKEN CURRY
Bengal, north-east India

Chachchori/charchori is a Bengali method of dry-frying, like a bhoona, but less spicy. The distinctly Bengali spicing can vary according to choice but usually includes at least some panch phoran, while turmeric and chilli are mandatory. White poppy seeds are sometimes present, and help to give the dish a crunchier texture. Little if any water should be used, and any ingredient can be cooked by this method. Serve with rice or bread and chutneys and/or pickles or serve alongside other curries.

Serves 4

3 tablespoons mustard-blend oil

$1/2$ teaspoon turmeric

1 teaspoon panch phoran (see page 62)

2 teaspoons white poppy seeds

25 g (1 oz) split and polished gram lentils (chana dhal)

$1/2$–1 teaspoon chopped dried red chillies

2 or 3 cloves garlic, finely chopped or puréed

225 g (8 oz) caramelized onions (see page 61)

2 tablespoons thin strips of red pepper

$1/2$–1 tablespoon chopped fresh red chilli

625 g (1 lb 5 oz) chicken breast, skinned and cut into 2 cm ($3/4$ inch) cubes

1 tablespoon finely chopped fresh coriander

salt, to taste

1 Heat the oil in a karahi or wok. Stir-fry the turmeric, panch phoran, poppy seeds, lentils and dried red chillies for 15 seconds. Add the garlic and stir-fry for about 1 minute more.

2 Add most of the fried onions, red pepper and fresh chilli and stir-fry for 2 more minutes. Set aside 2 tablespoons of this mixture for a garnish.

Stir-fried chicken curry

3 Add the chicken pieces, and stir-fry for about 15 minutes to make a fairly dry dish. Add a little water, if necessary, to prevent sticking.

4 Cut through one piece of chicken to ensure that it is fully cooked – it should be white right through with no hint of pink. Season the curry with salt and add the fresh coriander.

5 Serve garnished with the reserved onion, red pepper and fresh chilli mixture.

Koli Nallamalu
CHICKEN IN A DARK PEPPER SAUCE
Coorg, Karnataka, southern India

This chicken is slow cooked until the sauce is very dark and very aromatic with black pepper. The dish is unique to Coorg, or Kodagu, one of Karnataka's most beautiful hill regions and the source of the river Kauvery. The people of Coorg are a conglomorate of tribes – first Scythians, then Moplas and now Coorgs (or Kodvas). The Coorgs love to hunt and are known to be partial to partridge. Coorgs use kachampuli (Coorg vinegar – see page 122) but red wine vinegar is a good alternative.

Serves 4

3 tablespoons vegetable oil

4–6 cloves garlic, finely chopped or puréed

2.5 cm (1 inch) piece of fresh root ginger, shredded

225 g (8 oz) brown onion paste (see page 61)

1 spring or grilling chicken, about 1.5 kg (3 lb), skinned, or 4 partridges, 350–400 g (12–14 oz) each, skinned

4 tablespoons red wine vinegar

400 ml (14 fl oz) water or fragrant stock (see page 59)

1 bunch of coriander

salt, to taste

Masala 1

3–6 teaspoons finely ground black pepper

4 teaspoons ground coriander

2 teaspoons paprika

1/4–1 teaspoon chilli powder

Masala 2

1 or 2 green chillies, finely chopped

10–12 fresh or dried curry leaves (optional)

4 brown/black cardamoms

1 teaspoon black cumin seeds

1 Heat the oil in a karahi or wok. Stir-fry Masala 1 for 15 seconds. Add the garlic and stir-fry for about 30 seconds, then add the ginger and onion paste and stir-fry for 1 minute more. Set aside.

2 Place the chicken or partridges in a 2.25–2.75 litre (4–5 pint) lidded casserole dish and add the stir-fry, Masala 2, red wine vinegar and the water or stock. Place in a preheated oven, 190°C/375°F/Gas 5.

3 After 20 minutes, inspect, stir and taste. Add a little water if needed then return the casserole dish to the oven.

4 After a further 20 minutes inspect again. This time add the fresh coriander before replacing the casserole in the oven.

5 After a final 20 minutes, taste the dish. The chicken or partridge flesh should be tender. Season with salt and serve.

Kozhi Varattiyathu
DEEP-FRIED CHICKEN DRUMSTICKS

Malabar, Kerala, south India

In this Malabari recipe chicken drumsticks are marinated in a paste before being deep-fried.

Serves 4

8 chicken drumsticks, skinned

vegetable oil for deep-frying

Marinade

2 tablespoons gram flour (besan)

2 tablespoons plain white flour

10–12 curry leaves, finely chopped (optional)

2 or 3 cloves garlic, puréed

2.5 cm (1 inch) piece of fresh root ginger, puréed

2 tablespoons coriander seeds, crushed

3 green chillies, finely chopped

1 teaspoon peppercorns, crushed

1/4 teaspoon turmeric

2 tablespoons lemon juice

1–2 teaspoons chilli powder

1 teaspoon salt

1 Mix the marinade ingredients together in a bowl with just enough water to make a stiff paste.

2 Cut small gashes in the chicken drumsticks using a sharp knife and work the marinade into the flesh.

3 Put the drumsticks in a shallow non-aluminium bowl (see cook's tip page 77) with all the excess marinade. Cover and refrigerate for up to 24 hours.

4 To cook, heat the oil in a deep frying pan to 190°C/375°F. Add one drumstick to the hot oil. After a few seconds add the next, and continue until all the drumsticks are in. Fry for 10–12 minutes.

5 Remove the drumsticks from the pan using a slotted spoon. Shake off the excess oil and drain them on absorbent kitchen paper. Serve with dosa or an Indian bread.

Kori Gassi
MANGALOREAN CHICKEN CURRY
Mangalore, Karnataka, southern India

Kori is chicken, gassi is a mixture of coconut, red chillies, peppercorns, spices, tamarind and onion.

Serves 4

3 tablespoons sunflower or soya oil

2 or 3 cloves garlic, finely chopped

2.5 cm (1 inch) piece of fresh root ginger, shredded

225 g (8 oz) white onion paste (see page 61)

4 large chicken legs (thigh and drumstick), skinned

200 g (7 oz) fresh coconut flesh, grated

2 tablespoons tamarind purée (see page 62)

200 ml (7 fl oz) water or fragrant stock (see page 59)

salt, to taste

Masala
1 tablespoon coriander seeds

1 tablespoon cumin seeds

1 teaspoon chilli powder

1 tablespoon black peppercorns

1/2 teaspoon fenugreek seeds

1/2 teaspoon turmeric

2–4 dried red chillies

1 Heat the oil in a karahi or wok. Add the masala and stir-fry for 15 seconds. Add the garlic and stir-fry for about 30 seconds, then add the fresh ginger and onion paste and stir-fry for 1 minute more.
2 Mix this with the chicken pieces then place the chicken and the remaining ingredients in an oven tray. Cover with foil and cook in a preheated oven, 190°C/375°F/Gas 5, for 10 minutes.
3 Turn the chicken pieces over, baste with the sauce in the pan, cover again with foil and cook for 10 minutes more.

4 Using a sharp knife, cut to the bone to test that the chicken is fully cooked – the juices should run clear – then serve.

Maasah
SPICED STUFFED PEPPERS
Modern chef's recipe

In this recipe peppers are stuffed with a filling of chicken keema and rice, baked and then served with a sweet and sour sauce. This dish is from London chef Pital Gopal.

Serves 4

8 firm peppers, any colour

4 teaspoons sunflower oil

Filling
200 g (7 oz) minced chicken breast

200 g (7 oz) mashed potato

2 or 3 cloves garlic, finely chopped

2.5 cm (1 inch) piece of fresh root ginger, shredded

1–4 green chillies, finely chopped

2 teaspoons ground coriander

1/2 teaspoon salt

1/2 teaspoon chilli powder

pinch of asafoetida

1 Cut the stalk end off the peppers and reserve. Scoop out any pith and seeds from the pepper cavities, being careful not to break the skin.
2 Mix all the filling ingredients together then press the filling firmly into each pepper cavity until level with the top. Drizzle 1/2 teaspoon oil over the top of each stuffed pepper and cover with a cut-off stalk end.
3 Wedge the 8 peppers in a foil-lined oven dish so that they can all stand upright without falling over.
4 Bake in a preheated oven, 160°C /325°F/Gas 3, for 15–20 minutes. Serve with rice, and/or breads.

Makhani Murgh
BUTTER CHICKEN
Moghul origin, northern India

This dish yields a generous amount of rich sauce, which is an unexpected red colour due to its use of paprika and tomato. The British media claim that chicken tikka masala, a dish of clay oven-baked chicken in a red sauce is not an Indian dish, but a modern British invention. The French claim they invented cooking with garlic and butter. Both myths can be dispelled here. This dish was around in Moghul times, 450 years ago, long before chicken tikka masala hit the headlines and before French haute cuisine. Butter has been used in Indian cooking for over 600 years.

Serves 4

2 tablespoons ghee (see page 61)
4–6 cloves garlic, finely chopped or puréed
225 g (8 oz) onion masala sauce (see page 61)
200 g (7 oz) tinned tomatoes, puréed
1 tablespoon tomato purée
1 teaspoon garam masala (see page 60)
1 tablespoon chopped fresh coriander
24 cooked malai chicken tikka pieces (murgh malai tikka, see page 77)
50 g (2 oz) butter, any type
salt, to taste

Red Masala
2 tablespoons paprika
2 teaspoons ground coriander
1½ teaspoons ground cumin
chilli powder, to taste

Garnish
fresh coriander
almond flakes, toasted
single cream

1 Heat the ghee in a large wok. Stir-fry the garlic and the red masala for 30 seconds, then add the onion masala sauce and stir-fry for 2 more minutes.
2 Add the puréed tinned tomatoes, tomato purée, garam masala and coriander. Stir-fry for 5 minutes or so, until the oil separates.
3 Then add the cooked chicken and any spare cooked marinade. Simmer for a further 2 or 3 minutes, adding a little water if needed to prevent the ingredients sticking.
4 Season with salt. Add the butter and simmer for a few moments more.
5 Garnish with the coriander, toasted flaked almonds and a curl of cream.

Mirchwangan Korma
RED HOT CHILLI CHICKEN KORMA
Kashmir, extreme northern India

Korma is a style of cooking, and does not necessarily mean mild, as this seriously hot traditional dish from the Kashmir Maharajas firmly proves. On-the-bone chicken pieces are marinated in tomato purée, paprika, red wine, bottled beetroot, red chillies and red pepper, with an aromatic masala.

Serves 4

750 g (1½ lb) chicken drumsticks, skinned
3 tablespoons ghee (see page 61)
4 cloves garlic, finely chopped
225 g (8 oz) onion masala sauce (see page 61)
½ red pepper, sliced
20 fresh crimson (or dried) Kashmiri chillies, or 10 dried red chillies, any type
1 tablespoon garam masala (see page 60)
1 tablespoon finely chopped fresh coriander
salt, to taste

Butter chicken

Marinade

1 tablespoon paprika

1 teaspoon coriander

1 teaspoon cumin

1 tablespoon extra hot chilli powder

2 tablespoons tomato purée

1 unvinegared, cooked peeled beetroot, sliced

120 ml (4 fl oz) red wine

1 Put the marinade ingredients and the ground masala in a blender or food processor and 'pulse' to a pouring paste using water as needed.

2 Mix the marinade ingredients and chicken drumsticks in a large non-aluminium bowl (see cook's tip page 77). Cover and refrigerate for up to 48 hours.

3 To cook, heat the ghee in a large karahi or wok and stir-fry the garlic for 30 seconds.

4 Add the onion masala sauce and cook for 5 minutes. Then add the chicken and all of the marinade to the pan. Cook for 5 minutes, stirring as needed, and adding a little water if needed to prevent sticking.

5 Add the remaining ingredients and continue cooking for about 15 more minutes. Season with salt and serve.

Raan-e-Murgh
BAKED CHICKEN LEGS

Moghul origin, northern India

Here, chicken legs are marinated then baked and served with a uniquely flavoured sauce made from garlic, onion, spices and chilli. See the recipe for Raan on page 124 for the lamb version.

Serves 4

8 chicken drumsticks, skinned

Baked chicken legs

Marinade

about 120 ml (4 fl oz) milk

200 g (7 oz) plain yogurt

200 ml (7 fl oz) single cream

2 tablespoons vegetable oil

2 tablespoons fresh lemon juice

3 or 4 cloves garlic, chopped

2.5 cm (1 inch) piece of fresh root ginger, chopped

2 or 3 fresh red chillies, chopped

1 tablespoon finely chopped fresh coriander

2 tablespoons ground almonds

1 teaspoon salt

Masala

2 tablespoons ground coriander

1 tablespoon garam masala (see page 60)

2 teaspoons cardamom pods, ground

1 teaspoon fennel seeds

1 Adding the milk little by little, put all the marinade ingredients and the masala in a blender or food processor and 'pulse' to a pourable purée.

2 Cut small gashes in the chicken drumsticks using a sharp knife and work the marinade into the flesh.

3 Put the drumsticks in a shallow non-aluminium bowl (see cook's tip page 77) with all the excess marinade. Cover and refrigerate for up to 24 hours.

4 To cook, put the chicken drumsticks, topped by any excess marinade in an oven tray. Cover with foil and cook in a preheated oven, 190°C/375°F/Gas 5, for 10 minutes.

5 Turn the drumsticks over, baste with the marinade, cover again with foil and cook for 10 minutes more.

6 Using a sharp knife, cut to the bone to test that the chicken is fully cooked – the juices should run clear.

7 There will be a reasonable amount of cooked marinade in the oven tray. Place this in a saucepan and mix well. When simmering, pour it over the drumsticks to serve.

Murgh Masala

RICE-STUFFED ROASTED WHOLE CHICKEN

Maharaja and Moghul origin

This dish, also known as kurzi murgh, originated in ancient Persia, when peacock would have been the bird of choice. In this recipe a whole chicken is marinated then stuffed with cooked rice and roasted. A boned chicken makes the dish ultra-luxurious. Choose any of the rice recipes in Chapter 7 for stuffing the chicken. Note that cavity sizes vary from bird to bird.

Serves 4

about 1.75 kg (4 lb) roasting chicken

Marinade
500 g (1 lb 2 oz) natural yogurt
4 tablespoons vegetable oil
12 cloves garlic, finely chopped
5 cm (2 inch) piece of fresh root ginger, finely chopped
4–6 fresh red chillies
1 tablespoon garam masala (see page 60)

Stuffing
any of the rice recipes from Chapter 7, cooked
2 or 3 hard-boiled eggs

Masala 1
4 bay leaves
4–6 green cardamoms
8–10 cloves
1 teaspoon peppercorns

Masala 2
1/2–2 teaspoons chilli powder
2 teaspoons ground coriander
2 teaspoons cumin seeds
1/2 teaspoon turmeric

Sauce
2 tablespoons ghee (see page 61)
3 or 4 cloves garlic, finely chopped
5 cm (2 inch) piece of fresh root ginger, finely chopped
200 g (7 oz) brown onion paste (see page 61)
1 tablespoon tomato purée
400 g (14 oz) tinned tomatoes, puréed
2 tablespoons finely chopped fresh coriander
salt, to taste

1 Put all the marinade ingredients in a blender or food processor and 'pulse' to a pouring paste using water as needed.

2 Skin the chicken, keeping it whole, then wash it inside and out and remove all unwanted matter. Dry the chicken and cut gashes in the flesh using a sharp pointed knife. Rub the chicken all over, inside and out, with the marinade paste. Put it in a non-aluminium bowl (see cook's tip page 77), cover and refrigerate overnight, or for at least 12 hours.

3 To make the stuffing, mix the cooked rice and Masala 1 together then combine with the whole shelled hard-boiled eggs. Gently cram the chicken cavity with this mixture.

4 Carefully wrap the chicken in foil and place it on a rack above an oven tray in the oven. Roast in a preheated oven, 190°C/375°F/Gas 5, for a total of 1 1/2 hours for a 1.75 kg (4 lb) bird. Deduct or add 4 minutes per 100 g (4 oz) for weight under or over this.

5 Meanwhile, make the sauce. Heat the ghee in a karahi or wok. Add Masala 2 and stir-fry for 30 seconds. Add the garlic and stir-fry for another 30 seconds. Add the ginger and the onion paste and stir-fry for 30 seconds more. Add the tomato purée, puréed tinned tomatoes and the fresh coriander and simmer for 5 or 6 minutes. Season with salt.

6 After 20 minutes of roasting discard the foil around the chicken and baste the bird with one-third of the sauce.

7 Repeat the basting twice at 20-minute intervals. It will need further roasting according to step 4.

8 At the end of the cooking time, check that the chicken is cooked by inserting a meat thermometer into the flesh; it should read 73°C (163°F). Alternatively, push a small skewer into the flesh at one leg joint – if the juices run clear, the chicken is ready. If the juices are pink, continue cooking the chicken for a little longer.

9 Sprinkle the fresh coriander over the chicken then serve with any spare sauce and roasted root vegetables (see page 177).

Qasuri Methi ke Sag Murgh
FENUGREEK & SPINACH-FLAVOURED CHICKEN
Punjab, north-west India

The savoury flavours of fenugreek leaf and spinach make this the signature dish of the Punjab.

Serves 4

8 chicken drumsticks, skinned
3 tablespoons ghee (see page 61)
4–6 cloves garlic, coarsely chopped
5 cm (2 inch) piece of fresh root ginger, coarsely chopped
225 g (8 oz) onion masala sauce (see page 61)
2 or 3 tomatoes, coarsely chopped
1 tablespoon tomato purée
200 g (7 oz) tinned spinach purée
2 tablespoons dried fenugreek leaves
3 tablespoons coarsely chopped fresh coriander
salt, to taste

Marinade
175 g (6 oz) yogurt
50 ml (2 fl oz) single cream
1$\frac{1}{2}$ teaspoons paprika
1$\frac{1}{2}$ teaspoons ground coriander
1 teaspoon chilli powder

Masala
2 teaspoons paprika
1 teaspoon garam masala (see page 60)
2 teaspoons ground coriander
1 teaspoon ground cumin
1 teaspoon turmeric

1 Mix the marinade ingredients together in a bowl. Cut small gashes in the chicken drumsticks using a sharp knife and work the marinade into the flesh. Place in a shallow non-aluminium bowl (see cook's tip page 77) with all the excess marinade. Cover and refrigerate for up to 24 hours.

2 To cook, remove the chicken from the marinade, shaking off and reserving any excess, but ensuring that there is a liberal coating left on each piece. Place on an oven tray and bake in a preheated oven, 190°C/375°F/Gas 5, for 20 minutes, then remove and keep warm. Strain the liquid off the oven tray and reserve.

3 Heat the ghee in a karahi or wok. Stir-fry the masala for 15 seconds. Add the garlic and stir-fry for about 30 seconds, then add the ginger and stir-fry for 1 minute more. Add the onion masala sauce and continue stir-frying for another minute. Add the tomatoes, tomato purée, spinach, fenugreek and the coriander leaves and simmer for 5 or 6 minutes. Season with salt.

4 Add the cooked drumsticks and any juices to the sauce, mix well and serve with an Indian bread.

Rezala Morgh
RICH-TASTING HOT CHICKEN
Bengal, north-east India

The traditional Bengali rezala contains no red colours – a natural 'grey' look is acceptable, yellow is usual (thanks to the saffron and turmeric in this recipe). Fresh green chilli is mandatory. The unashamed richness of this dish comes from hand-stirred reduced milk called kisha, or koya, replicated here by the use of identically flavoured tinned evaporated milk. You can omit the sugar and raisins, a taste beloved by some Bengalis, if you like, but do use top-quality rosewater for a gorgeous fragrance.

Serves 4

4 tablespoons ghee (see page 61)
1 teaspoon turmeric
10–12 cloves garlic, very finely chopped
225 g (8 oz) caramelized onions (see page 61)
675 g (1 lb 6 oz) chicken breast, skinned and
    cut into 2 cm (3/4 inch) cubes
3 or 4 green chillies, sliced lengthwise
400 g (14 oz) tin evaporated milk
20–30 saffron strands (optional)
1 tablespoon raisins (optional)
2 teaspoons white granulated sugar (optional)
2 tablespoons chopped pistachio nuts
1 tablespoon ground almonds
1 teaspoon garam masala (see page 60)
1 tablespoon rosewater
salt, to taste

Masala
12 green cardamoms, crushed
3 or 4 pieces of cassia bark, each about
    5 x 1 cm (2 x 1/2 inch)
2 teaspoons panch phoran (see page 62)

1 Heat the ghee in a karahi or wok. Add the masala and stir-fry for 30 seconds. Reduce the heat and add the turmeric and garlic, stir-frying for about 1 minute.
2 Add the onion tarka and continue stir-frying for another 2 minutes.
3 Add the chicken and the chillies. When sizzling, add the evaporated milk and the saffron, if using.
4 Simmer for about 15 minutes, then add the remaining ingredients except the salt and the rosewater.
5 Simmer for a further 5 minutes. Cut through one piece of chicken to ensure that it is fully cooked – it should be white right through with no hint of pink. Season with salt and add the rosewater. Serve with plain rice.

Zeera Murgh
CHICKEN COOKED WITH CUMIN
Modern chef's recipe

The speciality of London chef Sanjay Anand, this recipe is probably one of the simplest dishes in this book, and also one of the tastiest. In it chicken chunks are stir-fried with butter, cumin and salt.

Serves 4

50 g (2 oz) unsalted butter
1 tablespoon cumin seeds
2 tablespoons cumin, ground
150 ml (5 fl oz) water or fragrant stock (see
    page 59)
500 g (1 lb 2 oz) chicken breast, skinned and
    cut into 2 cm (3/4 inch) cubes
salt, to taste

1 Heat the butter in a karahi or wok to quite a high heat. Add the cumin seeds and stir-fry for about 30 seconds. Add the ground cumin and stir-fry for a further 30 seconds, then add 3 or 4 tablespoons of the water or stock and stir-fry for 2 or 3 minutes.

2 Add the chicken pieces and stir-fry briskly for about 2 minutes, then reduce the heat slightly, and over the next 5 minutes add the remaining water or stock, stirring as needed.

3 To finish off, increase the heat and resume a brisk stirring for about 5 minutes to reduce the remaining liquid to form a dryish gravy and coating.

4 Cut through one piece of chicken to ensure that it is fully cooked – it should be white right through with no hint of pink. If not, continue stir-frying until it is. Season with salt then serve with Indian breads.

Bahn Morog Shikari
WILD FOWL CURRY
Bengal, north-east India

In this Bengali recipe, the bird would traditionally have been red jungle fowl, the ancestor of the modern chicken, but these are now in short supply. This version uses partridge or pheasant instead.

Serves 4

4 partridges, 350–400 g (12–14 oz) each, or
  2 female pheasants, about 1 kg (2¼ lb)
  each, weighed after skinning and removing all
  unwanted matter
2 tablespoons mustard-blend oil
1 teaspoon wild onion seeds
2 or 3 cloves garlic, chopped
200 g (7 oz) brown onion paste (see page 61)
350 ml (12 fl oz) water or fragrant stock (see
  page 59)
1–2 green chillies, finely chopped
1 tablespoon coarsely chopped fresh coriander
salt, to taste

Masala
6 cloves
3 or 4 brown/black cardamoms
1–3 pieces of cassia bark, each about
  5 x 1 cm (2 x ½ inch)
2 or 3 bay leaves

1 Skin the partridges or pheasants and cut each into joints, i.e. 2 drumsticks, 2 thighs, the back (halved) and 2 wings.

2 Heat the oil in a karahi or wok and stir-fry the wild onion seeds for 30 seconds, then add the garlic and stir-fry for 30 seconds more. Add the onion paste and stir-fry for 1 further minute.

3 Add the masala, water or stock, the partridge or pheasant pieces, chillies and coriander and simmer over a low heat for 15–20 minutes or until the water has been cooked out. Serve with plain rice.

Dopeyaja Harsh
ONION-SWEETENED DUCK
Moghul origin, northern India

Originating in Persia, this dish became a firm Moghul favourite. A 1590 book describing court life describes it as 'a meat dish cooked with ghee, spices, yogurt and a lot of onion'. Do meaning 'two' and peyaja (or piaza), meaning 'onions' gets its name from the double batch of onions that appear in the recipe, one in the initial fry, the other later in the cooking. The caramelized onions added at the end provide a natural sweet taste, which greatly suits duck breast.

Serves 4

3 tablespoons ghee (see page 61)
3 or 4 cloves garlic, finely chopped
225 g (8 oz) fried onions
4 tablespoons yogurt

675 g (1 lb 6 oz) duck breast, weighed after
    removing all unwanted matter, cut into 4 cm
    (1^1/$_2$ inch) cubes
100 g (4 oz) onion, thinly sliced
250 ml (9 fl oz) water or fragrant stock (see
    page 59)
2 or 3 fresh red chillies, shredded (optional)
2 tablespoons finely chopped fresh coriander
2 teaspoons garam masala (see page 60)
100 g (4 oz) caramelized onions (see page 61)
salt, to taste

Masala

2 teaspoons coriander seeds, roasted and
    ground
^{1}/$_2$ teaspoon cumin seeds, roasted and ground
1 teaspoon turmeric
1 teaspoon chilli powder

1 Heat the ghee in a karahi or wok and stir-fry the
garlic for 30 seconds. Add the masala and stir-fry
for 1 minute. Add the fried onions, yogurt and the
duck, mix well and stir-fry for 3 or 4 minutes
2 Transfer the contents of the pan to a
2.25–2.75 litre (4–5 pint) lidded casserole dish,
cover and put in a preheated oven,
190°C/375°F/Gas 5.
3 After about 15 minutes, inspect and add the
chopped onion strips, the water or stock and
chillies, if using. Return the casserole to the oven
for a further 20–25 minutes.
4 Inspect again, this time adding the fresh
coriander and garam masala. Return to the oven for
a final 20 minutes, or until the duck is tender and
the liquid reduced to a thick consistency, about half
its original volume.
5 Add the onion tarka and season with salt. Return
the casserole dish, lid off, to the oven. Switch off
and leave it for 10 minutes, before serving with dhal
and parathas.

Dum Pukht ke Titaar
SEALED PARTRIDGE
Lucknow, northern India

Dum pukht literally means 'containing the steam'.
The technique originated in ancient Persia and
involved filling a cast-iron vessel with meat and
spices, sealing a tightly fitting lid in place with
chupatti dough, and cooking it. The dish was
then unsealed at the table so that waiting diners
could enjoy the release of the cooking aroma (see
page 31). The method has enjoyed a recent revival
in modern India thanks to master chef Imtiaz
Qureshi, who took it to India's Sheraton Group.
Since dum pukht really is special, a special bird –
partridge (titaar) – is used here.

Serves 4

4 partridges, 350–400 g (12–14 oz) each,
    skinned
4 cloves garlic, whole
2.5 cm (1 inch) piece of fresh root ginger,
    shredded
200 g (7 oz) onion, cut into strips
2 or 3 green chillies, thinly sliced
1 tablespoon palm sugar (jaggery) or brown
    sugar
450 ml (15 fl oz) water or fragrant stock (see
    page 59)
1 green pepper, cut into strips
2 tablespoons coarsely chopped fresh coriander
2 teaspoons garam masala (see page 60)
1 teaspoon salt

Masala

2 teaspoons coriander seeds
1 teaspoon cumin seeds
2 pieces of cassia bark, each about 5 x 1 cm
    (2 x ^{1}/$_2$ inch)
6–8 cloves
1 teaspoon fennel seeds

1 Roast and grind the masala, following the instructions on page 60.

2 Combine all the ingredients in a 2.25–2.75 litre (4–5 pint) lidded casserole dish.

3 Cook the casserole, lid on, in a preheated oven, 190°C/375°F/Gas 5, for 1 hour, then serve with Indian bread or rice.

Kalia
PHEASANT IN A THIN RED SAUCE
Bengal, north-east India

Kalia (qalia/qaliya) is a curry made from water and/or milk, creating a thin sauce (whereas korma is an oil-based method where all water is reduced out of the cooking). This kalia is particular to Lucknow, Bengal and Bangladesh. Red colours are mandatory, from the chilli and tomato. Spicing includes white poppy seeds. The choice of pheasant (see cook's tip below) with its dark, gamey flesh, particularly suits kalia.

Serves 4

4 tablespoons ghee (see page 61)

2 cloves garlic, chopped

2.5 cm (1 inch) piece of fresh root ginger, very finely chopped

225 g (8 oz) caramelized onions (see page 61)

2 female pheasants, about 1 kg (2¼ lb) each, weighed after skinning and removing all unwanted matter

400 ml (14 fl oz) water or fragrant stock (see page 59)

1 or 2 fresh red chillies, sliced

2 teaspoons tomato purée

1 tablespoon tomato ketchup

100 g (4 oz) carrots, sliced

2 teaspoons garam masala (see page 60)

1 teaspoon finely chopped fresh coriander

salt, to taste

Masala

1 teaspoon white cumin seeds

½ teaspoon coriander seeds, crushed

2 pieces of cassia bark, each about 5 x 1 cm (2 x ½ inch)

2 or 3 bay leaves

1 teaspoon poppy seeds (posta dana)

½ teaspoon chilli powder

½ teaspoon turmeric

1 Heat the ghee in a karahi or wok. Add the garlic and stir-fry for 30 seconds. Add the ginger and cook for another 30 seconds. Add the masala and stir-fry for 30 seconds more. Add the onions and stir-fry for another 30 seconds.

2 Add the pheasants and stir-fry for 5 minutes.

3 Place the pheasants in a lidded casserole dish and add the water or stock, the contents of the karahi or wok, the chillies, tomato purée, ketchup and carrots. Cook the casserole in a preheated oven, 190°C/375°F/Gas 5.

4 After 15 minutes inspect and stir, adding a little more water if needed. Cook for 15 more minutes. Add the garam masala and fresh coriander and season with salt. Cook for a final 10 minutes or so, by which time the pheasants should be really tender. Using a sharp knife, cut to the bone to test that the pheasant is fully cooked – the juices should run clear.

5 Serve with a lentil and/or vegetable dish and a rice.

COOK'S TIP The young female pheasant provides the tenderest meat with the best flavour. It averages 1.25 kg (2½ lb) and should serve 3. The cock bird is slightly larger at 1.5 kg (3 lb) but its meat is generally tougher and drier and yields less.

Shikar ki Buttuck
WILD DUCK
Maharajah origin

This recipe, meaning 'hunted (of) duck' (or literally 'wild duck'), is typically found at the Maharajas' dining tables. The whole duck is casseroled in a yogurt, nut paste and spice mixture. Mallard, pintail, teal and widgeon are favourite wild duck, among others. There is quite a weight variation between species, and the largest (mallard) is considerably smaller than a domestic duck. A mallard at 1.25 kg (2½ lb) will just serve 2 to 3 people. A teal at 350 g (12 oz) is enough for a single portion.

My wife and I had this dish at a rather elegant Delhi dinner party. After the meal, another guest confided to my wife that he had just commited a 'faux pas' with the hostess. 'I told her I loved her buttuck,' he whispered. 'She misheard and thought I was referring to her posterior.'

Serves 4

2 wild ducks, about 1 kg (2¼ lb) each
2–3 cloves garlic, finely chopped
225 g (8 oz) onion, cut into long strips
400 ml (14 fl oz) water or fragrant stock (see page 59)
2 tablespoons coarsely chopped fresh coriander
1 tablespoon finely chopped fresh mint
2 teaspoons garam masala (see page 60)
salt, to taste

Marinade
100 g (4 oz) natural yogurt
3 tablespoons cashew nuts
1 teaspoon chopped fresh mint
2 or 3 fresh red chillies
2.5 cm (1 inch) piece of fresh root ginger
2 or 3 cloves garlic, finely chopped or puréed

1 Skin the ducks, removing as much fat as possible, and cut each into joints, i.e. 2 drumsticks, 2 thighs, the back (halved) and 2 wings.
2 Grind the marinade ingredients in a blender or food processor to make a pourable paste.
3 Coat the duck pieces with the marinade in a non-aluminium bowl (see cook's tip page 77). Cover and refrigerate for 24–60 hours.
4 To cook, place the duck pieces on a foil-lined oven tray. Pour any remaining marinade over each piece. Bake in a preheated oven, 190°C/375°F/Gas 5, for 15 minutes.
5 Transfer the duck to a 2.25–2.75 litre (4–5 pint) lidded casserole dish. Add the garlic, onion strips, water or stock then place the casserole, lid on, in the oven to cook.
6 After 15 minutes, inspect, stir and taste. Add a little water if needed to prevent sticking, then return the casserole to the oven.
7 After 10 minutes inspect again. This time add the fresh coriander, mint and garam masala. Replace the casserole in the oven again.
8 After a final 10 minutes, season with salt and serve.

Tak-a-Tan
CHOPPED TURKEY STIR-FRY
Modern chef's recipe

This fascinating dish is made on a huge, flat frying pan called a tava and derives its name from its special metal tools, shaped like flat, blunt-ended spoons. While a sauce base and the meat are cooking in the tava, the chef takes one tool in each hand and chops the ingredients with a rhythmic metallic clacking – 'taka-taka-taka-taka'. This version is from London chef Hardeep Singh.

Serves 4

Wild duck

4 tablespoons ghee (see page 61)

2 or 3 cloves garlic, finely chopped or puréed

2.5 cm (1 inch) piece of fresh root ginger, shredded

2 large onions, finely chopped

1/2 red pepper, cut into strips

1 or 2 fresh red chillies, finely chopped

1 tablespoon tamarind purée (see page 62)

4 tomatoes, chopped

625 g (1 lb 5 oz) turkey leg meat, skinned and cut into 2 cm (3/4 inch) cubes

2 tablespoons coarsely chopped fresh coriander

salt, to taste

Masala

1 teaspoon white cumin seeds

1 teaspoon black mustard seeds

1 teaspoon ground coriander

1 teaspoon paprika

1/2 teaspoon black peppercorns, crushed

1/2 teaspoon chilli powder

1/2 teaspoon fenugreek seeds

1/2 teaspoon turmeric

1 Heat the ghee in a karahi or wok. Stir-fry the masala for 15 seconds. Add the garlic and stir-fry for about 15 seconds more. Add the ginger and stir-fry for another 15 seconds.

2 Add the onions, red pepper, fresh chillies, tamarind and tomatoes and stir-fry for 5 minutes. Reserve 2 tablespoons of this mix for garnish.

3 Add the turkey pieces, and stir-fry for 18–20 minutes to make a fairly dry dish, although a little water may be needed to prevent the ingredients sticking to the pan.

4 Season with salt, and add the fresh coriander. Chop the turkey pieces smaller if you wish. Serve garnished with the 2 tablespoons of the mixture saved earlier.

Soola ka Battar

DESERT BARBECUED QUAIL

Rajasthan, north-west Indian desert

Chicken is not native to the sparse deserts of Rajasthan, but hunted wild bird is a luxury cooked over coals. The tiny quail originated in the Middle East but is now found in India and is the basis for this recipe, although wild pigeon or woodcock are also fair game. At just 100–150 g (4–5 oz) each, cooked whole, one quail will yield enough meat for 1 person for a starter or serve 2 quails per person for a main course.

Serves 4

8 quails, skin on

Marinade

50 g (2 oz) natural yogurt

2 or 3 cloves garlic

2.5 cm (1 inch) piece of fresh root ginger

2 teaspoons ground almonds

1 tablespoon soft cream cheese

2 tablespoons brown onion paste (see page 61)

1 or 2 green chillies, finely chopped

1 teaspoon gram flour (besan)

salt, to taste

1 Put the marinade ingredients in a blender or food processor and 'pulse' to a pouring paste using water as needed.

2 Coat the quails with the paste.

3 To cook, place the quails top-side up on a foil-lined oven tray. Bake in a preheated oven, 190°C/375°F/Gas 5 for 12 minutes, or barbecue them over hot coals, then serve.

3 | meat

It is virtually mandatory to eat meat on the bone in India. It gives the dish greater flavour and Indians love sucking out the juicy marrow. The bone in question is the leg. Some of the meat is cut away and used; the remaining meat stays on the bone and is cut into roughly 4 cm (1¹/₂ inch) pieces – this is a job for the butcher.

Traditionally, goat and mutton are the principal meats, since beef is not eaten by Hindus and pork is not eaten by Muslims. However, both these meats are eaten by other communities, and there are appropriate recipes here. Game, such as venison, hare, rabbit and even the more specialized wild boar, are also enjoyed by the affluent and by the tribes (see page 129).

Bakra Dahi Wala
GOAT CURRY COOKED IN YOGURT
Kashmir, extreme northern India

A purée of yogurt, garlic, ginger, onion, tomato and spices is used to marinate on-the-bone goat meat overnight. It is then casseroled to create a mild, very aromatic Kashmiri dish.

Serves 4

675 g (1 lb 6 oz) lean leg of goat or mutton, weighed after removing all unwanted matter, cut into 2.5 cm (1 inch) cubes
4 tablespoons ghee (see page 61)
1 tablespoon coarsely chopped fresh coriander salt, to taste

Marinade
225 g (8 oz) brown onion paste (see page 61)
2 or 3 cloves garlic, finely chopped or puréed
2.5 cm (1 inch) piece of fresh root ginger, shredded
100 g (4 oz) tinned tomatoes
225 g (8 oz) natural yogurt

Masala 1
1 bay leaf
2 brown cardamoms
3 cloves
2 or 3 pieces of cassia bark, each about 5 x 1 cm (2 x ¹/₂ inch)

Masala 2
1 teaspoon ground coriander
1 teaspoon ground cumin
¹/₂ teaspoon turmeric
¹/₂ teaspoon chilli powder
¹/₄ teaspoon ground black pepper

Masala 3
1 tablespoon dried fenugreek leaves
1 teaspoon garam masala (see page 60)

1 Put the marinade ingredients in a blender or food processor and 'pulse' to a pouring paste using water as needed.
2 Combine the marinade, Masala 1 and the meat in a non-aluminium bowl (see cook's tip page 77). Cover and refrigerate for up to 48 hours.
3 To cook, heat the ghee in a 2.25–2.75 litre (4–5 pint) lidded casserole dish and stir-fry Masala 2 for 30 seconds. Add the marinated meat, stir-frying it for about 5 minutes. Then put the casserole, lid on, in a preheated oven, 190°C/375°F/Gas 5.
4 After 20 minutes, inspect, stir and taste. Add a little water if needed to prevent sticking. Return the casserole to the oven.
5 Repeat after 20 minutes. This time add Masala 3 before replacing the casserole in the oven.
6 After a final 20 minutes, taste the meat – it should be tender. Add the fresh coriander and season with salt. Replace the casserole in the oven and turn off the heat. Serve after 10 minutes.

Erachi Olathiathu
BEEF COCONUT-FRY
Syrian Christian origin, Kerala, south India

In south India's state of Kerala, the politics is mostly Communism and the religion Hindu. However, thanks to a visit by a Syrian saint in 52AD, there is a small group of his descendant converts known as Syrian Christians. India's shores are awash with coconut, which commonly features in Syrian Christian cuisine. In this dish, also called erachi olittiyedu or gosht ulathiyathu, beef is floured, then sealed in a paste of coconut and spices and finally casseroled to a fairly dry result.

Serves 4

50 g (2 oz) coconut milk powder (see page 57)
2–4 dried red chillies, chopped
675 g (1 lb 6 oz) lean topside of beef, weighed after removing all unwanted matter, cut into 4 cm (1½ inch) cubes
3 tablespoons vegetable oil
2 cloves garlic, finely chopped or puréed
100 g (4 oz) brown onion paste (see page 61)
400 ml (14 fl oz) water or fragrant stock (see page 59)
75 g (3 oz) fresh coconut flesh, shredded or desiccated coconut
2 teaspoons tamarind purée (see page 62)
10–12 fresh or dried curry leaves (optional)
salt, to taste

Masala

2 tablespoons coriander seeds
¾ teaspoon cumin seeds
1 teaspoon fennel seeds
1 teaspoon black mustard seeds
3 cloves
3 green cardamoms
5 cm (2 inch) piece of cassia bark

1 Dry roast and grind the masala, following the instructions on page 60. Then add just enough water to make the ground masala into a paste.
2 Combine the coconut milk powder and dried chillies and place on a large plate. Dab the pieces of meat in it, ensuring they are lightly coated in the mixture.
3 Place the coated meat in a 2.25–2.75 litre (4–5 pint) lidded casserole dish.
4 Heat the oil in a karahi or wok. Stir-fry the masala paste for 30 seconds then add the garlic and stir-fry for another 30 seconds. Add the onion paste and continue stir-frying for 1 further minute, then add the mixture to the casserole and place in a preheated oven, 190°C/375°F/Gas 5.
5 After 15 minutes, inspect and stir in one-third of the water or stock plus the coconut, tamarind and curry leaves, if using.
6 Inspect again 20 minutes later, adding the remaining water or stock.
7 Cook for a further 20 minutes or until the meat is tender. The dish should be quite dry – if it is tender, but not dry enough, transfer the mixture to a karahi or wok and stir-fry until it becomes dry. Serve with plain rice.

Champ Bukhara
BAKED LAMB CHOPS
Modern chef's recipe

Here, lamb chops are marinated, then grilled or barbecued. This modern recipe first emerged at India's top tandoori restaurant, Delhi's Bukhara, where Alfred Prasaad worked before becoming executive chef at the highly regarded Tamarind restaurant in London, UK.

Serves 4

8 lamb chops, about 100 g (4 oz) each

Marinade
4 cloves garlic
2.5 cm (1 inch) piece of fresh root ginger, chopped
200 g (7 oz) natural yogurt
200 ml (7 fl oz) single cream
2 fresh red chillies, chopped
1 tablespoon tomato purée
1 teaspoon salt
2 teaspoons garam masala (see page 60)
1 teaspoon paprika
1/2 teaspoon chilli powder

1 Put the marinade ingredients in a blender or food processor and 'pulse' to a pouring paste using water as needed.
2 Mix the marinade and lamb chops in a non-aluminium bowl (see cook's tip page 77). Cover and refrigerate for up to 48 hours.
3 To cook, place the chops on a rack in a grill pan lined with foil to catch drips. Cook under a preheated medium grill – grilling times will depend on the size and thickness of chops, but 8–10 minutes should be sufficient.

Baked lamb chops

4 Turn the chops over, baste with any remaining marinade and grill for a further 5–8 minutes. Serve. Alternatively, you could cook the lamb chops on a barbecue.)

Do Peeaza Chukander
LAMB WITH ONION & BEETROOT
Maharajah origin

Originating in Persia, this dish, like Dopeyaja Harsh (onion-sweetened duck, see page 103), was another Moghul favourite. This recipe is based on one by the Maharajah of Sailana, gourmet chef and author of a fascinating cookery book called *Maharaja Sailana's Cookery Delights*. In it he states that dopeeaza is a Moghul term meaning any meat cooked with onions and/or a vegetable, in this case beetroot.

Serves 4

3 tablespoons ghee (see page 61)
3 or 4 cloves garlic, finely chopped or puréed
2.5 cm (1 inch) piece of fresh root ginger, shredded
225 g (8 oz) fried onions
675 g (1 lb 6 oz) leg or neck of lamb, weighed after removing all unwanted matter, cut into 4 cm (1 1/2 inch) cubes
100 g (4 oz) natural yogurt
100 g (4 oz) unvinegared, cooked peeled beetroot, finely chopped or minced
100 g (4 oz) onion, cut into long thin strips
200 ml (7 fl oz) water or fragrant stock (see page 59)
2 or 3 fresh red chillies, shredded (optional)
2 tablespoons finely chopped fresh coriander
2 teaspoons garam masala (see page 60)
4 tablespoons caramelized onions (see page 61)
salt, to taste

Masala

2 teaspoons chilli powder

2 teaspoons coriander seeds, roasted and
ground

1 teaspoon garam masala (see page 60)

1 Heat the ghee in a karahi or wok and stir-fry the
garlic for 30 seconds. Add the masala and stir-fry
for another 15 seconds. Add the ginger and fried
onions and the lamb. Mix well and stir-fry for
3 or 4 minutes. Stir in the yogurt and beetroot.
2 Tip the contents of the pan into a 2.25–2.75 litre
(4–5 pint) lidded casserole dish, cover and cook in
a preheated oven, 190°C/375°F/Gas 5.
3 After about 15 minutes, inspect the casserole and
add the chopped onion strips, the water or stock
and chillies, if using. Replace the casserole in the
oven.
4 Inspect again after 20–25 minutes, this time
adding the fresh coriander and garam masala.
Return to the oven for a final 20 minutes, or until
the lamb is perfectly tender and the liquid reduced
to a thick consistency, about half its original volume.
5 Add the onion tarka and season with salt. Return
the casserole, lid off, to the oven, now switched off,
and leave for 10 minutes, before serving with dhal
and parathas.

Dhansak
MEAT SIMMERED WITH
LENTILS & VEGETABLES

Parsee origin

Traditionally, dhansak always uses meat with up to
four types of lentil and slow cooking amalgamates
the flavours. During the cooking, a kind of
ratatouille of aubergine, tomato, spinach and fresh
chillies is added. Meat mixed with vegetables and
fruit is a typically Parsee recipe and shows its
Persian origins. Dhansak is probably the most
popular Parsee dish and has sweet and sour
flavours – the sweet comes from palm sugar

(jaggery) and the sour from a slight overtone of
fresh lime. The apt derivation of the name of this
dish comes from dhan, meaning 'wealthy' in
Gujarati, and sak, meaning 'vegetables'.
Pronounced slightly differently, dhaan means
'rice', which accompanies this sumptuous dish,
traditionally eaten as a Parsee Sunday special.

Serves 4

25 g (1 oz) split and polished gram lentils
(chana dhal)

25 g (1 oz) split and polished green lentils
(moong dhal)

25 g (1 oz) split and polished red lentils
(masoor dhal)

50 g (2 oz) split oily lentils (toovar/toor dhal)

4 tablespoons ghee (see page 61)

400 g (14 oz) lean lamb, weighed after
removing all unwanted matter, cut into 3 cm
(1¼ inch) cubes

225 g (8 oz) onions, finely chopped

2 or 3 cloves garlic, finely chopped or puréed

200 g (7 oz) tinned tomatoes, strained

1 tablespoon palm sugar (jaggery) or brown
sugar

3 or 4 pieces of red pepper, finely chopped

100 g (4 oz) aubergine, cut into bite-sized
cubes

100 g (4 oz) courgette, cut into bite-sized cubes

100 g (4 oz) fresh baby spinach, coarsely
chopped

1 or 2 green chillies, sliced

juice of 1 lime

2 tablespoons coarsely chopped fresh coriander

salt, to taste

Masala 1

1 teaspoon cumin seeds

1 brown cardamom

5 cm (2 inch) piece of cassia bark

½ teaspoon black mustard seeds

Masala 2

1 teaspoon turmeric
1 teaspoon ground coriander
1 teaspoon ground cumin
$1/4$ teaspoon fenugreek seeds, ground
$1/2$ teaspoon chilli powder

1 Mix the lentils together and soak them overnight in plenty of water.

2 To cook, place the drained lentils in a large saucepan and simmer in twice their volume of water for about 30 minutes, then coarsely mash them in the pan.

3 Heat 2 tablespoons of the ghee in a 2.25–2.75 litre (4–5 pint) lidded casserole dish, and fry the meat for about 5 minutes to seal it.

4 Heat the remaining ghee in a karahi or wok and stir-fry Masala 1 for about 30 seconds. Add just enough water to Masala 2 to make a paste then add it to the pan and stir-fry for about 1 minute. Add the onions and garlic and continue to stir-fry for about 2 minutes.

5 Add the contents of the pan to the meat and put the casserole, lid on, in a preheated oven, 190°C/375°F/Gas 5.

6 After 20 minutes, inspect, stir and taste. Add a little water if needed to prevent sticking. Replace the casserole in the oven.

7 Repeat after 20 minutes, and add the strained tinned tomatoes, sugar, mashed lentils, red pepper, aubergine, courgette and spinach.

8 Cook for another 20–30 minutes, or until the meat is tender. Add the fresh coriander and season with salt. Turn off the heat and leave the casserole in the oven for a further 10 minutes, or until ready to serve.

Gosht Tikkea Malai ke Bohris
BAKED MARINATED BEEF
Gujarat, west India

Gujarat is a largely Hindu vegetarian state, but not all Gujaratis are Hindus or vegetarians. The Bohris is a small community of Gujarati meat-eating Muslims. This is their signature dish: cubes of beef marinated in cream, garlic and ginger, then coated with breadcrumbs and baked.

Serves 4

675 g (1 lb 6 oz) lean beef, weighed after removing all unwanted matter, cut into 4 cm ($1^1/2$ inch) cubes
4 tablespoons vegetable oil
4 eggs, beaten
85 g (3 oz) dried breadcrumbs
3 tablespoons ghee (see page 61)
2 or 3 cloves garlic, finely chopped or puréed
50 g (2 oz) onions, finely chopped
salt, to taste
4 tablespoons caramelized onions (see page 61)

Marinade

500 ml (18 fl oz) thick pourable cream
2 or 3 cloves garlic, puréed
2.5 cm (1 inch) piece of fresh root ginger, puréed
1 tablespoon garam masala (see page 60)
1 tablespoon paprika
2 teaspoons ground coriander
1 teaspoon ground cumin
$1/2$ teaspoon turmeric

1 Mix the marinade ingredients together in a large non-aluminium bowl (see cook's tip page 77). Stir in the meat, cover and refrigerate for up to 24 hours.

2 Line an oven tray with foil and drizzle the oil over the foil.

3 Tip the beaten eggs into a large shallow bowl and the breadcrumbs onto a large plate. Remove the cubes of meat from the marinade. Dip each piece into the beaten egg then dab in the breadcrumbs to cover.

4 Place the breadcrumbed meat on the foil-lined tray, then bake in a preheated oven, 190°C/375°F/Gas 5, for 20–30 minutes.

5 Meanwhile, make the sauce. Heat the ghee in a karahi or wok. Stir-fry the garlic for 15 seconds, then add the onions and continue stir-frying for 5 minutes. Add the remaining marinade and simmer for about 5 minutes, stirring frequently. Add water as needed to loosen the mixture. Season with salt.

6 To serve, arrange the meat on individual plates, pour the sauce over the top and garnish with the onion tarka.

Horin Kofta
VENISON MEATBALLS
Kashmir, extreme northern India

The kofta, or meatball, was invented by the Arabs, who call it kafta. This Kashmiri recipe normally uses mutton or goat or occasionally, as here, venison, which is the meat of deer up to 2$\frac{1}{2}$ years in age, specially bred for the table. The meatballs are called either 'rista' or 'ghushtaba', depending on their size. Serve them with or without the sauce below.

Makes 6 or 10 meatballs

675 g (1 lb 6 oz) lean venison, coarsely chopped into 3 cm (1$\frac{1}{4}$ inch) cubes
6 cloves garlic, finely chopped or puréed
2.5 cm (1 inch) piece of fresh root ginger, shredded
1 egg yolk
1 teaspoon turmeric
3 or 4 tablespoons vegetable oil

Masala 1
4 brown/black cardamoms
6 green cardamoms
1 teaspoon black peppercorns
$\frac{1}{2}$ teaspoon black cumin seeds
3 or 4 pieces of cassia bark, each about 5 x 1 cm (2 x $\frac{1}{2}$ inch)

Masala 2
1 teaspoon turmeric
$\frac{1}{4}$ teaspoon asafoetida
1 teaspoon garam masala (see page 60)
1 teaspoon dried fenugreek leaves

Sauce
2 tablespoons ghee (see page 61)
2 or 3 cloves garlic, finely chopped or puréed
2.5 cm (1 inch) piece of fresh root ginger, shredded
350 g (12 oz) white onion paste (see page 61)
1 or 2 fresh red chillies, finely chopped
150 ml (5 fl oz) fragrant stock or water (see page 59)
large pinch of saffron
salt, to taste

1 Roast and grind the ingredients for Masala 1, following the instructions on page 60.

2 Grind the meat, garlic, ginger, egg yolk, turmeric and ground Masala 1 in a blender or food processor. This may have to be done in 2 batches, depending on the size of your motor.

3 Remove from the blender or food processor and mix thoroughly by hand, picking out all unwanted meat matter as you go. Re-run the mixture in the machine then, using your hands, form the mixture into equal-sized balls. To make larger meatballs divide the mixture into 6, to make smaller ones divide the mixture into 10.

4 To cook the meatballs, heat the oil in a frying pan. Add the meatballs and fry for different times according to their size: 20–25 minutes for larger meatballs, 12–15 minutes for smaller ones. Keep turning the meatballs to cook them evenly – you may have to cook them in batches depending on the size of your pan.

5 While the meatballs are cooking, make the sauce. Heat the ghee in a karahi or wok. Stir-fry Masala 2 for 30 seconds, then add the garlic and stir-fry for another 30 seconds. Add the ginger, onion paste and chillies and continue stir-frying for 1 minute more.

6 Simmer for the next 10 minutes or so, adding the stock or water little by little as the sauce thickens – it should be neither too thick nor too runny. Keep simmering, then add the meatballs and saffron and season to taste. Simmer for a further 2 minutes, but avoid vigorous stirring which will break up the meatballs.

Keema
MINCED BEEF CURRY
Punjab, north-west India

Minced meat is a fine ingredient and this spicy, savoury Punjabi recipe is one of India's finest.

Serves 4

675 g (1 lb 6 oz) lean beef, weighed after
  removing all unwanted matter, finely minced
5 tablespoons ghee (see page 61)
2 cloves garlic, finely chopped
5 cm (2 inch) piece of fresh root ginger, finely
  chopped
200 g (7 oz) fried onions
400 g (14 oz) tinned tomatoes, strained
1 tablespoon tomato ketchup
1 tablespoon red pepper, chopped
1 or 2 green chillies, chopped
1 teaspoon garam masala (see page 60)
1 tablespoon coarsely chopped fresh coriander
1 tablespoon chopped fresh mint
salt, to taste

Masala

1 tablespoon dried fenugreek leaves
2 teaspoons garam masala (see page 60)
1 teaspoon turmeric
1 teaspoon ground coriander
$1/2$–2 teaspoons chilli powder
4 cloves
1 brown/black cardamom
4 bay leaves

1 Put the mince in a 2.25–2.75 litre (4–5 pint) lidded casserole dish. Add 2 tablespoons of the ghee and stir-fry for about 10 minutes to seal the meat.

2 Heat the remaining ghee in a karahi or wok and stir-fry the masala for 30 seconds, then add the garlic, ginger and fried onion and cook for about 2 minutes. Add a little water if it dries up too much.

3 Add the contents of the pan to the casserole dish with the tinned tomatoes and ketchup. Cover and cook in a preheated oven, 190°C/375°F/Gas 5, for 20–30 minutes.

4 Take it out of the oven and stir in the red pepper, chillies and garam masala. Return to the oven and continue to cook for a further 30 minutes.

5 Switch off the oven. Stir in the coriander and mint and season with salt. Return the casserole to the oven for 10 minutes, then serve with puris or parathas.

Methi Gosht
PUNJABI-STYLE FENUGREEK-FLAVOURED MEAT CURRY

Punjab, north-west India

A Punjabi favourite, methi (fenugreek) gosht (meat) is robust, very savoury and very spicy, although not chilli hot.

Serves 4

4 tablespoons ghee (see page 61)

2 teaspoons ground coriander

2 or 3 cloves garlic, finely chopped or puréed

2.5 cm (1 inch) piece of fresh root ginger, shredded

250 g (9 oz) onion masala sauce (see page 61)

1 tablespoon tomato purée

675 g (1 lb 6 oz) lean leg of lamb or mutton, weighed after removing all unwanted matter, cut into 2.5 cm (1 inch) cubes

water or fragrant stock (see page 59), as needed

4 tablespoons dried fenugreek leaves

2 teaspoons garam masala (see page 60)

2 tablespoons coarsely chopped fresh coriander

salt, to taste

1 Heat the ghee in a 2.25–2.75 (4–5 pint) lidded casserole dish then stir-fry the ground coriander, garlic and ginger for 1 minute. Add the onion masala sauce and tomato purée and simmer for about 5 minutes to thicken the sauce a little.
2 Add the meat and put the casserole, lid on, in a preheated oven, 190°C/375°F/Gas 5.
3 After 20 minutes, inspect, stir and taste. Add a little water or stock if needed to loosen the mixture. Return the casserole to the oven.
4 Inspect again after another 20 minutes. Add the fenugreek, garam masala and fresh coriander and return the casserole to the oven.

5 After a final 20 minutes, taste the dish. The meat should be tender, again add more water or stock if needed. Season with salt. Switch off the oven, replace the casserole in the oven for 10 minutes, then serve with parathas and plain raita.

Jungli Maas
JUNGLE MEAT

Rajasthan, north-west Indian desert

Also called lal maas (simply 'red meat'), this Rajasthani dish was, and still is, traditionally cooked by hunting parties at the end of their hunting day and comprises any freshly caught game or wild fowl, cooked al fresco at the campsite. This recipe's list of ingredients is minimal: meat, ghee, red chillies and salt – all available in the remotest Indian village.

Serves 4

3 or 4 tablespoons ghee (see page 61)

675 g (1 lb 6 oz) lamb neck, weighed after removing all unwanted matter, cut into 4 cm (1½ inch) cubes

2–6 dried red chillies, chopped

1–2 teaspoons salt

1 Heat the ghee in a karahi or wok until quite hot. Add the meat and reduce the heat while it cooks.
2 After 10 minutes add the red chillies.
3 Add splashes of water every now and then to prevent burning or sticking.
4 When tender, allow the water to cook out so that the dish is dry and serve with Indian breads.

Pasanda
MARINATED VEAL ESCALOPE
Moghul origin, northern India

In this recipe strips of tender veal are gently beaten to create thin pieces (escalopes), known by the Moghuls as pasanda. They are then marinated in red wine and/or spiced yogurt overnight. The Portuguese introduced wine to the Moghul courts in the early 16th century and, although Muslim, some of the Moghul emperors were not above enjoying alcoholic beverages. Jehangir, in particular, became an alcoholic, blessing the wine so as to convert it to 'holy water' and thus avoid the rules of Islam.

Serves 4

4 x 175 g (6 oz) pieces of lean veal steak
300 ml (10 fl oz) red wine
3 tablespoons ghee (see page 61)
4 cloves garlic, finely chopped or puréed
2.5 cm (1 inch) piece of fresh root ginger, puréed
250 g (9 oz) white onion paste (see page 61)
1 tablespoon coconut milk powder (see page 57)
2 tablespoons ground almonds
1 tablespoon tomato purée
water or fragrant stock (see page 59), as needed
2 tablespoons coarsely chopped fresh coriander
1 teaspoon garam masala (see page 60)
salt, to taste

Masala
1 teaspoon turmeric
1 teaspoon ground cumin
1 teaspoon ground coriander
1 teaspoon paprika
1 teaspoon chilli powder
1 teaspoon poppy seeds

1 Using a wooden meat hammer, make the pasanda by beating the veal steaks to pieces less than 5 mm (1/4 inch) thick. Place them in a shallow bowl, cover with the red wine and leave overnight.
2 Heat the ghee in a karahi or wok. Add the masala and stir-fry for 15 seconds. Add the garlic and stir-fry for about 30 seconds, then add the ginger and onion paste and stir-fry for 1 minute more. Set aside.
3 Put the marinated meat in a lidded casserole dish. Mix the stir-fried ingredients, the coconut milk powder, ground almonds and tomato purée with the wine marinade and add to the casserole, ensuring the meat is well covered. Place the casserole in a preheated oven, 190°C/375°F/Gas 5.
4 After 30 minutes, inspect and stir. Add a little water or stock if it is too dry. Return the casserole to the oven.
5 After another 30 minutes, inspect and taste. The pasanda should be tender – add more water or stock if needed. Add the coriander and garam masala and season with salt. Switch off the oven, replace the casserole in the oven for 10 minutes, then serve.

Sufaid Korma Ke Khada Masle

VEAL IN A WHITE CREAMY AROMATIC SAUCE

Moghul, north India

Korma has been hijacked by curry restaurants where it is offered as the mildest curry, sometimes made sickly by the overuse of sugar, cream, nuts and creamed coconut block, an ingredient never used in India. Real korma is in fact a cooking method where the dish begins with frying. Water is involved only towards the end of cooking and must then be cooked out. To this day, there are many korma recipes, ranging from mild to piquante (see page 96). The use of only whole spices in this classic Moghul veal korma creates a mild but astonishingly tasty, aromatic dish. Not only that, it could be the recipe for the legendary white korma allegedly served by the emperor Shah Jehan at the Taj Mahal's inaugural party.

Serves 4

675 g (1 lb 6 oz) lean leg of veal, weighed after removing all unwanted matter, cut into 2.5 cm (1 inch) cubes
2 tablespoons ghee (see page 61)
6 cloves garlic, puréed
2.5 cm (1 inch) piece of fresh root ginger, shredded
250 g (9 oz) white onion paste (see page 61)
2 tablespoons ground almonds
175 ml (6 fl oz) single cream
1 teaspoon garam masala
water or fragrant stock (see page 59), as needed
salt, to taste

Veal in a white creamy aromatic sauce

Marinade

225 g (8 oz) natural yogurt
250 ml (8 fl oz) single cream
2 cloves garlic, puréed
12 raw shelled cashew nuts, ground
1 or 2 cinnamon sticks, each about 7.5 cm (3 inches)
10–12 green cardamoms
10–12 cloves
3 or 4 bay leaves
1 teaspoon fennel seeds

Masala

2 teaspoons ground coriander
2 teaspoons ground white pepper

Garnish

toasted flaked almonds
2 teaspoons coarsely chopped fresh coriander
a little edible silver leaf (vark) (optional) (see cook's tip)

1 Mix the marinade ingredients and masala together in a non-aluminium bowl (see cook's tip page 77). Immerse the cubes of veal then cover and refrigerate for 6–48 hours.
2 Heat the ghee in a karahi or wok then add the garlic, ginger and onion paste. Stir-fry for 5 minutes.
3 Combine the fried mixture with the marinated veal then place in a 2.25–2.75 litre (4–5 pint) lidded casserole dish. Cover and cook in a preheated oven, 190°C/375°F/Gas 5, for 25 minutes.
4 Remove the casserole from the oven, inspect and stir, then mix in the ground almonds and cream. Return to the oven for 20 minutes more.
5 Remove the casserole from the oven again, inspect, add the garam masala and, if the mixture looks too dry, add a little water or stock. Taste for tenderness and judge how much more cooking is required – it will probably need at least 10 minutes more to reach tenderness. Serve garnished with the toasted flaked almonds, the coriander and the vark.

COOK'S TIP Vark, pronounced varak, is edible silver or gold foil. It is made from a nugget of either pure gold or silver, which is hammered between leather pads by craftsmen until thinner than paper. The sheets are used on top of dishes such as biriani and sweets as an edible garnish. It is vegan, has no flavour, and is, of course, a major talking point. The concept of eating gold and silver was invented by who else but the 17th-century Moghul emperors (see page 24).

Nehari
LAMB SHANK
Lucknow, northern India

This recipe, also spelt niharhi, dates back to the time of the Nawaabs of Lucknow (see page 31). The lamb shank is first marinated, then baked until it is so tender that its flesh literally falls off the bone and you can eat it with your fingers. Its own marinade forms the sauce.

Serves 4

4 lamb knuckles, about 350 g (12 oz) each

Masala

2 tablespoons coriander seeds
1 tablespoon allspice
1 teaspoon green cardamom pods
1 teaspoon fennel seeds

Marinade

about 50 ml (2 fl oz) milk
250 g (9 oz) natural yogurt
2 tablespoons vegetable oil
2 tablespoons freshly squeezed lemon juice
8 cloves garlic
2.5 cm (1 inch) piece of fresh root ginger, chopped
2 or 3 fresh red chillies, chopped
1 tablespoon tomato purée (optional)
200 g (7 oz) tinned tomatoes, puréed (optional)

1 tablespoon chopped fresh coriander
2 tablespoons ground almonds
1/2 teaspoon salt

1 Roast and grind the masala, following the instructions on page 60.
2 Put the marinade ingredients and ground masala in a blender or food processor. Adding the milk little by little, 'pulse' to a purée that is easy to pour.
3 Pare away all the fat and skin membrane from each lamb knuckle, and scrape the top bone clean. Stab the flesh all over using a small knife then coat the meat with the marinade in a non-aluminium bowl (see cook's tip page 77). Cover and refrigerate for up to 24 hours.
4 To cook, shake off and reserve any marinade for step 6. Cover each knuckle with foil. Transfer to a roasting tin and roast in a preheated oven, 180°C/350°F/Gas 4, for about 1 hour. Remove the foil after about 40 minutes.
5 When really tender, the flesh should literally fall off the bone. Prior to serving let the knuckles rest for 10 minutes to relax the meat.
6 Meanwhile, mix together the reserved marinade from step 4 and any cooked marinade and juices from the roasting tin. Stir-fry this mixture until it darkens in colour and makes a thick sauce.
7 Pour the sauce over each knuckle and serve.

Pandi
HOT, SOUR & SPICY PORK CURRY
Coorg, Karnataka, southern India

Every Coorg meal must have at least one dish of meat, and there is no proscription on pork. It could be a succulent roast or, like this recipe, a stew that uses coconut for its creaminess, chilli for its heat and kokum (sour plum) or tamarind for its sourness. In the hills of Karnataka the Coorg people call kokum 'kachampuli', or Coorg vinegar.

Serves 4

4 tablespoons vegetable oil

6 or 7 cloves garlic, finely chopped or puréed

2.5 cm (1 inch) piece of fresh root ginger, shredded

250 g (9 oz) brown onion paste (see page 61)

1 or 2 red chillies, finely chopped

675 g (1 lb 6 oz) lean pork leg, weighed after removing all unwanted matter, cut into 2.5 cm (1 inch) cubes

300 ml (10 fl oz) water or fragrant stock (see page 59)

1 teaspoon tamarind purée (see page 62)

200 ml (7 fl oz) tinned coconut milk

salt, to taste

Masala

1 teaspoon cumin seeds, roasted and ground

1 teaspoon black mustard seeds, roasted and ground

1/2 teaspoon black peppercorns, crushed

1/2 teaspoon turmeric

1 Heat the oil in a karahi or wok. Add the garlic and stir-fry for about 30 seconds, then add the masala, ginger, onion paste and chillies and stir-fry for 1 minute.

2 Transfer this to a 2.25–2.75 litre (4–5 pint) lidded casserole dish and add the pork, stir-frying it for about 5 minutes. Add one-third of the water or stock, then place the casserole, lid on, in a preheated oven, 180°C/350°F/Gas 4.

3 After 20 minutes, inspect, stir and taste. Add another third of the water or stock, the kokum or tamarind and the coconut milk. Return the casserole to the oven.

4 After another 20 minutes inspect again. This time add the remaining water or stock before returning the casserole to the oven.

5 After a final 20 minutes, taste the curry – the meat should be tender. Season with salt. Switch off the oven, replace the casserole in the oven for 10 minutes, then serve.

Tabak Maz, or Mans

RIBS IN A RICH SAUCE

Kashmir, extreme northern India

Here, lamb ribs or chops are simmered in a milk-based spicy Kashmiri sauce, then fried to completion.

Serves 4

8 lamb chops, about 100 g (4 oz) each after trimming off excess fat

3 tablespoons ghee (see page 61)

2 teaspoons fennel seeds

100 g (4 oz) brown onion paste (see page 61)

100 g (4 oz) natural yogurt

1 or 2 green chillies, finely chopped

1 tablespoon coarsely chopped fresh coriander

pinch of saffron

Boiling mixture

350 ml (12 fl oz) milk

50 g (2 oz) onions, finely chopped

2 or 3 cloves garlic, chopped

2.5 cm (1 inch) piece of fresh ginger, chopped

2 teaspoons ground coriander

1 teaspoon chilli powder

1 teaspoon ground cumin

6 cloves

3 or 4 brown/black cardamoms

2 x 5 cm (2 inch) pieces of cassia bark

2 or 3 bay leaves

1 teaspoon salt

1 Place the ingredients for the boiling mixture in a karahi or wok and bring to a simmer.

2 Add the lamb chops and simmer for 10–12 minutes, so that the chops are virtually cooked. Remove from the liquid and set aside. Strain the remaining contents of the pan so as to retain the liquid and discard the solids.

3 Heat the ghee in the karahi or wok and stir-fry the

fennel seeds for 30 seconds, then add the onion paste and stir-fry for 1 minute.

4 Add the strained liquid, the yogurt, chillies and coriander and simmer until reduced in volume by about one-third.

5 Add the chops and saffron to the pan and simmer over a low heat until the liquid has been completely cooked out. Serve with plain rice.

Raan
AROMATIC ROAST LAMB

Moghul origin, northern India

Also known as kurzi gosht, this is an absolute Moghul delight. A leg of lamb is pared of fat, and remains whole on the bone. Marinated in a paste made from yogurt, oil, lemon juice, garlic, ginger, red chillies, fresh coriander, ground almonds and aromatic spices for at least 3 hours, it is then slow-roasted until so tender that the flesh literally falls off the bone.

Serves 4–6

2.25–2.75 kg (5–6 lb) leg of lamb

Marinade
200 g (7 oz) plain yogurt
2 tablespoons sunflower oil
2 tablespoons freshly squeezed lemon juice
3 or 4 cloves garlic, puréed
2.5 cm (1 inch) piece of fresh root ginger, puréed
2 or 3 fresh red chillies, finely chopped
1 tablespoon coarsely chopped fresh coriander
2 tablespoons ground almonds
1 teaspoon salt
about 120 ml (4 fl oz) milk

Masala
2 tablespoons coriander seeds
1 teaspoon cloves

1 teaspoon green cardamom pods
1 teaspoon fennel seeds
5 cm (2 inch) piece of cassia bark

1 Roast and grind the masala, following the instructions on page 60.

2 Put the marinade ingredients and the ground masala in a blender or food processor. Adding the milk little by little, 'pulse' the ingredients to a purée that is easy to pour.

3 Pare away all the fat and skin membrane from the meat. Stab the meat all over with a small knife and coat with the marinade in a non-aluminium dish (see cook's tip page 77). Cover and refrigerate for 24–60 hours.

4 Transfer the lamb and marinade to a roasting tin and slow-roast in a preheated oven, 180°C/350°F/Gas 4, for about 3 hours. When really tender the flesh should literally fall off the bone. Prior to serving let the raan rest for 10–20 minutes in a low oven.

5 Serve the meat in chunks rather than sliced, accompanied by Indian breads and a yogurt chutney.

Roghan Josh Gosht
SLOW-COOKED AROMATIC MEAT DISH

Kashmir, extreme northern India

Roghan josh gosht is an astoundingly aromatic Moghul meat dish, perfected in Kashmir centuries ago. There are two possible derivations of the word 'roghan'. In the Kashmiri language, it means 'red', in Persian it means 'clarified butter'. Josh means both 'juice' and 'heat', the latter describing the intense but slow heat required to get the most from this dish. None of these meanings are incorrect. The dish did originate in Persia as a slow-cooked meat dish. Much later, when the

Aromatic roast lamb

Moghuls retreated to the cool of the Kashmir mountains to escape the heat of the summer, it acquired highly aromatic Kashmiri spices, such as brown cardamoms and saffron. It also became red with the use of alkanet root and a strange indigenous plant called maaval (nickamed 'cockscomb' by the British for its appearance). As these are not readily available, I use beetroot as a non-traditional, but truly non-artificial colouring.

Serves 4

400 ml (14 fl oz) fragrant stock, cold
  (see page 59)
400 g (14 oz) natural yogurt
675 g (1 lb 6 oz) lean leg of lamb, goat or
  mutton, weighed after removing all unwanted
  matter, cut into 2.5 cm (1 inch) cubes
2 or 3 cloves garlic, finely chopped or puréed
2.5 cm (1 inch) piece of fresh root ginger,
  shredded
50 g (2 oz) unvinegared, cooked peeled
  beetroot, chopped
250 g (9 oz) white onion paste (see page 61)
milk for thinning
1 tablespoon coarsely chopped fresh coriander
2 teaspoons garam masala (see page 60)
20–25 saffron strands
salt, to taste

Red Oil

2 tablespoons ghee (see page 61)
2 tablespoons chilli oil
5 or 6 flakes alkanet root (optional)

Masala 1

6 green cardamoms
3 brown cardamoms
6 cloves
3 or 4 pieces of cassia bark, each about
  5 x 1 cm (2 x 1/2 inch)
4 bay leaves

Masala 2

2 teaspoons paprika
1 teaspoon coriander, roasted and ground
1/2 teaspoon chilli powder
1/2 teaspoon freshly grated nutmeg

1 Mix the cold fragrant stock with the yogurt in a jug and whisk thoroughly. Heat the mixture in a saucepan, continuing to whisk.
2 When it comes to the boil, reduce the heat and simmer until the mixture is reduced to about half its original volume. Remove from the stove – it should be an off-white colour.
3 To make the red oil, heat the ghee and chilli oil in a karahi or wok. Add the alkanet root, if using. As soon as the oil turns red, strain through a metal strainer, discarding the root and retaining the oil.
4 Add the meat to a saucepan of boiling water for just 1 minute. Drain the water. Cool the meat and rinse it in cold water.
5 Put the garlic, ginger and beetroot in a blender or food processor and 'pulse' to a purée. Combine this with the onion paste, the meat, cooked yogurt and Masala 1. Cover and refrigerate for 6–24 hours.
6 To cook the meat, heat the red oil in a 2.25–2.75 litre (4–5 pint) lidded casserole dish and stir-fry Masala 2 for 30 seconds. Add the meat and its marinade. Put the casserole, lid on, in a preheated oven, 190°C/375°F/Gas 5.
7 After 20 minutes, inspect and stir. If at any time the curry gets too dry, add a little milk to thin it. Return the casserole to the oven.
8 Inspect again after another 20 minutes. Add the fresh coriander, garam masala and saffron.
9 After a final 20 minutes, again inspect and taste the casserole. The meat should be tender, but add more milk if needed. Season with salt. Switch off the oven, replace the casserole in the oven for 10 minutes, then serve.

Sakarand ka Gosht
MEAT & SWEET POTATO STEW
Parsee origin

Two very popular dishes among the Parsee community are this meat stew, using sweet potato, and its variant – Papata Ma Gosht – which uses ordinary potatoes. The stew is fairly dry, and the sweet potatoes are first baked, then fried before being added to the dish at the end of cooking.

Serves 4

3 tablespoons vegetable oil
2 teaspoons cumin seeds
1/4 teaspoon coriander seeds
10–12 fresh or dried curry leaves (optional)
1 teaspoon turmeric
1/2 teaspoon asafoetida
225 g (8 oz) sweet potatoes, peeled (optional) and cut into bite-sized pieces
3 tablespoons ghee (see page 61)
2 or 3 cloves garlic, finely chopped or puréed
2.5 cm (1 inch) piece of fresh root ginger, shredded
250 g (9 oz) caramelized onions (see page 61)
1 tablespoon tomato purée
675 g (1 lb 6 oz) lean stewing meat, weighed after discarding unwanted matter
water or fragrant stock (see page 59), as needed
1–4 fresh red chillies, chopped
1 tablespoon brown sugar
75 g (3 oz) fresh peas, cooked or frozen peas, thawed
salt, to taste

Masala
4 cloves
2 or 3 green cardamoms
1 brown cardamom

2 or 3 pieces of cassia bark, each about 5 x 1 cm (2 x 1/2 inch)

Garnish
1 teaspoon cumin seeds, roasted
coarsely chopped fresh coriander

1 Roast and grind the masala, following the instructions on page 60.
2 Heat the oil in a karahi or wok. Add the seeds, curry leaves, if using, turmeric and asafoetida and stir-fry for 30 seconds. Turn off the heat, add the sweet potatoes and stir them with the mixture so that they appear golden.
3 Place the sweet potatoes on an oven tray so that they are closely packed together, one layer deep. Bake in a preheated oven, 190°C/375°F/Gas 5, for 25–30 minutes.
4 Meanwhile, heat the ghee in a 2.25–2.75 litre (4–5 pint) lidded casserole dish and stir-fry the masala, garlic and ginger for 1 minute, then add the fried onions and tomato purée and stir-fry for 2 minutes more. Add the meat, stir-frying it for about 2 minutes, then put the casserole, lid on, into the oven.
5 After 20 minutes, inspect and stir, adding a little water or stock if it becomes too dry – now or at any time – and return the casserole to the oven. As the casserole goes back in, remove the cooked sweet potatoes from the oven, and set aside.
6 Remove the casserole again 20 minutes later and add the chillies and sugar. Continue cooking for at least 20 minutes more until the meat is cooked to your liking.
7 Add the sweet potatoes and the peas. Season with salt. Switch off the oven, replace the casserole in the oven for 10 minutes, then serve garnished with the roasted cumin seeds and fresh coriander.

Sorportel
CHILLI-HOT PORK & OFFAL
Goa, Indian west coast

Sorpotel (sarpotel/sarpartal/sarapatel) is a Goan modification of the Portuguese offal dish 'sarabulho'. Here we use about 55 per cent pork meat and 15 per cent each lambs' liver, chicken heart and kidney, but you can change the ratio to your taste. The sauce contains plenty of red chilli, palm sugar (jaggery) and Goan todi vinegar (here we use rice vinegar and balsamic vinegar to simulate the taste). Sorportel is traditionally left for up to 4 days to mellow before eating, which can be done in the fridge or freezer.

Serves 4

100 ml (3½ fl oz) rice vinegar
1 tablespoon balsamic vinegar
400 g (14 oz) lean pork meat, off the bone, weighed after removing all unwanted matter, cut into 2.5 cm (1 inch) cubes
50 g (2 oz) lambs' liver, cut into strips
50 g (2 oz) chicken heart, cut into strips
50 g (2 oz) chicken kidney, cut into strips
2 tablespoons ghee (see page 61)
6–8 cloves garlic, puréed
2.5 cm (1 inch) piece of fresh root ginger, puréed
250 g (9 oz) brown onion paste (see page 61)
1–4 fresh red chillies, finely chopped
1 cup oil
1 teaspoon salt
1 tablespoon palm sugar (jaggery)

Masala
1 teaspoon cumin seeds
2 pieces of cassia bark, each about 5 x 1 cm (2 x ½ inch)
6 cloves
1 teaspoon turmeric

2 teaspoons chilli powder
2 teaspoons black peppercorns, crushed
2 teaspoons paprika
½ teaspoon asafoetida

1 Mix the vinegars, meat and offal in a mixing bowl. Cover and refrigerate for up to 6 hours.
2 Heat the ghee in a 2.25–2.75 litre (4–5 pint) lidded casserole dish. Add the masala and stir-fry for 15 seconds. Add the garlic and stir-fry for about 30 seconds, then add the ginger and onion paste and stir-fry for 1 minute more.
3 Add the meat, offal, its juices and the red chillies, then put the casserole, lid on, in a preheated oven, 190°C/375°F/Gas 5.
4 After 20 minutes, inspect, stir and taste. Add a little water if needed to prevent sticking, although the finished dish should be fairly dry. Return the casserole to the oven.
5 Repeat after 20 minutes, then replace in the oven.
6 After a final 20 minutes, taste the dish – the meat should be tender. Add the salt. Switch off the oven, replace the casserole in the oven for 10 minutes, then serve.

Sular Shikaari ke Lepcha
WILD BOAR CURRY
Sikkim, north-east India

Sikkim, a tiny Buddhist state in north-east India, neighbours with Bhutan, Nepal and Tibet. Buddhists do not kill animals, but Sikkim's original mountain tribe the Lepcha are not Buddhist and they are good hunters, catching fish in their clear mountain streams, and wild boar or deer in the jungles, both considered a Lepcha delicacy. The Sikkim area is perfect for wild boar, which thrive in humid conditions. Here the meat is available from specialist butchers. Young wild boar around 6 months old (called marcassin) is very tender, but the animal is normally between one and four years old to be suitable for the table. Note the Lepcha tipple – the tribe is partial to brews such as toddy made from coconut. In its absence substitute tequila.

Serves 4

675 g (1 lb 6 oz) lean leg of wild boar, weighed after removing all unwanted matter, cut into 2.5 cm (1 inch) cubes
4 tablespoons ghee (see page 61)
1 tablespoon chopped fresh mint
2 tablespoons finely chopped fresh coriander
2 teaspoons garam masala (see page 60)
    100 ml (3½ fl oz) coconut toddy or tequila (optional)
salt, to taste

Marinade
200 g (7 oz) natural plain yogurt
100 ml (3½ fl oz) tinned coconut milk
12 cloves garlic, chopped
200 g (7 oz) caramelized onions (see page 61)
1 or 2 fresh red chillies, finely chopped

Masala
1 tablespoon coriander seeds
1 teaspoon green cardamoms
1 teaspoon black mustard seeds
½ teaspoon panch phoran (see page 62)

1 Roast and grind the masala, following the instructions on page 60.
2 Put the marinade ingredients and the ground masala in a blender or food processor and 'pulse' to a pouring paste using water as needed.
3 Mix the marinade and meat in a non-aluminium bowl (see cook's tip page 77). Cover and refrigerate for up to 24 hours.
4 Heat the ghee in a 2.25–2.75 litre (4–5 pint) lidded casserole dish and add the marinated meat, stir-frying it for about 5 minutes. Then put the casserole, lid on, in a preheated oven, 190°C/375°F/Gas 5.
5 After 20 minutes, inspect, stir and taste. Add a little water if needed to prevent sticking. Return the casserole to the oven.
6 After another 20 minutes inspect again. Add the mint, coriander and the garam masala. Replace in the oven.
7 After a final 20 minutes, taste the dish – the meat should be tender. Add the toddy or tequila, if using, and season with salt. Switch off the oven, replace the casserole in the oven for 10 minutes, then serve.

Vindaloo
CHILLI-HOT PORK CURRY
Goa, Indian west coast

This dish was introduced to India by the Portuguese when they first arrived in Goa in 1497. Called vinha d'alhos (meaning 'wine with garlic') it consisted of pork marinated in red wine, vinegar and garlic (alho), and is still found in Portugal today. The local Goanese Indians were soon converted to Christianity, so had no qualms about consuming pork and wine. Not surprisingly, they found the dish bland so they increased the quantity of garlic and added spices, notably plenty of chilli, another newly arrived Portuguese import. The recipe name was simplified to vin-DAR-loo, with the emphasis, as in the Portuguese version, on the second syllable. Unchanged to this day, this subtly sour, hot dish bears no resemblance to the popular curry-house pastiche.

Serves 4

675 g (1 lb 6 oz) lean leg of pork, weighed after removing all unwanted matter, cut into 4 cm (1¹/₂ inch) cubes
3 tablespoons ghee (see page 61)
6 cloves garlic, chopped
225 g (8 oz) onions, chopped
water or fragrant stock, as needed (see page 59)
1 tablespoon coarsely chopped fresh coriander
4 fresh red chillies, finely chopped
salt, to taste

Marinade
200 ml (7 fl oz) red wine
50 ml (2 fl oz) rice vinegar
6 cloves garlic, puréed
3 or 4 fresh red chilles, puréed
1 teaspoon salt

Masala
10 cloves
6 green cardamoms
5 cm (2 inch) piece of cassia bark
1 teaspoon cumin seeds

1 Mix the meat and the marinade ingredients together in a large non-aluminium bowl (see cook's tip page 77). Cover and refrigerate for up to 24 hours.
2 Heat the ghee in a karahi or wok. Add the garlic and the masala and stir-fry for 1 minute, then add the onions and continue to stir-fry for 5 minutes.
3 Tip the contents of the pan into a 2.25–2.75 litre (4–5 pint) lidded casserole dish. Add the pork and its marinade and combine well. Place the casserole in a preheated oven, 190°C/375°F/Gas 5.
4 After 20 minutes, inspect and stir, adding a little water or stock if the curry is becoming too dry.
5 Repeat 20 minutes later, adding the remaining ingredients.
6 Cook for a further 20 minutes or until the curry is cooked to your liking.

Chilli-hot pork curry

Xacutti

LAMB WITH A CASHEW & COCONUT PASTE

Goa, Indian west coast

Pronounced 'zak-yoo-tee', this recipe is a popular Goan dish, especially at festival time. Chicken, fish, crab, or in this case, lamb, is cooked with a paste of roasted cashew nuts and fresh coconut with red chilli, tamarind, spices and a hint of sweet. There are two versions, the Goan Hindu version, as here, uses chilli and sugar, the Catholic version is less pungent and uses palm sugar (jaggery).

Serves 4

2 tablespoons ghee (see page 61)
6 cloves garlic, finely chopped or puréed
50 g (2 oz) onion, very finely chopped
675 g (1 lb 6 oz) lean lamb leg, weighed after
    removing all unwanted matter, cut into 2.5 cm
    (1 inch) cubes
6–8 fresh or dried curry leaves (optional)
1 tablespoon coarsely chopped fresh coriander
6–8 mint leaves, chopped
2 tablespoons garam masala
1 lemon
salt, to taste

Masala

3 teaspoons coriander seeds
2 pieces of cassia bark, each about 5 x 1 cm
    (2 x 1/2 inch)
1/2 teaspoon fenugreek seeds
1/2 teaspoon peppercorns
1/2 teaspoon green cardamoms
1/2 teaspoon cloves
1/2 teaspoon cumin seeds

Marinade

1 tablespoon raw shelled cashew nuts
8 dried red chillies, whole
6–8 green chillies, chopped
1 tablespoon tamarind purée (see page 62)
1 teaspoon sugar (optional)
water and flesh of 1 fresh coconut
1 teaspoon turmeric

1 Roast and grind the masala, following the instructions on page 60. Put this in a blender or food processor with the marinade ingredients and 'pulse' to a pouring paste using water as needed.
2 Heat the ghee in a 2.25–2.75 litre (4–5 pint) lidded casserole dish and add the paste, stir-frying it for about 30 seconds. Add the garlic and stir-fry for 30 seconds, then add the onion and stir-fry for a further 5 minutes. Add the meat, stir-frying it for about 3 minutes. Then put the casserole, lid on, in a preheated oven, 190°C/375°F/Gas 5.
3 After 20 minutes, inspect and stir. Add a little water if needed to prevent sticking. Return the casserole to the oven.
4 Repeat after 20 minutes. Add the curry leaves, if using, the fresh coriander, mint and garam masala. Replace in the oven.
5 After a final 20 minutes, taste the dish – the meat should be tender. Squeeze in the lemon juice and season with salt. Switch off the oven, replace the casserole in the oven for 10 minutes, then serve with plain rice.

4 | fish & shellfish

Balchao Burra Camarao
TANGY LOBSTER CURRY
Goa, Indian west coast

This Goan favourite uses a prawn pickle called balchao/balichao/balichow (see page 224). Used sparingly, the base works well with lobster or giant tiger prawns, plentiful enough in Goa to be regarded as day-to-day ingredients rather than luxuries. In the Goan language the masala mix is called jeerem-jeerem, literally 'cumin-pepper'.

Serves 4

2 whole cooked lobsters, any type, about 1 kg (2¼ lb) each
4 tablespoons ghee (see page 61)
1 teaspoon cumin seeds
6 cloves garlic, finely chopped
200 g (7 oz) white onion paste (see page 61)
1 or 2 fresh red chillies, finely chopped
4 fresh tomatoes, chopped
1 tablespoon tomato purée
1 tablespoon prawn pickle (see page 224)
65 ml (2½ fl oz) tinned coconut milk
25 ml (1 fl oz) rice vinegar
1 teaspoon balsamic vinegar
200 g (7 oz) cooked peeled prawns
1 tablespoon coarsely chopped fresh coriander
½ teaspoon ground black pepper
salt, to taste
cooked boiled rice, to serve

Masala (jeerem-meerem)
2 teaspoons ground cumin
2 teaspoons chilli powder
2 teaspoons ground black pepper
1 teaspoon turmeric
½ teaspoon ground cinnamon

Tangy lobster curry

Garnish
fresh root ginger, cut into julienne strips
fresh coriander

1 Carefully halve the lobster shells lengthwise and remove the meat. Chop the meat into small pieces. Wash the shells and reserve.
2 Add just enough water to the masala to make a paste thick enough to drop sluggishly off a spoon.
3 Heat the ghee in a karahi or wok. Add the cumin seeds and masala paste and stir-fry for 30 seconds. Add the garlic and stir-fry for 1 minute, then add the onion paste and stir-fry for 3 minutes.
4 Add the chillies, tomatoes, tomato purée, balchoa and coconut milk. Simmer until thickened.
5 Add the vinegars, lobster meat, prawns, coriander, pepper and a little salt and simmer until hot.
6 Arrange a cleaned lobster shell on each plate, on top of a bed of rice. Divide the curry equally among the lobster shells and pour any spare curry over the top of each portion. Garnish with fresh ginger and coriander and serve.

Caranguejos Konkani
GOAN CRAB CURRY
Goa, Indian west coast

Crabs are very popular in Goa. White meat is found in the claws and legs, and dark meat in the body shell. This recipe produces a chilli-hot, runny sauce.

Serves 4

4 x 450 g (1 lb) cooked crabs in their shells
3 tablespoons vegetable oil
1 teaspoon mustard seeds
1 teaspoon fennel seeds
100 g (4 oz) finely chopped onion
1 or 2 green chillies, finely chopped

8 cooked king prawns, shells on, about 65 g
   (2½ oz) each
10–12 fresh or dried curry leaves (optional)
salt, to taste

Paste
6 cloves garlic, crushed
1–3 fresh red chillies, chopped
most of the flesh of 1 coconut (reserve the rest
   for the garnish)
1 teaspoon coriander, ground
1 teaspoon turmeric

Garnish
caramelized onions (tarka) (see page 61)
slivers of red and green chilli

1 Put the paste ingredients in a blender or food
processor and 'pulse' to a pouring paste using water
as needed.
2 Extract all the flesh you can from the crab shells,
claws and legs, and chop. Discard the claws and
legs, wash the body shells and reserve.
3 Heat the oil in a karahi or wok and stir-fry the
seeds for 20 seconds. Add the onion and the
chillies, and stir-fry for 2 or 3 minutes. Add the
paste and stir-fry for 5 minutes.
4 Add the crab meat and king prawns, curry leaves,
if using, and sufficient water to keep the mixture
loose. When simmering and hot right through,
season with salt.
5 Remove the king prawns and strain the curry,
keeping the liquid for step 6. Fill each crab shell
with curry. Tip the remaining curry into a serving
bowl and place the filled crab shells and the prawns
decoratively on top.
6 Either pour the spare liquid into the bowl or serve
it separately. Garnish with onion tarka and slivers of
chilli to serve.

Fihunu Mas Lebai
GRILLED GARLIC RED MULLET
Andaman Islands

This recipe is the only one in this book from
India's Andaman Islands, the place where the
direct tribal descendants of the first humans to
enter India are found today, still speaking their
original language (see page 8). They have
always fished and used fire, and this recipe is
undoubtedly very ancient. Any round white fish
will do for this recipe – bass, cod, monkfish, John
Dory, whiting, grey mullet, perch, pollack or black
sea bream are all perfect. Here we use red mullet,
known in the Andamans as lebai.

Serves 4

4 whole red mullet, about 30 cm (12 inches)
   long, gutted, cleaned and dried
juice of 2 limes
1 teaspoon salt
2 teaspoons finely chopped fresh red chillies
8 cloves garlic
175 g (6 oz) raw cashew nuts, chopped
1 tablespoon coarsely chopped fresh coriander
2 or 3 green chillies, chopped
1 tablespoon sesame oil

Garnish
lime wedges
dark salad leaves

1 Using a small, sharp knife, make several slashes
on the sides of the fish.
2 Mix the lime juice, salt and red chillies together.
Coat the fish, inside and out with this mixture, cover
and refrigerate for 1 hour or so.
3 Put the garlic, cashews, coriander, green chillies

Grilled garlic red mullet

and oil in a blender or food processor and 'pulse', using water as needed, to a smooth and pourable paste.

4 Rub the paste into both sides of the fish, retaining any spare paste.

5 To cook, place the fish on a rack in a grill pan lined with foil to catch drips. Cook under a preheated medium grill for 8–10 minutes.

6 Turn the fish, baste with any remaining marinade and grill for a further 5–8 minutes.

7 Serve garnished with lime wedges and salad leaves.

Haakh Gadh
FRIED FISH WITH SPINACH
Kashmir, extreme northern India

Being land-locked, Kashmir has access to only freshwater fish – any fish that inhabits inland lakes, streams and rivers comes into this category. Choose from carp, perch, salmon trout (sea trout), brown trout, rainbow trout, or the smaller grayling, roach or rudd. The fish (gadh) is fried and the spinach cooked in spices before the two are combined and served. Kashmiri spinach (haakh) has a distinctive flavour, but it's fine to use normal spinach in this recipe.

Serves 4

2–3 tablespoons ghee (see page 61)
500 g (1 lb 2 oz) freshwater fish, weighed after removing all unwanted matter, cut into 2.5 cm (1 inch) cubes
3 or 4 cloves garlic, finely chopped
250 g (9 oz) white onion paste (see page 61)
400 g (14 oz) fresh spinach, coarsely chopped
salt, to taste

Masala
2 teaspoons paprika
1 tablespoon turmeric
1 teaspoon chilli powder
6 green cardamoms
1 teaspoon black cumin seeds

1 Heat the ghee in a karahi or wok. Add the pieces of fish and stir-fry for about 3 minutes, then remove the fish from the pan using a slotted spoon. Shake off the excess ghee and leave the fish to drain on absorbent kitchen paper.

2 Add the masala to the ghee left in the pan and stir-fry for 15 seconds. Add the garlic and stir-fry for about 30 seconds, then add the onion paste and stir-fry for 1 minute more.

3 Add the spinach and cook for about 5 minutes. Return the fish to the pan, along with enough water to keep the mixture loose. Season with salt and serve.

Huggo
GRILLED MACKEREL
Mangalore, Karnataka, southern India

Mangalore is a port and shipbuilding centre on the Malabar Arabian Sea coast in the state of Karnataka. With the city's backwaters formed by the local rivers, it is not surprising that fish plays a large part in the local diet – herring, pilchard, smelt or, as here, mackerel. These all come under the oily fish category, and contain the ultra-healthy omega-3 oil. In this recipe the mackerel is marinated in a sour hot paste, before being grilled or barbecued.

Serves 4

4 fresh mackerel, about 350 g (12 oz) each, gutted, cleaned and dried

Marinade

1 tablespoon tamarind purée (see page 62)
2 or 3 cloves garlic, puréed
1 or 2 fresh red chillies, finely chopped
3 tablespoons vegetable oil
1 teaspoon turmeric
1 teaspoon ground cumin
1 teaspoon salt

Garnish

lime wedges
onion rings
salad leaves

1 Mix the marinade ingredients together and use to coat each mackerel thoroughly. Cover and leave the fish to absorb the flavours for about 1 hour.
2 To cook, place the fish on a rack in a grill pan lined with foil to catch drips. Cook under a preheated medium grill for about 5 minutes.
3 Turn the fish, baste with any remaining marinade and grill for a further 5–8 minutes. (Alternatively, barbecue the mackerel after coating with the paste.)
4 Serve garnished with lime wedges, onion rings and salad leaves.

Khatti Machi Dum
FRIED TROUT IN A YOGURT SAUCE
Kashmir, extreme northern India

This recipe is an example of Kashmiri Pandit cuisine, its distinction being that it uses no garlic or onion. Highly religious, Pandits consider garlic and onion to be aphrodisiacs, and they are often denied to Hindu widows. Asafoetida, a flavouring from a giant herbaceous plant, is used as a substitute. However, this recipe is still exciting in flavour – a freshwater fish such as trout is first fried, then simmered in a sauce of spices, ginger and yogurt.

Serves 4

3 tablespoons vegetable oil
4 skinned trout fillets, about 175 g (6 oz) each
2.5 cm (1 inch) piece of fresh root ginger, puréed
250 g (9 oz) natural yogurt
2 green chillies, finely chopped
2 teaspoons finely chopped fresh coriander
juice of 1 lemon
salt, to taste

Masala 1

2 pieces of cassia bark, each about 5 x 1 cm (2 x $1/2$ inch)
1 teaspoon chopped dried red chillies
$1/2$ teaspoon fenugreek seeds
$1/2$ teaspoon fennel seeds
$1/2$ teaspoon cloves

Masala 2

1 teaspoon cumin seeds
1 teaspoon turmeric
$1/2$ teaspoon asafoetida

1 Roast and grind Masala 1, following the instructions on page 60.
2 Heat the oil in a karahi or wok. Stir-fry Masala 2 for 15 seconds. Turn off the heat. Add the trout fillets and coat with the golden oil. Remove the trout from the pan and place on a plate.
3 Keeping the oil hot in the karahi or wok, stir-fry Masala 1 for about 30 seconds. Add the ginger and stir-fry for about 30 seconds, then add the yogurt and chillies and stir-fry for 2 minutes more.
4 Add the trout and simmer until the fillets are cooked. This takes only 5–7 minutes, but you may need to add water to keep the sauce runny, which may increase the cooking time. Add the coriander and lemon juice towards the end of cooking. Season with salt.
5 Serve with plain rice and a raita from Chapter 8.

Chemeen Manga Karavali
PRAWNS WITH MANGO
Modern chef's recipe

Here, prawns (chemeen) are stir-fried with light spices and fresh mango strips. Karavali, or Konkan, is the name given to the rugged, beautiful coastline that stretches from southern Maharashtra to Mangalore in Karnataka. Karavali is also the name given to a Taj Group restaurant in Bangalore, which specializes in the cooking of that region under the direction of chef Aylur Shriram. This is his recipe.

Serves 4

675 g (1 lb 6 oz) raw king prawns, weighed after peeling and removing the heads but leaving the tails on
4 tablespoons sunflower oil
4–6 cloves garlic, finely chopped
150 g (5 oz) onion, thinly sliced
4 or more green chillies, shredded
200 ml (7 fl oz) tinned coconut milk
1–2 firm fresh mangoes, peeled and the flesh cut into thin strips
10–12 fresh or dried curry leaves (optional)
2 tablespoons fresh lime juice
salt, to taste
fresh coriander, to garnish

1 Inspect the prawns, remove the veins from their backs using a sharp knife and rinse them clean.
2 Heat the oil in a large frying pan. Add the garlic, onion and chillies and stir-fry for about 5 minutes.
3 Add the coconut milk, mango strips and curry leaves, if using, and, when simmering over a low heat, add the prawns. Cook for 8–12 minutes, depending on prawn size, turning once or twice. During this time, the coconut milk will reduce in volume, so compensate for this by adding water, little by little, to keep the mixture loose.

4 Sprinkle the lime juice over the top and season with salt.
5 Garnish with the coriander and serve with rice.

Kolmino Patio
HOT, SWEET & SOUR PRAWNS
Parsee origin

The Parsees developed the combination of hot, sweet and sour tastes many centuries ago. One dish that particularly suits the combination is fish curry (patia/patio), which contains all kinds of fish. Tamarind is the key to the essential sour taste, while the sweetness comes from palm sugar (jaggery). Tomato purée and ketchup, although not traditional, are used by today's Parsee cooks.

Prawns work supremely well in this curry, especially peeled prawns in brine since their briny taste contributes greatly to the end result. Alternatively, use tiny brown shrimps because although their shells are translucent when raw, their colour when cooked is browner than the pink of most crustaceans. Their shells are so soft and fiddly to peel that it is easier to consume them with their shells on. Indeed the slight resultant crunchiness improves their taste and texture.

Serves 4

675 g (1 lb 6 oz) cooked prawns (see above)
50 g (2 oz) natural yogurt
250 g (9 oz) onion masala sauce (see page 61)
6 cloves garlic, puréed
2.5 cm (1 inch) piece of fresh root ginger, puréed
4 tablespoons water
2 tablespoons vegetable oil
2 tablespoons palm sugar (jaggery)
1 tablespoon tomato purée

Prawns with mango

1 tablespoon tomato ketchup
2 tablespoons tamarind purée (see page 62)
salt, to taste

Masala 1

1/2 teaspoon mustard seeds
1/2 teaspoon fennel seeds
1/2 teaspoon cumin seeds
1/2 teaspoon fenugreek seeds

Masala 2

2 tablespoons paprika
2 teaspoons ground coriander
1/2 teaspoon ground cumin

1 Inspect the prawns and, if not too fiddly, remove the veins from their backs using a sharp knife then rinse them clean.

2 Combine the yogurt, onion masala sauce, garlic, ginger and water in a bowl to make a pourable paste.

3 Heat the oil in a karahi or wok and stir-fry Masala 1 for about 30 seconds. Add Masala 2 and cook for 1 minute. Add the yogurt paste and fry for about 10 minutes, until golden.

4 Add the palm sugar (jaggery), tomato purée, ketchup and tamarind to the fried mixture, and simmer until you have a thick and dark gravy (5 more minutes at most).

5 Add the prawns and season with salt. Simmer until hot right through, then serve with rice, chupatti and chutneys.

Kozambhu
CASSEROLED TAMARIND FISH

Chettinad, Tamil Nadu, south India

A fish and meat-eating community called Chettiyars have been resident in Chettinad near the Chennai (Madras) area in the south-eastern Indian state of Tamil Nadu since the earliest times. The arrival of the British East Indian Company elevated them from tribe to millionaires. The Company had an insatiable demand for teak for building ships and bungalows. Surrounded by teak, the Chettiyars soon became prime suppliers, acquiring large amounts of Burmese teak forests for the purpose.

Theirs is a distinctive style of cooking. This dish of fish in a sour sauce of tamarind and chillies is typical of Chettinad and suits oily fish, which contain the ultra-healthy omega-3 oil. Mackerel is ideal, but more fun is a tropical fish such as hilsa, a very bony type of herring; katla, a small Bengali carp; or the Mediterranean garfish, which is similar to mackerel except it has tiny bones that can be eaten.

Serves 4

4 fresh fish (see above), about 350 g (12 oz)
    each, gutted and cleaned
2–4 green chillies, whole
400 ml (14 fl oz) milk
1 tablespoon tamarind purée (see page 62)
200 ml (7 fl oz) tinned coconut milk
salt, to taste

Masala

1 teaspoon crushed mace
6–8 cloves
3 or 4 pieces of cassia bark, each about
    5 x 1 cm (2 x 1/2 inch)
4–6 green cardamoms
1/2 teaspoon freshly grated nutmeg

Garnish

2 tablespoons peanuts, pan-roasted (see page 86) and crushed

fresh coriander

1 Place the masala, fish and chillies in a 2.25–2.75 litre (4–5 pint) lidded casserole dish.

2 Bring the milk, tamarind and coconut milk to a simmer in a saucepan then pour over the fish and put the casserole, lid on, in a preheated oven, 190°C/375°F/Gas 5.

3 Cook for 15–20 minutes. Check that the fish is cooked – cooking times will vary according to fish size and type – then season with salt.

4 Garnish with the peanuts and coriander and serve.

Macchi Kadhi
COD IN YOGURT SAUCE

Gujarat, west India

Any dried flat fish fillet will work in this Gujarati recipe, but it tastes extra special if you use salted cod fillet, of which the best is Spanish bacalao or Goan bacalhau. The salting process uses young fillets which are lightly cured to give a soft texture. The yogurt sauce here is the typical Gujarati mixture of gram flour, yogurt and turmeric with a hint of sugar in a creamy, slightly sweet, golden sauce.

Serves 4

4 pieces of salted cod fillet (see above), dry weight about 150 g (5 oz) each

3 tablespoons vegetable oil

$1/2$ teaspoon turmeric

250 g (9 oz) natural yogurt

200 ml (7 fl oz) water

50 g (2 oz) gram flour (besan)

2–3 cloves garlic, finely chopped

225 g (8 oz) caramelized onions (see page 61)

sugar, to taste (optional)

salt, to taste

Masala

1 teaspoon garam masala (see page 60)

1 teaspoon turmeric

$1/2$ teaspoon black peppercorns, crushed

$1/4$ teaspoon asafoetida

Garnish

shreds of red and green chilli

shreds of fresh root ginger

1 Soak the fish fillets in plenty of water for 24 hours, then drain, wash, rinse and set aside – the fillets will have gained at least 20 per cent in weight.

2 To cook, heat the oil in a frying pan. Stir in the turmeric and after a few seconds add the fillets. Fry on each side for a few seconds each, then remove the pan from the heat.

3 Put the yogurt in a 2.75 litre (5 pint) saucepan. Whisk in the water. Bring to the simmer, whisking regularly, and continue simmering and whisking for about 5 minutes.

4 Mix the gram flour and masala with enough water to make a runny paste.

5 Heat the oil in a karahi or wok. Add the masala paste and stir-fry for 15 seconds. As it thickens, add the yogurt, little by little, whisking all the time as it thickens. Eventually it will stop thickening, but if it gets too thick, add a little water.

6 Now add the garlic, onions and sugar, if using, and simmer for 1 minute more.

7 Add the fillets and their oil. Cook for about 8 minutes or until they are cooked through. Garnish with shreds of chilli and ginger and serve with plain rice.

Maacher Jingha Sorse Jhal
MUSTARD-SPICED PRAWNS & MONKFISH

Bengal, north-east India

If any spices typify Bengali cooking they are mustard and nigella (wild onion) seeds, and if any main ingredient, it is seafood. This recipe is a combination of monkfish and prawns, cooked in a paste of mustard powder, turmeric and chilli, enhanced with mustard seed.

Not so long ago, the ugly-faced monkfish was the poor relation in the fish world, its firm, sweet flesh substituting for lobster. Times have changed, however, and monkfish now costs more per weight than lobster. Use middle to large-sized prawns (king prawns) in this recipe.

Serves 4

2 tablespoons sunflower or soya oil
2 or 3 cloves garlic, finely chopped or puréed
250 g (9 oz) white onion paste (see page 61)
about 200 ml (7 fl oz) water
350 g (12 oz) monkfish flesh, cut into bite-sized pieces
350 g (12 oz) raw king prawns, weighed after peeling and removing the heads, tails and veins
1 or 2 teaspoons chopped dried red chillies
1 or 2 green chillies, finely chopped
sugar, to taste (optional)
salt, to taste

Masala 1
2 tablespoons mustard powder
$1/2$ teaspoon chilli powder
$1/2$ teaspoon turmeric
$1/4$ fenugreek seeds, ground

Masala 2
1 teaspoon nigella (wild onion) seeds
1 teaspoon turmeric
1 teaspoon black mustard seeds

Garnish
2 or 3 dried red chillies, whole
white poppy seeds, to sprinkle

1 Mix enough water with Masala 1 to make a smooth paste.
2 Heat the oil in a karahi or wok. Add Masala 2 and stir-fry for 15 seconds. Add the garlic and stir-fry for about 30 seconds, then add the onion paste and stir-fry for 1 minute.
3 Stir in the water and, when simmering, add the monkfish, prawns, dried and fresh chillies.
4 Simmer for about 10 minutes or until cooked. Season with salt and a little sugar, if using, then garnish with the whole dried red chillies and some poppy seeds before serving.

Mustard-spiced prawns and monkfish

Macchi ka Salan
FISH IN A SPICY SAUCE
Hyderabad, central India

Macchi is the generic word for 'fish', ka means 'of' and 'salan' is a type of Urdu spicing, a speciality of Hyderabad. Fish from tropical waters are suited to this dish – they are increasingly available fresh or frozen. Choose from barracuda, croaker, bream, grouper, marlin, rayfish, snapper, swordfish or tuna.

Serves 4

2 tablespoons vegetable oil
2 or 3 cloves garlic, finely chopped
2.5 cm (1 inch) piece of fresh root ginger, shredded
50 g (2 oz) natural yogurt
4 dried red chillies, whole
2 tomatoes, chopped
150 ml (5 fl oz) water
250 g (9 oz) fried onions
1 tablespoon tamarind purée (see page 62)
200 ml (7 fl oz) tinned coconut milk
675 g (1 lb 6 oz) fish, weighed after removing all unwanted matter, cut into 2.5 cm (1 inch) cubes
salt, to taste

Masala
3 teaspoons coriander seeds
1 teaspoon cumin seeds
$1/2$ teaspoon red chilli powder
$1/4$ teaspoon turmeric

1 Heat the oil in a karahi or wok. Add the masala and stir-fry for 15 seconds then add the garlic and stir-fry for a further 30 seconds. Add the ginger and stir-fry for about 30 seconds more, then add the yogurt and chillies and stir-fry for 2 minutes more.
2 Add the tomatoes and chillies and 3 tablespoons of the water. Fry gently until most of the liquid evaporates.
3 Add the remaining water, onions, tamarind and coconut milk. When simmering, add the fish. Maintain the sauce at a gentle simmer, stirring occasionally, until the fish is cooked.

Mathi
FRIED OR BARBECUED SARDINES
Mangalore, Karnataka, southern India

This simple recipe is very Mangalorean. Small sardines, about 10 cm (4 inches) long are kept whole with heads and tails on. Dusted with spiced gram flour, they are then fried.

Serves 4

12 sardines, about 50 g (2 oz) each, cleaned and dried
3 or 4 tablespoons sunflower oil
salt, to taste
lime wedges, to serve

Masala
3 tablespoons gram flour (besan)
2 teaspoons ground coriander
1 teaspoon cumin seeds
1 teaspoon ground black pepper
1 teaspoon chilli powder
$1/2$ teaspoon turmeric
pinch of asafoetida

1 Mix the masala ingredients together, spread out on a large plate and keep dry.
2 Heat the oil in a large frying pan. Dab one fish in the masala then add it to the hot oil in the frying pan. Repeat with all the fish.
3 Cook each fish for about 10 minutes, turning them over in turn and removing them from the pan in the order they went in. Sprinkle with salt and serve hot with lime wedges.

Min Tuluka
CRISP SPICED WHITEBAIT
Tamil Nadu, south India

With a coastline of 7,500 km (4,700 miles) it is hardly surprising that fish is so popular all over India. Heaviest is the adult blue-fin tuna, which weighs more than a beef carcass at 560 kg (over half a ton) and measures 3 m (10 feet) long. Longest at 4.5 m (14 feet 9 inches) is the swordfish although it weighs less. At the other extreme are whitebait or sprats, the young of any round fish (usually the herring), which are a maximum of 3 cm ($1^1/_4$ inches) long and can be much smaller – these are enjoyed with as much relish as the giants. Here is a Tamil Nadu recipe for miniscule fish. Min (or meen) is fish and tulu is a local culinary style. Other regions have their variations, for example the recipe is known as murola in Bengal and motiallem in Goa.

Serves 4

675 g (1 lb 6 oz) whitebait or sprats, cleaned
  and dried
vegetable oil for deep-frying

Sauce
3 tablespoons sunflower oil
1 teaspoon turmeric
10–12 fresh or dried curry leaves (optional)
2–4 cloves garlic, finely chopped
100 g (4 oz) onions, finely chopped
1 or 2 green chillies, finely chopped
1 teaspoon chopped dried red chillies
4 tablespoons tinned coconut milk
1 tablespoon coarsely chopped fresh coriander
salt, to taste

Masala
3 tablespoons gram flour (besan)
2 teaspoons mustard seeds

2 teaspoons sesame seeds
1 teaspoon chilli powder
$1/_2$ teaspoon turmeric
pinch of asafoetida

Garnish
2 teaspoons mustard seeds, roasted
snipped chives
chilli powder

1 Start by making the sauce. Heat the oil in a karahi or wok. Add the turmeric and curry leaves, if using, and stir-fry for 15 seconds. Add the garlic and stir-fry for about 30 seconds, then add the onions and the fresh and dried chillies and stir-fry for 4 minutes.
2 Add the coconut milk and coriander, and a little water if needed to keep the mixture loose. Bring to a simmer and season with salt. Set aside in the pan.
3 Mix the masala ingredients together, spread out on a large plate and keep dry. Dust the whitebait with a little of this spiced flour.
4 Heat the oil in a deep frying pan to 190°C/375°F (chip-frying temperature).
5 Add one dusted whitebait to the hot oil. After a few seconds add the next, quickly (to prevent them from sticking together), and continue until the surface area of the pan is full but not crowded. This maintains the oil temperature. Fry for 5–6 minutes.
6 Remove the whitebait from the pan, shake off the excess oil, drain them on absorbent kitchen paper and keep warm. Repeat until all the whitebait are cooked.
7 To serve, place the crispy whitebait on individual plates. Pour the sauce on top and garnish with the roasted mustard seeds, snipped chives and a sprinkling of chilli powder.

Mooli Cheemen

MIXED SEAFOOD IN COCONUT SAUCE

Karnataka, southern India

Mooli (mollee/mouli) is a delicate dish from Karnataka, southern India, where fish, or in this case a mixture of crab claws (the juicy flesh from the claws), scampi (the meat from the langoustine tail), and both the white meat (the round muscle) and the attached coral pink roe of king scallops, are simmered in a lightly spiced, coconut-based sauce coloured golden with turmeric and saffron.

Serves 4

4 tablespoons sunflower oil
4–6 cloves garlic, finely chopped
150 g (5 oz) onion, thinly sliced
10–12 fresh or dried curry leaves (optional)
1–3 green chillies, shredded
400 ml (14 fl oz) tinned coconut milk
generous pinch of saffron
8 crab claws, about 25 g (1 oz) each after being
   cooked and shelled
8 king scallops, cooked, about 25 g (1 oz) each
16 scampi, cooked and peeled, about 15 g
   (1/2 oz) each
2 tablespoons rice vinegar
50 ml (2 fl oz) dry white wine
salt and ground black pepper, to taste

Masala
1 teaspoon turmeric
1 teaspoon black mustard seeds
1 teaspoon yellow mustard seeds

Garnish
fresh coriander
lime wedges

1 Heat the oil in a large flat frying pan. Add the masala and stir-fry for 30 seconds then add the garlic, onion, curry leaves, if using, and chillies and stir-fry for about 5 minutes.
2 Add the coconut milk and saffron to the pan and simmer over a low heat for 10–12 minutes. The coconut milk will thicken – compensate for this by adding a little water as needed to keep the mixture loose.
3 Add the crab claws, scallops and scampi, the vinegar, wine and salt and pepper to season. Garnish with fresh coriander and lime wedges and serve.

Parpu Konjan

PRAWNS OR SHRIMPS IN LENTILS

Tamil Nadu, south India

Parpu is the Tamil word for 'dhal' and konjan for 'prawn'. It is often assumed that shrimps are tiny versions of prawns. In the US they are indeed called shrimps until they reach about 6 cm (2½ inches) in length, after which the term 'king prawn' is used. Prawns and shrimps are one and the same thing, according to the professionals, who measure them by how many you get to 450 g (1 lb).

This recipe uses prawns which yield between 200 and 300 to 450 g (1 lb) and are known as 'common prawns'.

Serves 4

50 g (2 oz) split and polished green lentils
   (moong dhal)
50 g (2 oz) split oily lentils (toovar/toor dhal)
4 tablespoons vegetable oil
2 or 3 cloves garlic, finely chopped or puréed
100 g (4 oz) onions, finely chopped
10–12 fresh or dried curry leaves (optional)
1 or 2 fresh red chillies, finely chopped
175 ml (6 fl oz) tinned coconut milk

175 ml (6 fl oz) water

400 g (14 oz) cooked peeled prawns

salt, to taste

2 tablespoons finely chopped fresh coriander, to garnish

Masala

2 teaspoons mustard seeds

1 teaspoon turmeric

1/4 teaspoon asafoetida

1 Mix the lentils together and soak them overnight in plenty of water.

2 To cook, place the drained lentils in a large saucepan and simmer in twice their volume of water for about 30 minutes, then coarsely mash them in the pan.

3 Heat the oil in a karahi or wok. Add the masala and stir-fry for 15 seconds. Add the garlic and stir-fry for about 30 seconds, then add the onion and stir-fry for 5 minutes.

4 Add the curry leaves, if using, chillies, coconut milk and water and bring to a simmer. Add the prawns and the mashed lentils and cook until heated through.

5 Season with salt and serve garnished with fresh coriander.

Piri Piri Diabole Mankyo
DEVILLED SQUID RINGS

Goa, Indian west coast

The Portuguese stumbled across the chilli in Brazil in 1500. Although they believed that chilli was the work of the devil (they nicknamed chilli 'diabole', meaning devil) they introduced it to the world via their former African coastal colony of Mozambique. The African word for chilli is piri piri, literally 'hot-hot'. Goan chilli-hot dishes are also called piri piri, hence the name of this dish, piri piri diabole – made here with mankyo (squid). When my grandparents lived in Agra they had a Hindu cook called Thumbi. The Raj were partial to devilled items: devilled kidneys, devilled mushrooms, even devilled ham, which Thumbi was required to cook from time to time. Being a believer in many gods and many devils, Thumbi thought it circumspect not to tempt fate by cooking one, so had Thumbi been cooking it, the dish would simply have been called chilli squid.

Serves 4

25 g (1 oz) butter

4 cloves garlic, sliced

2.5 cm (1 inch) piece of fresh root ginger, cut into strips

4 tablespoons brown onion paste (see page 61)

1 tablespoon tomato purée

2 tablespoons puréed fresh red chilli

500 g (1 lb 2 oz) squid rings, cleaned

fresh lime juice, to taste

salt, to taste

Garnish

fresh coriander

fresh mint

1 Heat the butter in a karahi or wok. Add the garlic and stir-fry for about 30 seconds, then add the ginger and onion paste and stir-fry for 1 minute.

2 Add the tomato purée, chilli and a little water, then add the squid rings and stir-fry briskly to ensure they are evenly coated in the red sauce. Season with salt.

3 Squeeze lime juice liberally over the squid, garnish with fresh coriander and mint and serve.

COOK'S TIP Instead of using squid try making this recipe with 4 x 200 g (7 oz) cleaned octopus tentacles. These make an impressive presentation on the plate if kept whole.

Peixe Reachado
SPICY STUFFED FISH
Goa, Indian west coast

Peixe is the Portuguese and Goan generic word for 'fish'. Reachado (recheado/reichado) means 'stuffed'. Fish is eaten nearly every day in Goa – indeed, a day without fish is a bad day – and stuffed fish is regarded as supreme. The traditional Goan stuffing is a hot, sweet and sour paste, also called red masala.

Choose a thick, bone-free fillet cut from large fish such as cod, hake, ling, monkfish, halibut, catfish, tuna, shark, pike or salmon. The recipe below uses skate wings, the best of which are called 'middle-cut' by the fishmonger. They are at least 5 cm (2 inches) thick. Ask your fishmonger to cut a deep slit or pouch in each wing, into which you can insert the stuffing. Note the use of Szechwan pepper (telfa/teflam), a Chinese spice used nowhere else in Indian cooking but in Goan fish dishes.

Serves 4

3 tablespoons vegetable oil

1 teaspoon turmeric

4 skate wings, 'middle-cut' and pre-slit (see
   above), each weighing about 200 g (7 oz)

200 g (7 oz) finely chopped onion

2 tablespoons finely chopped fresh coriander

Stuffing Paste

2 tablespoons rice vinegar

1 teaspoon balsamic vinegar

1 or 2 fresh red chillies, chopped

4 cloves garlic, chopped

2.5 cm (1 inch) piece of fresh root ginger,
   chopped

1 tablespoon palm sugar (jaggery)

1 teaspoon salt

Masala 1

1 teaspoon garam masala (see page 60)

1 teaspoon turmeric

1/2 teaspoon Szechwan pepper

1/2 teaspoon black peppercorns, crushed

1/4 teaspoon asafoetida

Masala 2

1 teaspoon ground cumin

1 teaspoon ground black pepper

1 teaspoon ground cloves

1 teaspoon ground cinnamon

1 teaspoon turmeric

1 Put the stuffing paste and Masala 1 ingredients in a blender or food processor and 'pulse' to a pouring paste using water as needed. Set aside.

2 Heat half the oil in a frying pan. Stir in the turmeric and after a few seconds add the fish. Fry on each side for a few seconds to give it an even golden colour. Remove the fish from the pan using a slotted spoon, shake off the excess oil and leave to rest in a cold oven tray.

3 To make the stuffing, heat the remaining oil in a karahi or wok. Add Masala 2 and stir-fry for 15 seconds. Add the onion, the reserved paste and the coriander and stir-fry for 5 minutes, then set aside until cool enough to handle.

4 Carefully insert one-quarter of the stuffing into each fish pouch. Place the fish in the oven tray and cook in a preheated oven, 190°C/375°F/Gas 5, for 10 minutes. Serve, Goan style, with baguette-like bread.

Spicy stuffed fish

Ramus
CRISP-FRIED WILD SALMON
Parsee origin

Salmon (ramus, or rawas) is an unusual fish for India, but it does exist as a luxury item. Here, salmon is spread with a light spicy paste and simply fried the Parsee way.

Serves 4

4 wild salmon steaks, 150–175 g (5–6 oz) each, cleaned and dried
6 tablespoons vegetable oil
lemon wedges, to serve

Masala
3 teaspoons cornflour
2 teaspoons chilli powder
2 teaspoons turmeric
1 teaspoon salt

1 Combine the masala ingredients together and mix with enough water to make a paste.
2 Coat each piece of fish with the masala paste and set aside for 1 hour.
3 Heat the oil in a frying pan. Place the coated salmon steaks in the pan and fry for about 4 minutes on each side for a crispy texture. Serve with wedges of lemon.

Patrani Machli
BAKED HERB POMFRET
Parsee origin

This is a Parsee masterpiece. A filleted white fish, such as pomfret, cod or plaice, is coated with a green herb and coconut paste. In Mumbai (Bombay) where the dish originated, the fish is wrapped in a banana leaf before being baked. Foil works well as a substitute for the leaf, but will not produce the same delight on unwrapping.

Serves 4

4 pieces of filleted pomfret or cod steak, about 225 g (8 oz) each
3 tablespoons vegetable oil
2 tablespoons white distilled vinegar

Coating
90 g (3¹/₂ oz) onion, peeled and coarsely chopped
2 bunches of fresh coriander and tender stalks, chopped
1 teaspoon bottled mint sauce
1–4 green chillies, coarsely chopped
2 cloves garlic, chopped
1 tablespoon coconut milk powder (see page 57)
¹/₂ teaspoon salt
1 teaspoon ground cumin
1 lemon, freshly squeezed

Garnish
desiccated coconut
1 lemon, cut into wedges

1 Place all the coating ingredients in a blender or food processor and grind to a thick porridge-like paste. If the paste is too thin transfer it to a sieve to drain; if it is too thick, add a little water.
2 Lay each fish steak on a large piece of foil, then cover the fish completely with the paste, using it all up. Wrap the fish tightly in the foil.
3 Put the oil and vinegar in an oven tray then place the tray in a preheated oven, 190°C/375°F/Gas 5. When hot, put the foiled fish in the tray and bake for 20 minutes.
4 To serve, carefully unwrap and discard the foil. The coating should have adhered to the fish and should be quite moist. Pour all or some of the liquid in the pan over the dish. Garnish the fish with the desiccated coconut and lemon wedges and serve.

Maachi Jhol
FRAGRANTLY SIMMERED FISH
Bengal, north-east India

Bengal has a river system is about six times longer than its coastline. With so much natural water, hundreds of fish species thrive such as rui, boal, magur, shing, bekti, hilsa, katla and pomfret. All work in this recipe, but any firm white fish will do. 'Jhal' and 'jhol' are Bengali cooking terms. Jhal dishes require dry-frying with virtually no water (see page 145), while jhol ingredients require enough water to simmer them to completion.

Serves 4

1 teaspoon turmeric
1/2 teaspoon salt
4 x 200 g (7 oz) halibut (or other firm white fish) steaks
4 tablespoons mustard-blend oil
1 teaspoon panch phoran (see page 62)
6 tablespoons onion masala sauce (see page 61)
175 ml (6 fl oz) water or fragrant stock
1 tablespoon chopped fresh coriander, to garnish

1 Mix the turmeric and salt into a runny paste with a tiny drop of water, and spread over the fish. Traditionally, this is supposed to both enhance the flavour of the fish and reduce the odour during cooking.
2 Heat the oil in a large pan, then fry the panch phoran for 1 minute. Add the fish pieces, and fry each side for 2 minutes, turning once. Add the onion masala sauce, shake the pan to mix, and simmer for 2 minutes.
3 Add enough water or stock to just cover the fish. Simmer for 10 minutes, always shaking the pan rather than stirring, which can break up the fish.
4 Remove the fish from the pan and serve with a little of the sauce, garnished with fresh coriander.

Vevichathu Surmai
KERALAN SOURED KINGFISH CURRY
Syrian Christian origin, Kerala, south India

Vevichathu is a Keralan Syrian Christian fish curry, which is red in colour and flavoured with chilli and kodam puli (kudam pulli). Kodam puli is a small, very sour fruit (botanical name *Garcinia indica*, about the size of a small plum and very dark purple in colour. The rind, skin and flesh are dried by wood-smoking. The fruit is reconstituted by soaking in water for an hour, after which it can be chopped or ground to obtain a virtually black, sour-tasting agent. Kodam puli is most popularly found in Keralan cooking and especially fish dishes, as in this recipe. As for the fish, kingfish steaks (surmai) are ideal.

Serves 4
2 tablespoons vegetable oil
1/2 teaspoon mustard seeds
1/2 teaspoon fenugreek seeds
7 or 8 cloves garlic, finely chopped
2.5 cm (1 inch) piece of fresh root ginger, shredded
200 g (7 oz) brown onion paste (see page 61)
10–12 fresh or dried curry leaves (optional)
2 tablespoons tinned coconut milk
4 or 5 pieces of kodam puli, soaked (see above) or 1 tablespoon tamarind purée (see page 62)
200 ml (7 fl oz) water
4 kingfish steaks, about 200 g (7 oz) each, cleaned and dried
salt, to taste

Masala
2 teaspoons coriander seeds
1–2 teaspoons chopped dried red chillies
1/2 teaspoon fenugreek seeds
1/2 teaspoon turmeric

1 Roast and grind the masala, following the instructions on page 60.

2 Heat the oil in a karahi or wok. Add the mustard and fenugreek seeds and stir-fry for 15 seconds. Add the masala and garlic and stir-fry for about 30 seconds, then add the ginger and stir-fry for 30 seconds more. Add the onion paste and stir-fry for 2 or 3 minutes.

3 Add the curry leaves, if using, the coconut milk, kodam puli or tamarind and water and, when simmering, add the fish.

4 Simmer for 8–10 minutes or until the fish is tender. Season to taste and serve with plain rice.

Zawb Tempeirada
TEMPERED MUSSELS WITH TENDLIM

Goa, Indian west coast

In this Goan recipe, any type of mollusc can be tempered (temperado/tempeirada) in a fried spicy paste. Clams work well, as do mussels. If using mussels, as here, they are best bought live. Get the fishmonger to discard any mussel shells that are open – all shells must be tightly closed. Also get the mussels cleaned, there may be a 'beard' and other matter on the shell. This recipe is best if you use the mussels at once. If that's not possible place the mussels in cold water in the fridge overnight and, the next day, discard any mussels that have opened or are floating as these are dead.

Serves 4

3 tablespoons vegetable oil
2 teaspoons black mustard seeds
2–4 cloves garlic, minced
5 cm (2 inch) piece of fresh root ginger, grated
100 g (4 oz) onions, chopped
1 or 2 fresh red chillies, finely chopped
water and flesh of 1 fresh coconut, the flesh finely grated

200 ml (7 fl oz) fish stock
200 ml (7 fl oz) dry white wine
2 tablespoons coarsely chopped fresh coriander
675 g (1 lb 6 oz) live mussels (see above), cleaned
salt, to taste
lime wedges, to serve

Masala

2 teaspoons ground cumin
1 teaspoon ground coriander
1 teaspoon mango powder
1–3 teaspoons chilli powder
$1/2$ teaspoon turmeric

Garnish

red and green chillies, cut into thin strips

1 Add just enough water to the masala to make a paste thick enough to drop sluggishly off a spoon.

2 Heat the oil in a 2.25–2.75 litre (4–5 pint) lidded saucepan and add the mustard seeds. Stir-fry for 10 seconds then add the masala and stir-fry for 15 seconds. Add the garlic, ginger, onions and chillies and stir-fry for a further 5 minutes or so.

3 Add the coconut water and flesh, and the fish stock and wine, and season with salt. Stir well. When simmering, add the fresh coriander and finally the mussels.

4 Cover the pan and simmer for about 10 minutes, keeping the sauce fairly runny by adding water as needed.

5 At the end of the cooking time discard any mussels that have remained closed. Garnish with strips of chilli and serve with lime wedges.

5 | vegetables

Al Yakkhn
WINTER VEGETABLE CURRY
Kashmir, extreme northern India

I once spent a week on one of the exquisite sandalwood houseboats on a stunning lake in Kashmir's capital, Srinagar. Each boat is a floating, four-bedroomed hotel, housing two to eight guests, a butler, two cooks and several other servants. Being made of sandalwood, which is indigenous to Kashmir, the boats have a marvellous aroma. Trading on the lakes has to be seen to be believed. Traders arrive on small punts on which they display their wares. The traders invariably climb aboard, uninvited, and harangue the beleaguered tourist to purchase their wares. On one occasion I had seven punt owners selling souvenirs, pots and pans, fruit and vegetables, flowers and books, all on board in my lounge and all shouting at once. Oblivious to all of this, the cooks and butlers simply choose their ingredients, and for this recipe it was kohlrabi and lotus. Kohlrabi, or knol-kohl, is a bulbous vegetable with lush green leaves and a white or purple root resembling a turnip, which tastes of turnip and cauliflower. A hardy vegetable, it thrives in the mountainous districts of Kashmir. The bulb and leaves are used in this recipe, and are teamed here with another Kashmir resident, the lotus. This rather extraordinary perforated aquatic root grows freely in the Srinagar lakes. It is available tinned, and occasionally fresh, from specialist Asian greengrocers.

Serves 4 as an accompaniment

200 g (7 oz) kohlrabi or baby spinach
250 g (9 oz) lotus root, peeled and sliced into
   rounds
250 g (9 oz) kohlrabi root, peeled and cubed
2 tablespoons mustard-blend oil
1/2 teaspoon asafoetida

2 tablespoons black mustard seeds
2–4 cloves garlic, cut into thin julienne strips
225 g (8 oz) onion, cut into thin julienne strips
5 cm (2 inch) piece of fresh root ginger, cut into
   thin julienne strips
100 ml (3 1/2 fl oz) cup water
1–2 teaspoons chopped dried red chillies
salt, to taste

1 Steam, microwave or boil the kohlrabi or baby spinach for 2 or 3 minutes until cooked.
2 Do the same, separately, for the kohlrabi and the lotus, cooking them for about 4 minutes.
3 Heat the oil in a karahi or wok. Add the asafoetida, mustard seeds and garlic and stir-fry for 1 minute. Add the onion and ginger and stir-fry for 2 minutes.
4 Add the water and the chillies and bring to a simmer.
5 Add the drained leaves and vegetables, and stir-fry until the mixture returns to simmering point. Season with salt and serve.

Aloo Ghobi Methi
FENUGREEK-FLAVOURED POTATO & CAULIFLOWER
Punjab, north-west India

Originating in the Middle East, cauliflower is made up of a short stem with a number of florets, which are normally off-white, but can be green, yellow or red. Combine cauliflower with potato for a dish with robust savoury flavours that is essentially Punjabi.

Serves 4 as an accompaniment

1/2 teaspoon turmeric
2 large potatoes, peeled, cooked and quartered
12 cauliflower florets
3 tablespoons ghee (see page 61)
1 teaspoon cumin seeds

2 cloves garlic, finely sliced

2.5 cm (1 inch) piece of fresh root ginger,
   finely sliced

100 g (4 oz) fried onions

2 or 3 fresh tomatoes, halved

1 teaspoon dried fenugreek leaves

1 or 2 green chillies, sliced lengthwise

1/2 teaspoon garam masala (see page 60)

1 tablespoon chopped fresh coriander

salt, to taste

Masala

2 teaspoons ground coriander

1 teaspoon ground cumin

1 teaspoon turmeric

1/2 teaspoon chilli powder

1 Add the turmeric to a large saucepan of boiling water. Add the potatoes and boil for about 10 minutes until cooked. Drain and set aside.
2 Meanwhile, blanch the cauliflower florets in a saucepan of boiling water for 3 minutes, then drain.
3 Add just enough water to the masala to make a paste thick enough to drop sluggishly off a spoon.
4 Heat the ghee in a karahi or wok. Add the cumin seeds and fry for 20 seconds. Add the masala paste and stir-fry for 30 seconds. Add the garlic and stir-fry for another 30 seconds. Add the ginger and stir-fry for 30 seconds more. Add the fried onions and continue to stir-fry for 2 minutes more.
5 Add the tomatoes, fenugreek and chillies, and stir-fry for 2 minutes more.
6 Add the cauliflower florets and just enough water to keep the mixture loose. Simmer for about 3 minutes, or until the florets are tender.
7 Stir in the potato, garam masala and coriander. When hot, season with salt and serve.

Avial

COCONUT, YOGURT & MANGO MIXED VEGETABLES

Malabar, Kerala, south India

Avial is known as the 'Malabar masterpiece'. The authentic recipe must contain yogurt, sour green mango and coconut, and no garlic, ginger or onion – asafoetida, a garlic/onion flavoured substitute is used instead. Traditionally, the vegetables in the recipe include all or some of the following: ash gourd, aubergine, carrot, cucumber, drumstick gourd (see page 204), karela bitter gourd, plantain, potato, pumpkin, snake gourd, spinach and yam. Avial is prepared at festival time at the great temples of southern India in vast brass urns, 1.5 m (5 feet) high and 3 m (10 feet) in diameter, to feed the entire local population. This tradition goes back to the time when the Cholas built the temples in the first millennium AD (see page 21).

Serves 4 as an accompaniment

450 g (1 lb) exotic mixed vegetables (see above)

1 teaspoon turmeric

10–12 fresh or dried curry leaves (optional)

4 tablespoons vegetable oil

coconut milk powder for thickening, if needed
   (see page 57)

salt, to taste

Paste

water and flesh of 1 fresh coconut

2–4 green chillies, coarsely chopped

1 small sour mango, peeled and the flesh
   chopped

50 g (2 oz) natural yogurt

2 teaspoons cumin seeds

1 teaspoon black mustard seeds

1/2 teaspoon chilli powder

1/2 teaspoon asafoetida

1/2 teaspoon turmeric

1 Prepare and trim the vegetables, as appropriate – the tradition is to cut some into thinnish diamond-shaped slices.
2 Put the paste ingredients in a blender or food processor and 'pulse' using water as needed until it is smooth and pourable.
3 Add the turmeric to a large saucepan of boiling water then add the vegetables and blanch for 3–4 minutes. Strain, leaving enough blanching water in the pan to cover the vegetables. Add the curry leaves, if using, and bring back to a simmer.
4 Meanwhile, heat the oil in a karahi or wok. Add the paste and stir-fry for about 2 minutes.
5 Add the fried paste to the vegetables and simmer for 3 or 4 minutes until they are cooked. The sauce should not be too thick. If it is very watery (controllable at step 3), add some coconut milk powder to thicken it. Season with salt and serve.

Baigan Burtha
SMOKY AUBERGINE PURÉE
Orissa, east India

Burtha literally means a mash or purée of any vegetable. Here it is the aubergine, which is first slightly charred by baking and grilling. This not only helps in the removal of the skin, it also greatly enhances the smoky flavour much loved in Bengal and in Orissa.

Serves 4 as an accompaniment

2 deep purple oblong aubergines, each about
   15 cm (6 inch) long
2 tablespoons sunflower oil
1 or 2 green chillies, sliced
1/2 teaspoon chopped dried red chillies
1 tablespoon chopped fresh coriander
4 tablespoons natural yogurt (optional)
salt, to taste

1 Make a few small slits in each aubergine to allow steam to escape and prevent bursting, then cook in a preheated oven, 190°C/375°F/Gas 5, for at least 30 minutes.
2 Place the cooked aubergines under a preheated medium grill for 5 minutes. They should look wrinkled and darker and be slightly charred on the surface but not badly burned. Leave to cool.
3 Scoop out the aubergine flesh into a mixing bowl, discarding the skins. Mash the flesh with a fork.
4 Heat the oil in a karahi or wok. Add the fresh and dried chillies and the coriander and stir-fry for 2 minutes. Add the aubergine mash and the yogurt, if using. When hot, season with salt.
5 Serve hot as an accompaniment or serve cold as a relish.

Baigan ka Salan
HYDERABADI-SPICED AUBERGINE
Hyderabad, central India

The aubergine originated in south-east Asia and belongs to the nightshade family, as do tomatoes and potatoes. It is oblong and pear- or egg-shaped, hence its alternative name, eggplant. It is a fleshy, berry fruit, generally deep purple in colour and ranging in size from 6 to 30 cm (2½–12 inches) long. This is the traditional Hyderabai spicing.

Serves 4 as an accompaniment

8 small purple oblong aubergines, about 75 g
   (3 oz) each after the stem is removed
4 tablespoons vegetable oil
2 or 3 cloves garlic, finely chopped or puréed
2.5 cm (1 inch) piece of fresh root ginger,
   shredded
200 g (7 oz) caramelized onions (see page 61)
400 ml (14 fl oz) water or fragrant stock (see
   page 59)
10–12 fresh or dried curry leaves (optional)
175 g (6 oz) natural yogurt

1 tablespoon tamarind purée (see page 62)

1 or 2 green chillies, finely chopped

1 tablespoon red pepper, thinly sliced

1/2 tablespoon green pepper, thinly sliced

1/2 tablespoon yellow pepper, thinly sliced

salt, to taste

Masala

2 teaspoons cumin seeds

2 teaspoons poppy seeds

2 teaspoons sesame seeds

1 teaspoon coriander seeds

1 teaspoon turmeric

20–25 raw cashew nuts

50 g (2 oz) desiccated coconut

1–2 teaspoons chopped dried red chillies

1 Roast and grind the masala, following the instructions on page 60.

2 Slit each aubergine lengthwise about three-quarters of the length without separating the flesh at the stem end. Carefully discard the pith and seeds in the centre.

3 Heat the oil in a karahi or wok. Fry the aubergines lightly then remove and set aside.

4 Using the same oil, add the masala and stir-fry for about 15 seconds. Add the garlic and stir-fry for about 30 seconds, adding a few spoonfuls of water if needed to prevent sticking. Then add the ginger and onions and stir-fry for 1 minute.

5 Add the aubergines and the water, curry leaves, if using, yogurt, tamarind, chillies and peppers to the pan and simmer for 10 minutes, stirring occasionally.

6 Season with salt and serve.

Bemla Kauvery

BAMBOO SHOOT CURRY

Coorg, Karnataka, southern India

Although bamboo is generally associated with both pandas and Chinese cooking, some edible bamboo species grow quite freely in north-east India, Nepal and the cooler areas of southern India. Fresh whole bamboo shoots are sometimes available from Asian stores.

Serves 4 as an accompaniment

400 g (14 oz) fresh bamboo shoots, peeled, or tinned shoots, drained and rinsed

2 tablespoons black mustard seeds

2 tablespoons mustard, sunflower or soya bean oil

1–2 teaspoons chopped dried red chillies

10–12 fresh or dried curry leaves (optional)

100 g (4 oz) onions, thinly sliced

salt, to taste

Masala

2 tablespoons ground coriander

2 teaspoons ground cumin

1 teaspoon turmeric

1 teaspoon chilli powder

1/2 teaspoon asafoetida

1 Cut the bamboo shoots into 2 cm (3/4 inch) pieces.

2 Dry-fry the mustard seeds in a wok for 30 seconds and set aside.

3 Heat the oil in a karahi or wok. Add the masala, dried chillies and curry leaves, if using, and stir-fry for 30 seconds. Add the onions and stir-fry for 5 minutes or so.

4 Add the bamboo shoots and stir-fry briskly for a few minutes, sprinkling with water as needed to prevent sticking.

5 Add the mustard seeds, season with salt and serve immediately.

Bendakka, or Vendaikai
TAMIL STIR-FRIED OKRA
Tamil Nadu, south India

Okra, also known as bindi, is a green, tapering seed capsule, with a pointed tip and grooves along its length. Native to Africa and Asia, it ranges in size from about 6 cm to as much as 25 cm ($2^1/_2$–10 inches). Select soft, not scaly, specimens, no more than 11 cm ($4^1/_2$ inches) long.

Serves 4 as an accompaniment

6 tablespoons mustard-blend oil
2 teaspoons black mustard seeds
$^1/_2$ teaspoon black cumin seeds
4 tablespoons chopped onion
2 tomatoes, finely chopped
1 tablespoon strips of green pepper, sliced
   lengthwise
2–3 green chillies, sliced lengthwise
1 teaspoon sugar
450 g (1 lb) okra, left whole and untrimmed
juice of 1 lemon
1 tablespoon chopped coriander
salt, to taste

Masala
1 teaspoon ground cumin
1 teaspoon coriander seeds, ground
1 teaspoon ground cassia bark
$^1/_2$ teaspoon chilli powder
$^1/_2$ teaspoon green cardamom seeds, ground
$^1/_2$ teaspoon turmeric

1 Heat the oil in a karahi or wok, add the seeds and stir-fry for 30 seconds, then add the masala and onion and stir-fry for 5 minutes.
2 Add the tomatoes, green pepper, chillies and sugar and stir-fry for 5 minutes.
3 Add the okra to the pan and stir-fry for 5 minutes. Stir gently – if the okra gets bruised or cut it will go very sappy. Add water by the spoonful to keep the mixture loose.
4 Add the lemon juice and the chopped coriander.
5 Stir-fry for 5 minutes more. If the okra were tender initially they should now be cooked perfectly. Season with salt and serve at once. Do not refrigerate or freeze this dish – it will go sappy and mushy.

COOK'S TIP Okra combines well with a vegetable called tendli (Hindi), tendlim (Konkani/Goan), tindori (Marathi) or potol (Bengali) – it has no English name. A tiny member of the marrow family, it resembles the gooseberry in colour, markings and size, but is oval in shape. It has a similar limited flavour as marrow but, like courgette, its outer case is also edible. Tendli are sometimes called 'gentleman's toes', while okra are cutely known as 'ladies' fingers'. So, if you want 'fingers and toes', use 225 g (8 oz) okra and 225 g (8 oz) tendli and follow the recipe above, adding the tendli, whole, at step 4.

Bindi
CRISP OKRA
Modern chef's recipe

Okra can produce a sticky sap, but in this clever recipe from London chef Vikram Sunderam, the okra is dabbed in spiced gram flour, deep-fried and served at once. The process makes it so crunchy, it could be a stand-alone titbit, as well as an accompaniment dish.

Serves 4 as an accompaniment

vegetable oil for deep-frying
450 g (1 lb) okra
salt, to taste

Tamil stir-fried okra

Coating

25 g (1 oz) gram flour (besan)
1 teaspoon chilli powder
1 teaspoon ground cumin
1 teaspoon salt
1/2 teaspoon asafoetida

1 Mix the coating ingredients together in a mixing bowl.
2 Heat the oil in a deep frying pan to 190°C/375°F (chip-frying temperature).
3 Once it is hot, cut half the quantity of okra into 1 cm (1/2 inch) slices. Dab the rounds in the spiced flour mixture, then add to the oil, one at a time, but rapidly until the surface area of the pan is full but not crowded. This maintains the oil temperature. Fry for 4–5 minutes.
4 Remove the okra from the pan using a slotted spoon. Shake off the excess oil and drain on absorbent kitchen paper.
5 Repeat steps 3–4 until all the okra are cooked. Sprinkle with salt and serve at once.

Dhaaba Wallah Ande ka Tarkari
EGG & PEA CURRY

Throughout India

A favourite curry, hard-boiled eggs with peas is popular fare at the countless dhaabas distributed throughout India. These roadside eateries (transport cafés) are made of whatever materials are to hand – tin sheets, thatch or tarpaulin. The dhaaba wallah cooks on a primitive flame, often in full view of customers. Dhaabas offer a limited menu (nothing written down, of course) including dhals, omelettes, vegetable and mutton curries, the ubiquitous char (tea) and soft drinks. Seating is usually a charpoy (a rope-strung cot) in the open air in front of the eatery. Some operate all night and vertical neon tubes are their night-time beacon.

Serves 4 as an accompaniment

6 tablespoons vegetable oil
200 g (7 oz) fried onions
200 g (7 oz) tinned tomatoes and their liquid
1 tablespoon tomato purée
100 g (4 oz) fresh peas, cooked or frozen peas, thawed
coarsely chopped fresh coriander
4–8 hard-boiled eggs (depending on size and appetite), halved if liked
salt, to taste

Masala

1 teaspoon turmeric
1 teaspoon ground cumin
1 teaspoon garam masala (see page 60)
1 teaspoon ground coriander
1/2 teaspoon chilli powder

1 Add just enough water to the masala to make a paste thick enough to drop sluggishly off a spoon.
2 Heat the oil in a karahi or wok and fry the masala paste for 30 seconds.
3 Add a little water to prevent it from sticking, then add the onions, tomatoes and tomato purée.
4 Add the peas and coriander, and simmer for a further 3 or 4 minutes, then add enough water to achieve the texture of sauce that you require. Season with salt.
5 Add the hard-boiled eggs, whole or halved and simmer until hot. Serve immediately.

Chowgra
YOGURT-BASED VEGETABLE CURRY
Hyderabad, central India

Hyderabad is in Andra Pradesh, a southerly state with a very hot climate, but several factors differentiate it from the other southern states around it. Firstly, its population is 40 per cent Muslim. Secondly, and because of this, it is a largely meat-eating area; and thirdly, the people love yogurt, an ingredient more commonly associated with the north rather than the south. Chowgra vegetables in a yogurt-based curry sauce typifies the flavours of Hyderabad.

Serves 4 as an accompaniment

100 g (4 oz) green beans
100 g (4 oz) aubergine
100 g (4 oz) pumpkin
100 g (4 oz) sweet potato
100 g (4 oz) broad beans
2 tablespoons vegetable oil
2 or 3 cloves garlic, finely chopped or puréed
2.5 cm (1 inch) piece of fresh root ginger, shredded
200 g (7 oz) fried onions
1 or 2 green chillies, finely chopped
400 ml (14 fl oz) water or fragrant stock (see page 59)
50 g (2 oz) natural yogurt
1 tablespoon lemon juice

Masala 1
2 green cardamoms
4 cloves
1 bay leaf
1 cinnamon stick
1/4 teaspoon black cumin seeds

Masala 2
1 teaspoon turmeric
1/2 teaspoon asafoetida
2 teaspoons cumin seeds
1 teaspoon lovage seeds
10–12 fresh or dried curry leaves (optional)

1 Prepare and trim the vegetables, cut into in any shape you like.
2 Roast and grind Masala 1, following the instructions on page 60.
3 Add just enough water to Masala 2 to make a paste thick enough to drop sluggishly off a spoon.
4 Heat the oil in a karahi or wok. Add Masala 2 and stir-fry for 30 seconds. Turn off the heat then add the vegetables and stir to coat them with the mixture so that they look golden.
5 Setting the karahi or wok aside for further use, transfer the vegetables and their oil to an oven tray so that they are closely packed together, one layer deep. Bake in a preheated oven, 190°C/375°F/Gas 5, for 25 minutes.
6 Using a slotted spoon so as to leave the oil in the oven tray, transfer the vegetables to a bowl.
7 Tip the oil from the oven tray into the karahi or wok and heat. Add the garlic and stir-fry for 15 seconds. Add the ginger and stir-fry for about 30 seconds, then add the onions and stir-fry for 1 minute more.
8 Mix in Masala 1, the chillies, water or fragrant stock and yogurt and bring to a simmer.
9 After 5 minutes, add the roasted vegetables. When simmering add the lemon juice and serve hot.

Kari, or Karikai
MIXED VEGETABLE CURRY
Tamil Nadu, south India

Kari in Tamil means 'pepper', and writings from around 300AD tell of a dish cooked with pepper that was called kari or thallikari. This later evolved into the spicy stew found in Tamil Nadu to this day under the same name – kari, kuri, turkari or turkuri (see page 196). A similar dish is also called karikai, or kurikai. The *Oxford English Dictionary* attributes the word 'curry' to the Tamil word kari and the early English voyagers to India would have encountered this dish. Any vegetables can be used along with turmeric, garlic, coconut, black lentils (urid dhal) and dried red chillies. Omit the chilli for a more authentic dish; alternatively, you can omit the pepper. Heat-lovers should retain both.

Serves 4 as an accompaniment

1 teaspoon turmeric
450 g (1 lb) peeled and trimmed vegetables of
    your choice, such as green beans, sweet
    potato, parsnips and carrots, cut into 1 cm
    ($^1/_2$ inch cubes)
1 tablespoon mustard-blend oil
2 or 3 cloves garlic, finely sliced into rounds
150 g (5 oz) finely chopped onion
10–12 fresh or dried curry leaves (optional)
2 green chillies, sliced lengthwise
water and flesh of 1 fresh coconut, the flesh
    shredded
salt, to taste
4 tablespoons caramelized onions (tarka)
    (see page 61), to garnish

Masala 1
1 tablespoon split and polished black lentils
    (urid dhal)
1–2 teaspoons chopped dried red chillies
1 teaspoon black peppercorns
1 teaspoon cumin seeds
$^1/_2$ teaspoon black mustard seeds
$^1/_2$ teaspoon yellow mustard seeds

Masala 2
1 teaspoon ground white pepper
1 teaspoon turmeric
$^1/_2$ teaspoon asafoetida

1 Dry-fry Masala 1 in a karahi or wok for about 30 seconds then set aside.
2 Bring plenty of water to the boil in a 2.25–2.75 litre (4–5 pint) saucepan. Add the turmeric and the vegetables and simmer for about 5 minutes. Strain, retainining the cooking water.
3 Heat the oil in the karahi or wok. Add Masala 2 and stir-fry for 30 seconds, then add the garlic and stir-fry for another 30 seconds. Add the onion, curry leaves, if using, chillies and coconut flesh and water, and continue stir-frying for a further 1–2 minutes.
4 Add Masala 1 and the vegetables, together with enough of the retained cooking water to enable them to simmer without sticking.
5 When the vegetables are tender and heated through, season with salt. Heat the onion tarka then use it as a garnish. Serve at once with Kitchri (rice with lentils, see page 208) or plain rice.

Mixed vegetable curry

Dilruba Sabzi
VEGETABLES IN A CREAMY SAUCE
Moghul origin, northern India

This combination of crumbled paneer (Indian cheese), cream, eggs, nuts and vegetables has Iranian or Persian roots, and this rich recipe is a treasured Moghul vegetable dish.

Serves 4 as an accompaniment

3 tablespoons ghee (see page 61)
1–3 teaspoons finely chopped garlic
200 g (7 oz) onion masala sauce (see page 61)
150 ml (5 fl oz) single cream
450 g (1 lb) cooked, chopped vegetables of your choice, such as fresh or frozen peas, green beans, tinned sweetcorn
1 tablespoon very finely chopped fresh coriander
2 or 3 tablespoons crumbled paneer (see page 62)
2 hard-boiled eggs, chopped
1 tablespoon raw pistachio nuts, slightly crushed
2 teaspoons garam masala (see page 60)
salt, to taste

Masala
3 teaspoons ground coriander
1 teaspoon ground cumin
1 teaspoon turmeric
1/2 teaspoon chilli powder

1 Add just enough water to the masala to make a paste thick enough to drop sluggishly off a spoon.
2 Heat the ghee in a karahi or wok and fry the masala paste for 30 seconds. Add the garlic and stir-fry briskly for 20–30 seconds. Add the onion masala sauce and keep stirring for another minute.
3 Add the cream and the vegetables and simmer until hot right through, adding just enough water to keep a thickish texture.

4 Add the remaining ingredients, including salt to season, and continue cooking and stirring for 1 final minute or so. Serve with pullao rice (see page 207).

Foogath
GOURD, PLANTAIN & CASHEW CURRY
Goa, Indian west coast

Foogath originated in Goa, its name deriving from the Portuguese word refogar, meaning 'to stew in seasoning'. Once the Goans got hold of it, they interpreted the seasoning to mean chilli and the stewing to be as quick as possible. Put another way, it's a really quick-to-make spicy, lightly cooked vegetable dish, often using gourds, with two other Goan specialities, cashew nuts and plantains. Goans like slight sour tastes for which they use Goan vinegar made from coconut toddy, here substituted with rice and balsamic vinegars. The dish is also found in the Kerelan Malabar area. (See page 171 for details on gourd types.)

Serves 4 as an accompaniment

2 tablespoons mustard-blend oil
2 teaspoons yellow mustard seeds
3 or 4 cloves garlic, finely chopped
200 g (7 oz) fried onions
200 g (7 oz) plantains, weighed after peeling and sliced into rounds
1–4 green chillies, finely chopped
1–2 teaspoons chopped dried red chillies
1/2 red pepper, sliced
200 g (7 oz) bottle gourd or butternut squash, weighed after peeling and cut into cubes
2 tablespoons rice vinegar
1 teaspoon balsamic vinegar
4 tablespoons tinned coconut milk
20–30 cashew nuts, fried (see page 87)
salt, to taste

1 Heat the oil in a karahi or wok and stir-fry the seeds for about 30 seconds. Add the garlic and onions and continue cooking for another 2 minutes.
2 Add the plantains, chillies and red pepper. Then add enough water to cover, and simmer for about 5 more minutes.
3 Add the gourd or squash, vinegars and the coconut milk and keep simmering, adding just enough water to keep the mixture loose. Add the cashews and season with salt. Toss gently and serve immediately.

Kootu Kazhani
HOT & SOUR VEGETABLES
Chennai, Tamil Nadu, south India

A traditional south Indian dish, kootu/kootoo is a mixed-vegetable hot and sour curry, containing chilli, tamarind, sesame and coconut. This typical Madrassi dish is found in local homes, where it is slow-cooked in a mud pot over a wood fire. It was cooked in the same fashion 1,100 years ago and was then called melogra. Kazhani means 'rice-washed water', created by soaking the rice for a few minutes in water – the starchy stock is regarded as highly nutritious and imparts flavour to the gravy. It is served with that rice.

Bananas and plantains grow in clusters on long stems which hang down from palm trees. At the bottom of the stems, at a certain time of year, are the plant flowers. The 'flower' grows to about 20 cm (8 inches) in length and is an elongated heart-shape, surrounded by purple-brown leaves. Beneath the leaves are florets and yellow stigma. The flowerets are edible and highly prized. Cooked like cauliflower, they have a somewhat spongy texture. Banana flowers are occasionally available from Thai and Asian stores. They may be an acquired taste, but try this dish at least once for a true authentic taste of south India.

Serves 4 as an accompaniment

2 banana flowers, whole (see above)
4 tablespoons sunflower or soya oil
4–6 cloves garlic, sliced into rounds
225 g (8 oz) finely chopped red onion
2–4 fresh red chillies, finely chopped
10–12 fresh or dried curry leaves (optional)
200 ml (7 fl oz) tinned coconut milk
2 tablespoons tamarind purée (see page 62)
salt, to taste
red onion slices, to garnish

Masala
2 teaspoons sesame seeds
1 teaspoon ground coriander
1 teaspoon ground black pepper
1 teaspoon black mustard seeds
1/2 teaspoon black cumin seeds

1 Pull off the first leaf from each banana flower, revealing the many long thin soft baby flowers. Pluck all these, discard the leaf, and continue like this until all the flowers are picked. Then chop most of them coarsely, keeping a couple for garnishing.
2 Heat the oil in a karahi or wok, add the masala and stir-fry for 30 seconds, then add the garlic and stir-fry for 30 seconds more. Add the red onion and continue stir-frying for about 5 minutes.
3 Add the chillies and curry leaves, if using, and after 1 minute or so add the coconut milk and tamarind.
4 Add the banana flowers. Simmer for about 10 minutes, adding water only if the mixture reduces too much. Season with salt. Garnish with a few fresh banana flowers and red onion slices and serve with various colourful chutneys.

Khumbi
MUSHROOMS
Assam, north-east India

There are literally hundreds of edible mushroom species to choose from, the most familiar of which include field, cup, button and flat. Other less familiar cultivated varieties include beefsteak fungus, parasol, cep, blewit, pleurotte and oyster. Each has a distinctive flavour. Peel and wash them only if necessary, then cut as required. This dish from the humid tea-growing area of Assam uses a mixture of mushrooms.

Serves 4 as an accompaniment

3 tablespoons ghee (see page 61)
2 or 3 cloves garlic, finely chopped
seeds from 6–8 green cardamom pods
2 tablespoons water
450 g (1 lb) mushrooms, any type or
    combination, cleaned and thinly sliced
salt, to taste
1 tablespoon chopped chives

Masala
3 teaspoons paprika
1 teaspoon ground coriander
1/2 teaspoon chilli powder

1 Add just enough water to the masala to make a paste thick enough to drop sluggishly off a spoon.
2 Heat the ghee in a karahi or wok. Add the masala paste and stir-fry for 30 seconds, add the garlic and cardamom seeds and continue stir-frying for 30 seconds. Stir in the water.
3 Add the mushrooms and stir carefully, initially. Soon they will soften and yield some juices. Season with salt, garnish with the chive leaves and serve.

Mushrooms

Kurass ke Phul
STIR-FRIED CELERY
Modern chef's recipe

Celery is a herbaceous plant and a member of the umbelliferae family, as are cumin and fennel, both of which are used in this dish along with cream. Until its adoption by modern Indian chefs, celery was rarely used in India. This recipe comes from London restaurateur Cyrus Todiwallah.

Serves 4 as an accompaniment

225 g (8 oz) celery, trimmed of leaves and end
    stub, cleaned and cut into 2.5 cm (1 inch)
    pieces
4 tablespoons vegetable oil
2 or 3 cloves garlic, finely chopped or puréed
2.5 cm (1 inch) piece of fresh root ginger,
    shredded
4–6 fresh tomatoes, chopped
50 ml (2 fl oz) single cream
salt, to taste

Masala
1 teaspoon cumin seeds
1 teaspoon fennel seeds
1 teaspoon wild onion seeds
1 teaspoon coriander seeds
1 teaspoon turmeric
1/2–1 teaspoon chilli powder

1 Steam, microwave or blanch the celery until cooked but still crisp.
2 Heat the oil in a karahi or wok. Add the masala and stir-fry for about 1 minute. Add the garlic and ginger and stir-fry for 1 further minute.
3 Add the tomatoes and, when sizzling and soft, add the cooked celery and cream and mix well. The mixture should be quite dry, but add a little water to prevent burning while it heats up.
4 Season with salt and serve at once.

Bom Chount
KASHMIRI CURRIED APPLE
Kashmir, Extreme Northern India

Apple is an unexpected ingredient in this chapter on vegetables, and this is an unexpectedly good Kashmiri recipe. The apple is probably the world's most popular fruit and records of its cultivation go back to the ancient Egyptians. In Britain and India apples are known to have existed in the Stone Age, some 5,000 years ago.

Serves 4 as an accompaniment

3 tablespoons ghee (see page 61)
450 g (1 lb) cooking apples, peeled, cored and
  quartered
250 ml (9 fl oz) boiling water
8–10 green cardamoms
4 cinnamon sticks
4 tablespoons brown onion paste (see page 61)
1 teaspoon black salt (kala namak) or white sea
  salt, to taste (see page 58)
1 tablespoon tamarind purée (see page 62)
1 teaspoon black cumin seeds

Masala
2 tablespoons paprika
1 teaspoon turmeric
1/2 teaspoon ground ginger

1 Heat the ghee in a karahi or wok, add the masala and stir-fry for 30 seconds, then add the apples and stir-fry for 2 minutes.
2 Add the boiling water to a saucepan and return to the boil.
3 Add the cardamoms, cinnamon, onion paste, salt and tamarind and the fried apples with their ghee.
4 Cover the pan and cook the apples for about 5 minutes. Sprinkle with the black cumin seeds, mix well and serve.

Coquiero Caldine
GOAN MILD VEGETABLE STEW OR CURRY
Goa, Indian west coast

The word 'caldine' is derived from the Portuguese word 'caldeira', meaning a 'boiling pan' or 'cauldron' (caldo meaning 'soup'), although it has evolved into a more solid dish, using any main ingredients, which in this version are cabbage (couve), mung bean sprouts (ganthi) and snap peas. Coconut is mandatory, and coquiero means a 'coconut tree'. This recipe came from one of Goa's best and longest established restaurants, O Coquiero (The Coconut Tree) in Povorim north of Margoa. Being unknown to tourists, it is a frequent haunt of Goan locals.

Serves 4 as an accompaniment

2 tablespoons coconut oil
6 or 7 cloves garlic, finely chopped
2.5 cm (1 inch) piece of fresh root ginger,
  shredded
200 g (7 oz) caramelized onions (tarka)
  (see page 61)
water and flesh of 1 fresh coconut, puréed
  together
1 teaspoon palm sugar (jaggery)
1 teaspoon tamarind purée (see page 62)
200 g (7 oz) white cabbage, shredded
1 or 2 green chillies, whole
150 g (5 oz) snap peas, whole
150 g (5 oz) fresh bean sprouts
50 ml (2 fl oz) dry sherry
salt, to taste

Masala
1 teaspoon black peppercorns, crushed
1 teaspoon cumin seeds
1/2 teaspoon coriander seeds
1/2 turmeric

1 Heat the oil in a karahi or wok. Add the masala and stir-fry for 30 seconds, then add the garlic, ginger and fried onions and stir-fry for 3 minutes.
2 Add the coconut purée, palm sugar (jaggery) and tamarind and enough water to keep the mixture loose. Simmer for 2 minutes.
3 Add the cabbage and chillies, and continue to simmer for 5 minutes.
4 Add the snap peas, bean sprouts and sherry. Simmer for 2 or 3 minutes longer then season with salt and serve.

Looki Kalia
PUMPKIN CURRY
Bengal, north-east India

The kalia style of curry cooking is described on page 105. This Bengali dish includes white poppy seed as an intriguing spice and gourds such as pumpkin or bottle gourd. The gourd family is thought to have originated in Bengal, although it is so ancient that wild species developed in the Americas before continental drift caused the tectonic plates to separate. Anything called squash is Native American such as butternut squash, snake squash, custard squash and spaghetti squash and the pumpkin and chayote (christophene). In the Old World, the gourd family includes cucumber, marrow (which originated in Persia and grows to quite huge dimensions, averaging 30 cm/12 inches), and a whole range of exotic gourds from India, including ribbed gourd (looki), bottle gourd (doodi), round gourd (papdi), drumsticks (sajjar), bitter gourd (kerela) and snake gourd. The soft flesh is high in water content so requires minimal cooking and supplies relatively little nutrients.

Serves 4 as an accompaniment

450 g (1 lb) pumpkin or other gourds, weighed after step 1
100 g (4 oz) carrot, cut into equal-sized pieces
4 tablespoons ghee (see page 61)
200 ml (7 fl oz) tinned coconut milk
1 or 2 fresh red chillies, sliced
1 tablespoon tomato purée
1 tablespoon tomato ketchup
2 teaspoons garam masala (see page 60)
1 teaspoon finely chopped fresh coriander
salt, to taste

Paste
2 or 3 cloves garlic
2.5 cm (1 inch) piece of fresh root ginger
225 g (8 oz) onion, coarsely chopped
1 tablespoon white poppy seeds
25 g (1 oz) almond flakes, toasted

Masala
1 teaspoon panch phoran (see page 62)
5 cm (2 inch) piece of cassia bark
2 or 3 bay leaves
1/2 teaspoon chilli powder

1 Cut open the pumpkin or gourds. Scoop out the stringy centre and seeds and discard. Cut away the flesh, then cut it into bite-sized pieces.
2 Steam, microwave or boil the pumpkin and/or gourds and carrot pieces separately until tender.
3 Put the paste ingredients in a blender or food processor and 'pulse' using water as needed until it is smooth and pourable.
4 Heat the ghee in a karahi or wok. Add the masala and stir-fry for 30 seconds. Add the paste and stir continuously for about 5 more minutes, using some of the coconut milk to keep the mixture loose.
5 Add the remaining coconut milk, the chillies, tomato purée and ketchup and, when simmering, mix in the cooked pumpkin or gourds and carrots, the garam masala and coriander. When hot, season with salt and serve.

Dandal
BROCCOLI STEMS
Punjab, north-west India

This favourite Punjabi dish uses an ingredient often discarded – soft broccoli stems. A type of brassica with short fleshy green buds clustered in a single head, broccoli was developed in Italy in the 1500s. It resembles cauliflower, with which it can be substituted or combined in this recipe. Cut off the florets and keep them for another use.

Serves 4 as an accompaniment

2 tablespoons ghee (see page 61)
2 or 3 cloves garlic, finely chopped
1 cm (1/2 inch) piece of fresh root ginger, shredded
250 g (9 oz) white onion paste (see page 61)
350 g (12 oz) broccoli stems, cut into 4 cm (1 1/2 inch) pieces
1 or 2 green chillies, finely chopped
salt, to taste
2 teaspoons roasted cumin seeds, to garnish

Masala
1 teaspoon turmeric
1 tablespoon mango powder
1 tablespoon ground coriander
1/2 teaspoon lovage seeds

1 Heat the ghee in a frying pan. Add the masala and stir-fry for 15 seconds. Add the garlic and stir-fry for about 30 seconds, then add the ginger and onion paste and stir-fry for 1 minute more.
2 Add the broccoli stems and chillies and stir-fry for 2 minutes.
3 Add enough water to just cover the stems. Reduce the heat and simmer until the dish is quite dry and the stems are darker in colour. Season with salt.
4 Garnish with the roasted cumin seeds and serve.

Mattar Valor
PEA & GREEN BEAN CURRY
Delhi and Haryana, north-west India

Fresh peas are available in season and make a refreshing change from the ubiquitous frozen items, although it should be said that the frozen pea is one of the best frozen products. The pea is an excellent source of protein, sugar and starch and it contains numerous minerals. It contains small amounts of lectin, the toxin present in all pulses, so should ideally be cooked before eating. Green beans are closely related to peas, except that the seeds are tiny and the pods edible, so they make an ideal combination, as in this light curry of peas and beans from the state of Haryana.

Serves 4 as an accompaniment

225 g (8 oz) fresh peas, cooked or frozen peas, thawed
225 g (8 oz) fresh valor or Kenyan beans, chopped
2 tablespoons sunflower or soya oil
1/2 teaspoon lovage seeds
1 tablespoon sweet mango chutney, finely chopped
salt, to taste
3 or 4 tablespoons caramelized onions (see page 61), to garnish

1 Steam, microwave or boil the peas and beans separately until cooked.
2 Heat the oil in a karahi or wok. Add the seeds and stir-fry for 20 seconds. Add the peas and beans and continue stir-frying for 1 further minute, until mixed and hot.
3 Stir in the chutney, season with salt and serve when hot, garnished with caramelized onions.

Pea & green bean curry

Mirchi ka Salan
HYDERABADI CHILLI CURRY
Hyderabad, central India

My very good friend Karan Bilimoria, founder of Cobra beer, chose this as a star dish at his wedding feast in Secunderbad, Hyderabadi, where it is a signature dish. I make no apologies for the fact that this dish is seriously hot. It is deliciously tasty – I know because I was there. So taken was I with it, that the family gave me their recipe. Incidentally, the beans are to bulk it out, but heat-lovers may wish to omit them and double up on the chilli content.

Serves 4 as an accompaniment

20–30 Kenyan green beans, cut into 7.5 cm (3 inch) pieeces
2 tablespoons vegetable oil
10–12 fresh or dried curry leaves (optional)
20–30 green cayenne chillies, stems removed and halved and slit on one side
3 or 4 large dried red chillies, whole
salt, to taste

Masala
2 teaspoons poppy seeds
2 teaspoons sesame seeds
2 teaspoons coriander seeds
1¹/₂ teaspoons cumin seeds
1 teaspoon black mustard seeds
¹/₄ teaspoon fenugreek seeds

Paste
200 g (7 oz) onion
2 or 3 cloves garlic
2.5 cm (1 inch) piece of fresh root ginger
1 tablespoon palm sugar (jaggery)
4 tablespoons desiccated coconut
4 tablespoons raw shelled peanuts
3 tablespoons tamarind purée (see page 62)

1 teaspoon chilli powder
¹/₂ teaspoon turmeric

Garnish
scrapings of fresh coconut flesh (optional)
black mustard seeds
shreds of fresh red and green chilli

1 Roast and grind the masala, following the instructions on page 60.
2 Put the paste ingredients in a blender or food processor and 'pulse' using water as needed until it is smooth and pourable.
3 Steam, microwave or boil the beans until cooked. Set aside.
4 Heat the oil in a karahi or wok. Add the masala and stir-fry for 30 seconds. Add the paste and continue stir-frying for a further 2 or 3 minutes, adding water as necessary to keep the mixture loose.
5 Add the curry leaves, if using, and the chillies and cook for 5 minutes or so.
6 Add the cooked beans and cook for a further 2–3 minutes until the dish has a thickish consistency.
7 Season with salt, garnish and serve.

Navrattan Korma
NINE-JEWEL VEGETABLE CURRY
Moghul origin, northern India

A short distance from Agra is the city of Fatephur Sikri. It is completely deserted, but totally intact. Built by the Moghul emperor Akbar, it was abandoned 14 years later for want of a decent water supply. There are two places of special interest here. One is the harem kitchen, which still carries the smoke stains of the last cooking done there in the 16th century. Nearby is a vast alfresco chess board (India invented chess) where Akbar sat playing the game with servants dressed as the chess pieces making the moves on the board. His 'opponent' would be one of his inner court advisors, who was careful enough never to win. There were nine permanent advisors, known as Akbar's navrattan or 'nine jewels'. Each was at the top of his profession: vizeer, general, iman, poet, musician, philosopher, artist, Akbar's biographer and one other, which legend has it was his head chef. Perhaps it was he who created this delightful dish containing any nine colourful ingredients.

Serves 4 as an accompaniment

50 g (2 oz) carrot
50 g (2 oz) green beans
3 tablespoons vegetable oil
2 or 3 cloves garlic, puréed
2.5 cm (1 inch) piece of fresh root ginger, puréed
200 g (7 oz) white onion paste (see page 61)
300 ml (10 fl oz) milk
pinch of saffron
1 or 2 green chillies, finely chopped
1 tablespoon coarsely chopped fresh coriander
2 teaspoons garam masala (see page 60)
50 g (2 oz) tinned sweetcorn kernels
50 g (2 oz) tinned red kidney beans, drained and rinsed
50 g (2 oz) tinned chickpeas, drained and rinsed
50 g (2 oz) frozen peas, thawed
50 g (2 oz) golden sultanas
50 g (2 oz) fresh pistachio nuts
200 ml (7 fl oz) single cream
salt, to taste
toasted almond flakes, to garnish

Masala

1 teaspoon fennel seeds
1 teaspoon green cardamoms
$1/2$ teaspoon black cumin seeds
5 cm (2 inch) piece of cassia bark

1 Blanch the carrot and green beans then dice them into 1 cm ($1/2$ inch) cubes and set aside
2 Heat the oil in a karahi or wok. Add the masala and stir-fry for 30 seconds then add the garlic and stir-fry for 30 seconds more. Add the ginger and the onion paste and stir-fry for 5 more minutes.
3 Add the milk, saffron, chillies, coriander and garam masala and simmer for 3 or 4 minutes.
4 Add the blanched carrot and green beans, the tinned sweetcorn and its liquid, kidney beans, chickpeas, peas, sultanas, pistachio nuts and the cream. When simmering again, season with salt, garnish with toasted almond flakes and serve.

Niramish Butta
VEGAN SWEETCORN CURRY
Modern chef's recipe

This Bengali dish, also known as lubra, can be made with any vegetable. Here sweetcorn kernels are combined with baby corn in a modern twist of a Kolikot (Calcutta) recipe, adapted by executive chef Stephen Gomes of the Café Naz group. Not only is it vegan, it contains no garlic, ginger or onions. It gets its interesting flavour from five-spice mixture (panch phoran) and a crunchy texture from the roasted lentil garnish.

Serves 4 as an accompaniment

8 fresh baby sweetcorn, chopped into 1 cm ($1/2$ inch) lengths
2 tablespoons mustard-blend oil
1 teaspoon panch phoran (see page 62)
$1/2$ teaspoon asafoetida
1 or 2 green chillies, finely chopped
250 g (9 oz) tinned, drained or fresh, cooked sweetcorn kernels
pinch of sugar (optional)
1 tablespoon split and polished gram lentils (chana dhal)
salt, to taste

1 Steam, microwave or boil the baby sweetcorn until cooked.

2 Heat the oil in a karahi or wok. Add the panch phoran and asafoetida and stir-fry for 20 seconds, then add the chillies and continue stir-frying for 30 seconds more.

3 Add the sweetcorn kernels and stir-fry for about 2 minutes.

4 Add the sugar, if using, and season with salt.

5 Dry-dry the lentils in a heated dry wok for about 1 minute. Use to garnish the curry and serve at once.

Oonbhariu
PARSEE ROAST ROOT VEGETABLES
Parsee origin

This dish (also called umberio, or oberu) brings a whole new meaning to Indian vegetables, which are often stewed, and even overcooked. A slow-baked Parsee vegetable dish from Gujarat, it evolved from the stew called Undhui (see page 195). In the absence of the modern oven (still unavailable to many Indians) a pit is dug in the earth and lined with charcoal. When the coals are white hot, the lidded pan is lowered onto them, covered with more burning charcoal and left to slowly 'bake' for several hours. Parsees consider this dish their masterpiece to which they often add meat and especially quail. A selection of vegetables from plantain, mooli (white radish), sweet potato, baby aubergine, gourd, courgette, shallot, whole garlic, new potato, parsnip and carrot are stir-fried in a base of lovage seeds, cumin seeds, asafoetida and turmeric. This coats the vegetables with a golden glaze – note the ruby-like beetroot, added after the coating to enhance the already superb appearance. The dish is then oven-roasted, making it arguably the best Parsee vegetable speciality.

Parsee roast root vegetables

Serves 4 as an accompaniment

450 g (1 lb) exotic mixed vegetables (see above), weighed after preparation (see step 1)
4 tablespoons vegetable oil
1 teaspoon lovage seeds
2 teaspoons cumin seeds
10–12 fresh or dried curry leaves (optional)
1 teaspoon turmeric
$1/2$ teaspoon asafoetida
1 unvinegared, cooked peeled beetroot, cut into 4 cm ($1^{1}/_{2}$ inch) cubes
2–4 green chillies, whole with stems removed (optional)
salt, to taste

1 Prepare and trim the vegetables, cut into in any shape that you like. The baby aubergines look nice when cut lengthwise, but kept in one piece (so that the stem end is still whole).

2 Heat the oil in a karahi or wok. Add the seeds, curry leaves, if using, turmeric and asafoetida and stir-fry for 30 seconds. Now turn off the heat and add all the vegetables except the beetroot, and stir to coat them with the mixture so that they look golden. (This can be done a couple of hours before step 3.)

3 To cook, place the vegetables in an oven tray so that they are closely packed together, one layer deep. Place the beetroot at random across the tray. Roast in a preheated oven, 190°C/375°F/Gas 5, for 25–35 minutes. You may need to baste the vegetables with oil from the bottom of the oven tray, and roast a while longer.

4 Sprinkle the vegetables with salt and serve straight from the oven tray if it is attractive enough.

Papri

LENTIL DUMPLINGS WITH VEGETABLES

Gujarat, west India

Since 1983 I have had the privilege of organizing and leading tours to India. On my first tour I invited the late Meera Tanjeja to be the group's guide. Her delightful personality and enthusiasm for India's food is still remembered by those who came on that tour. At the time she was a prolific writer of Indian regional cookery books. As a tribute I am publishing a recipe she gave me years ago. Papri is simply the Gujarati word for vegetables, which can be of your choice. The light, gram flour dumplings are mandatory, however.

Serves 4 as an accompaniment

2 tablespoons vegetable oil, plus extra for
   deep-frying
2 or 3 cloves garlic, finely chopped
100 g (4 oz) runner beans, trimmed and cut
   into 2.5 cm (1 inch) pieces
4 baby aubergines, cut into 2.5 cm (1 inch)
   pieces
4 large potatoes, peeled and quartered
100 g (4 oz) yam, peeled and cut into 2.5 cm
   (1 inch) cubes
200 g (7 oz) caramelized onions (tarka)
   (see page 61)
400 ml (14 fl oz) water or fragrant stock (see
   page 59)
8 cherry tomatoes, whole
1 teaspoon sugar (optional)
salt, to taste
1 tablespoon coarsely chopped fresh coriander,
   to garnish

Masala

1 teaspoon cumin seeds
1 teaspoon turmeric

10–12 fresh or dried curry leaves (optional)
1/2 teaspoon lovage seeds
1/2 teaspoon asafoetida
1/2 teaspoon chilli powder

Dough

50 g (2 oz) gram flour (besan)
25 g (1 oz) all-purpose or strong white flour
100 g (4 oz) fresh fenugreek leaves, cleaned
   and chopped or 1 tablespoon dried fenugreek
   leaves
1 tablespoon vegetable oil
1/2 teaspoon chilli powder
1/2 teaspoon ground cumin
1/2 teaspoon salt
pinch of bicarbonate of soda

1 Heat the 2 tablespoons oil in a karahi or wok. Add the masala and stir-fry for 30 seconds. Add the garlic and stir-fry for 30 seconds more. Now turn off the heat and add the runner beans, aubergines, potatoes and yam, stirring to coat them with the mixture so that they look golden. (This can be done a couple of hours before step 2.)

2 Place the vegetables in an oven tray so that they are closely packed together, one layer deep. Bake in a preheated oven, 190°C/375°F/Gas 5, for 25–35 minutes.

3 Meanwhile, mix the dough ingredients with a little water to make a stiff dough. Shape the dough into 16 small balls.

4 Heat the oil in a deep frying pan to 190°C/375°F (chip-frying temperature).

5 Add one ball to the hot oil. After a few seconds add the next, and continue until the surface area of the pan is full but not crowded. This maintains the oil temperature. Fry for 5–7 minutes.

6 Put the cooked vegetables, fried onions, water or stock, cherry tomatoes, the deep-fried balls and the sugar, if using, in a saucepan and simmer for 5 minutes or so. Season with salt, garnish with fresh coriander and serve.

Payari Moong Upkari
GREEN BEANS WITH LENTILS
Southern India

This simple curry (upkari) accompaniment dish features beans (payari) and green lentils (moong dhal). It is quite dry, so needs a gravy-based curry to accompany it.

Serves 4 as an accompaniment

4 tablespoons vegetable oil
1/2 teaspoon turmeric
1 teaspoon mustard seeds
10–12 fresh or dried curry leaves (optional)
75 g (3 oz) onions, finely chopped
2–4 green chillies, chopped
350 g (12 oz) cooked french beans, cut into
   5 cm (2 inch) pieces
150 g (5 oz) cooked green lentils (moong dhal)
100 ml (3 1/2 fl oz) tinned coconut milk
100 ml (3 1/2 fl oz) water or fragrant stock (see
   page 59)
salt, to taste

Garnish
fresh chopped coriander
chopped dried red chillies, roasted

1 Heat the oil in a karahi or wok. Add the turmeric, mustard seeds, curry leaves, if using, onions and chillies and stir-fry for 1 minute.
2 Add the beans, dhal, coconut milk and water. When simmering, season with salt, garnish with chopped coriander and dried red chillies and serve.

Porial Kadama
FESTIVAL VEGETABLES
Tamil Nadu, south India

At New Year India's most southern state, Tamil Nadu, holds a festival called Pongal. The great temple complex in Madurai, essential visiting for all Hindus, is a major focal point for the festival. Food is closely associated with Hindu religious festivals and the temples specialize in cooking for the masses and dispensing it liberally to all-comers. The vegetables – fennel, kohlrabi and celeriac bulbs – in the recipe are shredded, along with that extraordinary south Indian native vegetable, the mooli (or white radish), which can grow as long as 60 cm (2 feet) and then resembles the tusks of the much-loved temple elephants.

Serves 4 as an accompaniment

1 fennel bulb
1 kohlrabi bulb
1 celeriac bulb
15 cm (6 inch) piece of mooli (white radish)
2 tablespoons mustard-blend oil
100 g (4 oz) chopped onion
120 ml (4 fl oz) tinned coconut milk
1 large potato, peeled, cooked and cut into
   small cubes
1 large firm mango, peeled and the flesh
   chopped
a few fresh pineapple chunks
2–4 fresh red chillies, chopped
1 tablespoon coarsely chopped fresh
   coriander
salt, to taste
1 tablespoon whole black lentils (urid dhal),
   to garnish

Masala

1 teaspoon black mustard seeds

1 teaspoon cumin seeds

1 teaspoon sesame seeds

10–12 fresh or dried curry leaves (optional)

1 teaspoon coriander seeds

1/2 teaspoon black cumin seeds

1/2 teaspoon turmeric

1 Peel the fennel, kohlrabi, celeriac and mooli, discarding unwanted matter. Shred them using a grater or a food processor attachment.

2 Heat the oil in a karahi or wok. Add the masala and stir-fry for 20 seconds, then add the onion and stir-fry for 5 minutes.

3 Add the coconut milk and the shredded vegetables and simmer for a few minutes until tender.

4 Add the potato, mango, pineapple, chillies and chopped coriander. Stir-fry for a few minutes until cooked to your liking, adding a little water if necessary to keep the mixture loose. Season with salt.

5 Meanwhile, dry-fry the lentils in a heated dry wok for about 1 minute. Sprinkle them over the vegetables to garnish and serve at once.

Rangalu Kanchkaladom
SWEET POTATO & GREEN BANANA

Bengal, north-east India

Both banana (kala) and the cooking species, plantain (kanch kala), originated in south-east Asia. When the green skin of the latter is peeled (and discarded), it reveals a firmer flesh than banana, which can be sliced or diced and cooked.

Serves 4 as an accompaniment

4 tablespoons ghee (see page 61)

2–4 tablespoons finely chopped garlic

100 g (4 oz) onion masala sauce (see page 61)

2 tablespoons tomato purée

150 ml (5 fl oz) milk

vegetable oil for deep-frying

225 g (8 oz) plantains, peeled and sliced into rounds

225 g (8 oz) sweet potatoes, peeled and cut into potato chip shapes

salt, to taste

Masala

2 tablespoons ground coriander

1 teaspoon ground cumin

1 teaspoon turmeric

1 teaspoon garam masala (see page 60)

1 teaspoon paprika

2 teaspoons dried fenugreek leaves

1 Add just enough water to the masala to make a paste thick enough to drop sluggishly off a spoon.

2 Heat the ghee in a karahi or wok. Add the masala and stir-fry for about 30 seconds. Add the garlic and the onion masala sauce and stir-fry for another 30 seconds

3 Stir in the tomato purée then add the milk, little by little – it will give a good, creamy gravy-like consistency if done slowly. Set aside.

4 Heat the oil in a deep frying pan to 190°C/375°F (chip-frying temperature). Add the pieces of plantain and sweet potato to the hot oil, one by one, to prevent the pieces sticking together. Fry for about 5 minutes, until evenly golden. Remove them from the oil and drain on absorbent kitchen paper.

5 Add the deep-fried plantains and sweet potatoes to the gravy, and reheat it to simmering. Add a little water to thin the sauce slightly if necessary. Season with salt and serve.

Porial Bagada Ottakuddi
SHREDDED BAMBOO SHOOTS
Ootakamund, Karnataka, south India

Ootakamund was a hill station built by the British in the Nilgiri Hills, the blue mountains, in Karnataka. It had a church, complete with spire made from corrugated iron, rose-lined cottages, a race course, a hunt complete with red jackets and one of the most exclusive clubs in India. Stanley Baldwin and Winston Churchill (both to become British prime ministers) were members in the late 19th century. And it was here that snooker was invented and the word 'black-balled' used to veto certain undesirables wishing to become members. Not for nothing was Ootakamund nicknamed 'snooty Ooty'. But the real inhabitants of the Nilgiri Hills were the Badaga tribe, who had lived there for millennia, and still do. The Badagas grow bamboo shoots and enjoy this simple recipe. It is served with what the Badagas delightfully call koo (plain basmati rice).

Serves 4 as an accompaniment

400 g (14 oz) fresh bamboo shoots, peeled, or
   tinned, sliced shoots, drained and rinsed
4 tablespoons ghee (see page 61)
2 teaspoons black mustard seeds
2 or 3 dried red chillies, chopped
20 fresh or dried curry leaves (optional)
salt, to taste

1 Shred the bamboo shoots.
2 Heat the ghee in a karahi or wok. Add the mustard seeds and as soon as the seeds start popping, add the chillies and curry leaves, if using.
3 Almost at once add the bamboo shoots. When hot, season with salt and serve.

Poro Mirchi
CHILLI OMELETTE
Parsee origin

Parsees love eggs – boiled, scrambled (ekuri) and as omlettes. They also love chillies, and this combination is excellent at any meal.

Serves 1

1 tablespoon vegetable oil
1 teaspoon black mustard seeds
1–3 green chillies, finely chopped
1 tablespoon chopped onion
2 eggs
salt, to taste

1 Heat the oil in a frying pan. Add the mustard seeds and stir-fry for 10 seconds. Add the chillies and onion, and stir-fry for about 2 minutes.
2 Briskly beat the eggs with a whisk or fork, then pour over the fried items. Twist the pan deftly and swiftly so that the egg rolls right around it and covers the base of the pan.
3 Fry over a medium heat until just firm then slide it out of the pan. Season with salt and serve the omelette flat, not folded.

RAILWAY STATION VEGETABLE CURRY

Throughout India

This is the only recipe in this book to have no Indian name. The British established India's railway network as a top-priority, no-expense-spared project after the 1854 Lucknow uprising. Never again would they be unable to mobilize troops quickly. The Indian railway is still one of the largest networks in the world. My mother travelled very long distances on it as a child in the 1920s, travelling between home and boarding school. One of the highlights was the ubiquitous curry which has been served at all Indian railway stations from the 1850s to this day. Indian trains do not have restaurants on board, so you order at one station and your curry and rice is delivered to your seat, as if by magic, at the next station.

Serves 4 as an accompaniment

3 tablespoons vegetable oil
2 or 3 cloves garlic, finely chopped or puréed
300 g (11 oz) onion masala sauce (see page 61)
200 g (7 oz) tinned tomatoes, mashed
1 teaspoon garam masala (see page 60)
1 tablespoon coarsely chopped fresh coriander
8 large potatoes, peeled, cooked and cut into bite-sized pieces
2 or 3 large carrots, peeled, cooked and finely diced
50 g (2 oz) fresh peas, cooked or frozen peas, thawed
salt, to taste

Masala
2 teaspoons ground coriander
2 teaspoons dried fenugreek leaves
1 teaspoon cumin seeds
1 teaspoon turmeric
$1/2$–2 teaspoons chilli powder
$1/2$ teaspoon mango powder
salt, to taste

1 Add just enough water to the masala to make a paste thick enough to drop sluggishly off a spoon.
2 Heat the oil in a karahi or wok. Add the masala paste and stir-fry for 30 seconds. Add the garlic and stir-fry for another 30 seconds. Add the onion masal sauce and continue to stir-fry for 1 or 2 minutes.
3 Add the tomatoes, garam masala and the chopped coriander and simmer for 5 or 6 minutes.
4 Add the potatoes, carrots and peas. When hot, season with salt and serve.

Rasa Karela chi-Bhaji
TASTY FRIED BITTER GOURD

Kerala, south India

Ayurvedic philosophy states that the Indian meal must have six rasas (tastes): sweet, salty, bitter, pungent, sour and spicy. Not every non-Indian would agree with pungency, presuming that means piquancy, nor with bitterness. But the bitter taste is so important to India that I would be derelict in my duties if I did not include just one dish with a bitter ingredient. Unless you have an Asian store near you, the ingredient I have chosen may be beyond your reach. It is the aptly named bitter gourd, or karela, which averages about 15 x 4 cm (6 x 1$1/2$ inches) and has sharp pointed ends. I was given this recipe by Brian George, a schoolteacher who regularly visits India on teaching exchanges. Of karela he says: 'As with fine malt whisky, the first taste often repels, but equally like malt one grows to love it. Certainly, I developed a taste for it and would always recommend it be given a try.'

Serves 4 as an accompaniment

3 or 4 bitter gourds (karela), weighing about
   400 g (14 oz) in total
2 tablespoons mustard-blend oil
1 teaspoon mustard seeds
10–12 fresh or dried curry leaves (optional)
200 g (7 oz) fried onions
300 g (11 oz) natural yogurt
salt, to taste

Masala
1/2 teaspoon ground cumin
1/2 teaspoon ground coriander

1 Wash the karela, trimming off any hard skin, and chop into bite-sized slices. Cook in a saucepan of boiling water for about 10 minutes then drain.
2 Heat the oil in a karahi or wok. Add the mustard seeds, curry leaves, if using, and masala and stir-fry for 10 seconds, then add the onions and stir-fry for about 1 minute more.
3 Add the yogurt, and allow the mixture to reduce and thicken a little.
4 Finally, add the drained karela to the yogurt. When heated through, season with salt. Serve hot or cold.

Ravaiya
STUFFED BABY AUBERGINE
Gujarat, west India

This is the gastronomic jewel in Gujarat's crown. The choice of aubergine is crucial for this recipe. You need deep-purple baby aubergines, no longer than 10 cm (4 inches) and bottle shaped (not spherical). The stuffing is your choice, but here I advocate a true Gujarati stuffing containing many tasty items including gram flour and crushed peanuts. For a full Gujarati experience, serve the aubergines with Kadhi Shorba (curry soup, see page 66), Khitchri (rice with lentils, see page 208) and Khatta Puda (savoury gram flour pancakes, see page 220).

Makes 8

8 baby aubergines, no more than 10 cm
   (4 inches) long (see above)
2 teaspoons vegetable oil

Stuffing
8 tablespoons mashed potato
1 tablespoon finely chopped onion
1 tablespoon gram flour (besan)
about 30 peanuts, pan-roasted (see page 86)
   and crushed
4 cloves garlic, finely chopped
1 cm (1/2 inch) piece of fresh root ginger,
   shredded
1 tablespoon coarsely chopped fresh coriander
1 teaspoon garam masala (see page 60)
1 teaspoon turmeric
1 teaspoon chilli powder
1/2 teaspoon ground coriander
1/2 teaspoon ground cumin
1/2 teaspoon cumin seeds
1/2 teaspoon lovage seeds
1 teaspoon salt

1 Mix the stuffing ingredients together in a bowl.
2 Wash the aubergines, leaving the stems on. Using a small sharp knife, carefully cut down the length of one side of each aubergine to make a slit, but do not cut through to the other side. Carefully scoop out and discard the pith and seeds.
3 Stuff the aubergines with the mixture and line them up, side by side, on a greased oven tray.
4 Brush the aubergines with a little oil then bake them for a minimum of 15 minutes in a preheated oven, 190°C/375°F/Gas 5, until tender. They may need a few minutes more baking depending on their size.

Tamarta, Bhare Sag Palak

BEEF TOMATOES STUFFED WITH CHEESE & SPINACH

Modern chef's recipe

Beefsteak tomatoes are ideal for stuffing and baking. This stuffing is a traditional mix of spinach and paneer, and an innovative twist is to top it with Gruyère or mozzarella cheese to obtain the golden crust of a gratin.

Makes 4

4 firm beefsteak, or marmade, tomatoes, about 9 cm (3¹/₂) inches in diameter
4 tablespoons grated Gruyère or mozzarella cheese

Stuffing

225 g (8 oz) cooked fresh, frozen or tinned spinach, well drained
2 cloves garlic, finely chopped
2 tablespoons finely chopped spring onions
120 g (4¹/₂ oz) paneer, crumbled (see page 62)
1 tablespoon finely chopped fresh coriander
1 tablespoon chopped fresh mint
1 or 2 green chillies, finely chopped
1 teaspoon garam masala (see page 60)
1 teaspoon cumin seeds
1 teaspoon mustard seeds
¹/₂ teaspoon mango powder
1 teaspoon salt

1 Mix the stuffing ingredients together until the stuffing is soft and mouldable and set aside.
2 Cut the top off each tomato and discard. Without making a hole in the sides of the tomatoes, carefully scoop out and discard the seeds and central pulp.
3 Spoon the stuffing mixture into the tomato cavities and place them on a sheet of foil on an oven tray. Top each tomato with 1 tablespoon cheese then bake in a preheated oven, 160°C/325°F/Gas 3, for 15–20 minutes. Serve hot.

Salnoo

PARSEE POTATOES

Parsee origin

In this recipe parboiled quartered potatoes are fried in mustard seeds, curry leaves, if using, and turmeric, then finished off with a little water. It is hard to believe that the potato, probably the world's most popular vegetable was not 'discovered' until the 16th century in the Americas. There are numerous varieties of potato, but in general terms most large red potatoes are best for roasting. Most large whites have the best texture for frying and boiling, and therefore currying. New potatoes are best scrubbed unpeeled, and boiled whole, and are superb in curries.

Serves 4 as an accompaniment

2 tablespoons mustard-blend oil
1 teaspoon mustard seeds
10–12 fresh or dried curry leaves (optional)
2 or 3 cloves garlic, finely chopped
100 ml (3¹/₂ fl oz) water
¹/₂ teaspoon turmeric
1 or 2 green chillies, finely chopped
450 g (1 lb) potatoes, peeled, cooked and quartered
2 tablespoons finely chopped fresh coriander
salt, to taste

1 Heat the oil in a karahi or wok. Add the seeds and curry leaves, if using, and stir-fry for 30 seconds. Add the garlic and stir-fry for a further 30 seconds.
2 Add the water, turmeric and the chillies and bring to a simmer.
3 Add the potatoes and the fresh coriander and when hot, season with salt.

Beef tomatoes stuffed with cheese & spinach

Sag Mattar Paneer
SPINACH WITH PEAS & CHEESE
Throughout India

The dark green, creamy textured spinach contrasts with the bright green spheres of the peas and the golden white of the fried paneer (Indian cheese). This extraordinary classic originated in north-west India, but is now found all over the country.

Serves 4 as an accompaniment

500 g (1 lb 2 oz) baby spinach, chopped
2–4 cloves garlic, finely chopped
50 g (2 oz) natural yogurt
1 tablespoon coarsely chopped fresh coriander
2–4 green chillies, finely chopped
3 tablespoons ghee (see page 61)
225 g (8 oz) paneer, fried (see page 88)
100 g (4 oz) fresh peas, cooked or frozen peas, thawed
water or fragrant stock (see page 59)
salt, to taste

Masala

2 tablespoons dried fenugreek leaves
1 tablespoon coriander seeds
1 teaspoon cumin seeds
2–4 brown cardamoms
4–6 cloves

1 Roast and grind the masala, following the instructions on page 60.
2 Put the masala, 2 tablespoons of the spinach, the garlic, yogurt, fresh coriander and chillies, if using, in a blender or food processor and 'pulse' to a smooth paste using water as needed.
3 Heat the ghee in a karahi or wok and add the paste. Stir-fry for 6–8 minutes, adding enough water to prevent sticking.
4 Add the remaining spinach and stir-fry until it is softened.

5 Add the paneer and peas and mix in gently (so as not to break the paneer). Season with salt. The dish will be fairly dry by now, so add water or fragrant stock if you want a runnier texture. Serve when heated through.

Sangri Kair
RAJASTHANI STRING BEANS WITH BERRIES
Rajasthan, north-west Indian desert

Rajasthan, literally 'land of the kings', is renowned for its palaces and forts, and for its vast tracts of desert interspersed with rocks, lakes and sparse jungle, where rain can be absent for years. Such harsh conditions result in specialized crops such as millet, gram, oil seeds and lentils such as mooth and moong. No rice or root vegetables grow in the desert, but mushrooms, beans and berries are nurtured where there is sufficient water. Typical of these are sangri (Prosopis cinararia), leguminous fruit pods, and kair (Cappris deciduas), small sour green berries. Both are occasionally available in Asian stores.

Serves 4 as an accompaniment

6 tablespoons gram flour (besan)
1–2 fresh red chillies, chopped
1/4 teaspoon asafoetida
300 g (11 oz) sangri or runner beans, washed, stringed and cut diagonally
75 g (3 oz) kair or gooseberries
2 tablespoons vegetable oil
salt, to taste

Masala

1 teaspoon mustard seeds
1 teaspoon cumin seeds

Garnish

caramelized onions (tarka) (see page 61)
fresh coriander

1 Combine the gram flour, chillies and asafoetida in a bowl and add just enough water to make a paste thick enough to drop sluggishly off a spoon.
2 Steam or microwave the sangri and kair separately for about 3 minutes to soften them.
3 Heat the oil in a karahi or wok, add the masala and stir-fry for 20 seconds.
4 Add the gram flour paste and stir-fry it until it goes a little darker, using more water if necessary to keep the mixture loose.
5 Add the softened sangri and kair and gently stir-fry to mix in.
6 Season with salt. Garnish with the onion tarka and coriander and serve with Rajasthani bread (see page 219) and natural yogurt.

Sevian Tamatar
GRAM FLOUR VERMICELLI NOODLES IN A TANGY TOMATO GUJARATI CURRY SAUCE

Gujarat, west India

This is one of the few Indian noodle dishes. It uses crispy sev, factory-made noodles from gram flour dough, which is pushed through a device called the 'murukus press' via a plate with small holes to make thin noodles of vermicelli thickness. These are dropped straight into the deep-fryer to make short, crisp, golden-yellow, thread-like sticks. These are cooled, packed and sold in Asian stores as ready-to-eat crispy nibbles. In this recipe they are immersed in a tangy sauce, whereupon they become soft like noodles.

Serves 4 as an accompaniment

3 tablespoons vegetable oil
1 teaspoon white cumin seeds
$1/2$ teaspoon coriander seeds
3 or 4 cloves garlic, finely chopped
2.5 cm (1 inch) piece of ginger, finely chopped
4–6 spring onions, leaves and bulbs, finely chopped
1–3 green cayenne chillies, chopped
400 g (14 oz) tin tomatoes
2 tablespoons coconut milk powder (see page 57)
50 g (2 oz) natural yogurt
2 teaspoons garam masala (see page 60)
1–2 tablespoons lemon juice
200 g (7 oz) packet sev (see above)
salt, to taste

Masala

1 teaspoon ground coriander
$1/2$ teaspoon turmeric
$1/2$ teaspoon mango powder
$1/2$ teaspoon paprika

Garnish

fresh coriander
1 fresh red chilli, cut into thin rings

1 Heat the oil in a karahi or wok. Add the seeds and stir-fry for 10 seconds, then add the masala and stir-fry for 20 seconds more. Add the garlic and ginger and stir-fry them for 30 seconds. Now add just enough water to cool things down and create a lightly sizzling paste. Stir in the spring onions (scallions) and chillies, and continue to stir-fry for a further 2 minutes, adding dashes of water as needed.
2 Add the tinned tomatoes and their juice, the coconut milk powder, yogurt and garam masala. Mix well until simmering for a couple of minutes. Season with salt and add the lemon juice.
3 Just before serving, stir in most of the sev. Garnish with the remaining sev, some fresh coriander and chilli rings, then serve at once.

Thakkali Chugander
TOMATO & BEETROOT
Tamil Nadu, south India

An edible tuber, beetroot (chugander) has been
cultivated since ancient times. The British brought
it to India in the 1800s, which makes it one of the
later ingredients to enter Indian cuisine. Its
relatively late arrival makes it a minor ingredient in
Indian cooking, but it appears from time to time,
as in this Tamil recipe, where it is accompanied by
another great 'modern' – as far as India is
concerned – immigrant from the New World, the
tomato.

Serves 4 as an accompaniment

6–8 plum tomatoes
100 g (4 oz) beetroot leaves or red spinach,
  washed
2 tablespoons sesame oil
1 teaspoon aniseeds
$1/2$ teaspoon black cumin seeds
325 g ($11^1/2$ oz) boiled beetroot, peeled and
  cut into 2 cm ($3/4$ inch) cubes or slices
1 tablespoon garam masala (see page 60)
salt, to taste

1 Briefly steam, microwave or blanch the tomatoes
so that you can remove the skins easily without
making the tomatoes too mushy. Cut the skinned
tomatoes into halves or quarters.
2 Remove any tough stems from the leaves then
shred the leaves coarsely.
3 Heat the oil in a karahi or wok. Add the seeds
and stir-fry for 30 seconds. Add the tomato and the
beetroot and stir-fry until hot. Add a sprinkling of
water and the leaves. Continue to stir-fry for
2–3 minutes as they soften and almost melt into the
mixture.

Tomato & beetroot

4 Add the garam masala and season with salt.
Serve hot.

Thakkali Mulakittathu
HOT-TEMPERED TOMATO CURRY
Mangalore, Karnataka, southern India

Tomato (tamata in Hindi or thakkali in
Malalayam) belongs to the nightshade family, as
does the chilli and the potato. The tomato and
potato were initially largely ignored by Moghuls,
Indians and British alike, who believed them to be
deadly poisonous. Not so the chilli, which was
immediately accepted when the Portuguese
introduced it to India in the 16th century. They
failed with potatoes and tomatoes, however, which
gained only limited acceptance in Indian cuisine
until American missionaries reintroduced them in
the 19th century. This explains the absence to this
day of potato and tomato in many traditional
recipes, which predate the discovery of the New
World. This colourful, red Malalayam Mangalore
recipe, however, does the tomato justice. Note the
use of Masala 2 – it is a common south Indian
technique called tempering, whereby items are
fried and placed on hot, wet dishes at the table to
create a sizzle.

Serves 4 as an accompaniment

225 g (8 oz) tomatoes, any type
3 tablespoons sunflower oil
1 teaspoon cumin seeds
1 teaspoon yellow mustard seeds
1–2 teaspoons chopped dried red chillies
4 tablespoons split and polished gram lentils
  (chana dhal)
6 cloves garlic, thinly sliced
5 cm (2 inch) piece of fresh root ginger, finely
  sliced
100 g (4 oz) brown onion paste (see page 61)
2 tablespoons tamarind purée (see page 62)

1 or 2 green chillies, finely chopped

10–12 fresh or dried curry leaves (optional)

2 tablespoons mustard-blend oil

salt, to taste

Masala 1

1 teaspoon ground cumin

1 teaspoon ground coriander

1/2 teaspoon paprika

1/2 teaspoon turmeric

1/4 teaspoon mango powder

1/4 teaspoon asafoetida

Masala 2

8 fresh or dried curry leaves (optional)

2 teaspoons split and polished gram lentils
   (chana dhal)

1 teaspoon whole black lentils (urid dhal)

1/2 teaspoon cumin seeds

1/2 teaspoon yellow mustard seeds

1/2 teaspoon chopped dried red chillies

1 Briefly steam, microwave or blanch the tomatoes so that you can remove the skins easily without making the tomatoes too mushy. Cut the skinned tomatoes into halves or quarters.

2 Add just enough water to Masala 1 to make a paste thick enough to drop sluggishly off a spoon.

3 Heat the oil in a karahi or wok. Add the seeds and stir-fry for 10 seconds. Add the Masala 1 paste, dried chillies and gram lentils and stir-fry for 45 seconds. Add the garlic and stir-fry for 30 seconds more, then add the ginger and the onion paste, and a little water if necessary, and continue to stir-fry for 3 or 4 minutes.

4 Add the skinned tomatoes, the tamarind, green chillies and curry leaves, if using, and stir for 5 minutes. Add water as necessary to create a gravy, then season with salt.

5 Meanwhile, heat the mustard-blend oil in a frying pan. Add Masala 2 and stir-fry for 30 seconds.

6 To serve, take the tomato curry to the table, then garnish it with the hot fried Masala 2, which will sizzle as it comes into contact with the wet curry (see above).

Thoran

SHREDDED CABBAGE & CARROT WITH COCONUT

Southern India

A member of the brassica family, cabbage is one of the most ancient known vegetables, originating in Asia Minor and the eastern Mediterranean. Cultivation has created its crisp, tightly packed leaves, whose colours range through all hues of green, white and red. This lightly spiced dish probably originated in Kerala over 2,000 years ago but is now popular all over southern India. It is called porial (see pages 179 and 181) in Tamil Nadu, thoora in Andhra Pradesh and palya in Mysore. Ingredients nearly always include fresh coconut and shredded cabbage, with additional items varying from place to place. For example it can include the green pod of the lobia bean, and/or plantains or, as here, carrot.

Serves 4 as an accompaniment

4 tablespoons split and polished black lentils
   (urid dhal)

6 tablespoons mustard-blend oil

2 tablespoons mustard seeds

250 g (9 oz) white cabbage, shredded

250 g (9 oz) carrot, shredded

salt, to taste

Paste

water and 1/2 the flesh of 1 fresh coconut

20 raw cashew nuts

3 or 4 dried red chillies

2.5 cm (1 inch) piece of fresh turmeric or
   1/2 teaspoon ground turmeric

1 Soak the lentils in plenty of water for up to 2 hours. Drain well.
2 Put the paste ingredients in a blender or food processor and 'pulse' to a pouring paste using water as necessary.
3 Heat the oil in a karahi or wok then stir-fry the mustard seeds and the drained soaked lentils for 2–3 minutes.
4 Add the paste and stir-fry until simmering, adding just enough water to make it easily mobile.
5 Then add the cabbage and carrot (which don't need preblanching). Simply stir them around for the few minutes it takes to cook to a firm texture. Then season with salt and serve at once.

Tondak
GOAN MUSHROOMS
Goa, Indian west coast

Before 1983 one had to make a river crossing aboard a rather delightful antiquated car ferry to reach one of Taj Hotels' flagship properties at Fort Aguada. Alongside this well-preserved old Portuguese sea defence, and long before the area became the tourist trap it is now, Taj had built an attractive hotel. In those days, that palm-fringed coastline was virtually devoid of humanity and was so beautiful that Mrs Indira Ghandi decided to hold the 1983 Commonwealth prime ministers' conference there. Taj built a number of plush, luxury villas for the heads of state, of which Mrs Ghandi and Margaret Thatcher were two. The Indian government built a huge bridge for the occasion, to replace the ferry, and Goa's pace of life was never the same. This dish, unchanged for centuries, was on the special Goan banquet menu masterminded by Taj chefs.

Serves 4 as an accompaniment

3 tablespoons coconut oil
100 g (4 oz) brown onion paste (see page 61)
4 tablespoons puréed fresh coconut flesh
1 tablespoon tamarind purée (see page 62)
450 g (1 lb) mushrooms, any type or mixture, cleaned
salt, to taste

Masala
2–4 teaspoons chilli powder
1 teaspoon ground cinnamon
1 teaspoon ground coriander
$1/2$ teaspoon ground black pepper
$1/2$ teaspoon turmeric

1 Add just enough water to the masala to make a paste thick enough to drop sluggishly off a spoon.
2 Heat the oil in a karahi or wok. Add the masala paste and stir-fry for 1 minute. Add the onion paste and stir-fry for 1 or 2 minutes.
3 Add enough water to make the mixture into a medium-thickness sauce. When it is simmering, add the coconut and tamarind, season with salt, then add the mushrooms. Serve as soon as they are hot.

Ugavela Moong
CURRIED BEANSPROUTS
Southern India

Beansprouts are one of nature's miracles. Almost any dried bean or lentil, no matter how old, will sprout when water is applied under the correct conditions. An important Chinese vegetable from time immemorial, beansprouts occasionally appear in Indian cuisine, either raw or, as in this recipe from southern India, lightly spiced.

Serves 4 as an accompaniment

2 tablespoons mustard-blend oil
450 g (1 lb) beansprouts
4 tablespoons water
100 g (4 oz) caramelized onions (see page 61)
2 tablespoons vegetable oil
salt, to taste

Masala 1
1 tablespoon ground coriander
1 teaspoon turmeric
1 teaspoon chilli powder
1/2 teaspoon asafoetida

Masala 2
8 fresh or dried curry leaves (optional)
2 teaspoons split and polished gram lentils
  (chana dhal)
1 teaspoon whole black lentils (urid dhal)
1/2 teaspoon cumin seeds
1/2 teaspoon yellow mustard seeds
1/2 teaspoon chopped dried red chillies

1 Add just enough water to Masala 1 to make a paste thick enough to drop sluggishly off a spoon.
2 Heat the mustard-blend oil in a karahi or wok. Add the masala paste and stir-fry for 30 seconds. Add the beansprouts and the water and when hot right through, add the onions and season with salt.

3 Meanwhile, heat the vegetable oil in a frying pan. Add Masala 2 and stir-fry for 30 seconds. Use this to garnish the beansprouts then serve.

Took Aloo
SINDHI POTATO
Punjab, north-west India

Since 1947, Rajasthan and the Punjab have shared their western borders and the Thar Desert with the Pakistani state of Sind. Food shares no borders, however, and a Sindi dish that transcends politics is this potato dish enjoyed by many Punjabis and Rajasthanis. Potatoes are coated in oil, coloured golden with turmeric, then baked and finally deep-fried until crisp – a little effort for a rewarding result.

Serves 4 as an accompaniment

3 tablespoons vegetable oil
1 lb (450 g) potatoes, peeled and cut into 4 cm
  (1 1/2 inch) cubes
vegetable oil for deep-frying

Masala
1 1/2 teaspoons turmeric
1/2 teaspoon asafoetida

1 Heat the oil in a karahi or wok. Add the masala and stir-fry for 30 seconds. Now turn off the heat and add the potatoes. Stir to coat them in the spices so that they look golden.
2 Place the potatoes in an oven tray so that they are closely packed together, one layer deep. Bake in a preheated oven, 190°C/375°F/Gas 5, for about 20 minutes.
3 Remove from the oven and allow to cool a little, then press each potato into a disc shape.

Curried beansprouts

4 Heat the oil in a deep frying pan to 190°C/375°F (chip-frying temperature).

5 Add one potato to the hot oil. After a few seconds add the next, and continue until the surface area of the pan is full but not crowded. This maintains the oil temperature. Fry for 3 or 4 minutes.

6 Remove the potatoes from the pan, shake off the excess oil and drain them on absorbent kitchen paper.

7 Let stand for a short time while they become crisp, then serve.

Undhui
GUJARATI FIVE-VEGETABLE STEW
Gujarat, west India

A Gujarati favourite dish, this traditionally contains five vegetables – here, plantain, white radish, aubergine, pumpkin or gourd and courgette – which are cooked in a sauce made from gram flour, asafoetida and yogurt. Undui is often served with gram flour vegetable kofta balls in it, or you could use pakora balls (see page 87), adding them to the stir-fry with the gram flour paste at step 4. From undhui evolved the Parsee oonbhariu (see page 177) where the vegetables are baked dry.

Serves 4 as an accompaniment

100 g (4 oz) plantain
100 g (4 oz) white radish
100 g (4 oz) aubergine
100 g (4 oz) pumpkin or gourd flesh
100 g (4 oz) courgette
3 tablespoons vegetable oil
$1/2$ teaspoon lovage seeds
4 cloves garlic, finely chopped
225 g (8 oz) brown onion paste (see page 61)

1 green chilli, chopped
6 tablespoons gram flour (besan)
milk, as needed
200 g (7 oz) natural yogurt
juice of 1 or 2 limes
salt, to taste

Masala
2 tablespoons ground coriander
2 teaspoons ground cumin
1 teaspoon turmeric
1 teaspoon chilli powder
$1/2$ teaspoon asafoetida

1 Prepare the plantain, white radish, aubergine, pumpkin or gourd and courgette then steam, microwave or boil them separately until soft. When cooked, cut them into bite-sized pieces.

2 Add just enough water to the masala to make a paste thick enough to drop sluggishly off a spoon.

3 Heat the oil in a karahi or wok. Add the seeds and stir-fry for 30 seconds. Add the chopped garlic and cook for 30 seconds more, then add the masala paste, the onion paste and chilli and stir-fry for a further 2 or 3 minutes.

4 Combine the gram flour with just enough milk to make another paste that is thick enough to drop sluggishly off a spoon. Add this paste to the stir-fry, and briskly mix the ingredients together, adding enough milk to keep the mixture loose until it stops thickening.

5 Add the yogurt and the vegetables to the pan. Continue to add milk as needed to keep the stew suitably mobile. Cook until simmering. Add the lime juice and season with salt. Serve with bread and chutneys.

Gujarati five-vegetable stew

Turkari

SOUTH INDIAN VEGETABLE CURRY

Southern India

Turkari is a spicy, seasoned stew, which is also a method of cooking using plentiful liquid and slow cooking. In northern India it is called kalia, elsewhere in India it is called ishtoo (because of the difficulty in pronouncing the letters 's' and 't' together). Turkari simply means 'vegetables' in southern India. Here is a typical dish.

Serves 4 as an accompaniment

600 ml (20 fl oz) water or fragrant stock (see page 59)
2–4 cloves garlic, quartered
2 or 3 fresh red chillies, whole
100 g (4 oz) green beans, chopped and cooked
100 g (4 oz) aubergines, chopped and cooked
100 g (4 oz) pumpkin flesh, chopped and cooked
100 g (4 oz) sweet potato, peeled if liked, chopped and cooked
100 g (4 oz) broad beans, chopped and cooked
salt, to taste
2 tablespoons black/brown mustard seeds, to garnish

Masala
3 or 4 bay leaves
5 cm (2 inch) piece of cassia bark
4–6 green cardamoms
2 star anise
3 or 4 dried red chillies
2.5 cm (1 inch) piece of fresh turmeric or 1 teaspoon ground turmeric

1 Put the water or stock in a 2.25–2.75 litre (4–5 pint) saucepan. Add the masala, garlic and chillies and simmer for about 3 minutes.
2 Add the cooked vegetables, season with salt and serve at once with plain rice, garnished with the mustard seeds.

6 | lentils

Aloo Chole
POTATO & CHICKPEA CURRY
Punjab, north-west India

Potato (aloo) and chickpea (chole) are a formidably good combination, especially when curried as in this benchmark dish from the Punjab.

Serves 4 as an accompaniment

250 g (9 oz) dried chickpeas (kabli chana)
2 litres (3½ pints) water
2 tablespoons ghee (see page 61)
1 large onion, chopped
1–4 green chillies, finely chopped
1 tablespoon tomato purée
1 tablespoon tomato ketchup
6–8 small potatoes, peeled and boiled
4 firm tomatoes, quartered
2 tablespoons chopped fresh coriander
salt, to taste

Masala

1 teaspoon ground cumin
1 teaspoon chilli powder
1 teaspoon mango powder
½ teaspoon ground coriander
½ teaspoon turmeric
¼ teaspoon ground black pepper
2 cloves, ground
2 bay leaves, ground
½ teaspoon black Indian rock salt (see page 58)

1 Soak the chickpeas overnight in plenty of water to allow them to swell and soften.
2 Drain and rinse the chickpeas well. Bring the water to the boil in a 3.5 litre (6 pint) saucepan.

Add the chickpeas and simmer until tender – about 45 minutes. Drain and set aside.
3 Mix the masala with enough water to make a pourable paste.
4 Heat the ghee in a karahi or wok. Add the masala and stir-fry for about 1 minute. Add the onion and the chillies, and continue to stir-fry for a further 3 or 4 minutes.
5 Add the tomato purée and ketchup, the potatoes and tomatoes. When well mixed in, add the cooked chickpeas and stir carefully until heated through. Season with salt and garnish with fresh coriander. Serve hot or cold.

COOK'S TIP A quicker alternative to soaking and cooking dried chickpeas is to use a 400 g (14 oz) tin of chickpeas, with their liquid, too, if liked. If you are serving the curry cold, it is not necessary to heat the tinned chickpeas in step 5.

Dhal Bukhara (Dhal Makhni)
CREAMY BROWN LENTILS
Modern chef's recipe

This chestnut brown-coloured dish takes its name from the famous Bukhara Tandoori restaurant at Delhi's Maurya Sheraton Hotel. It is a modern development of the classic north Indian lentil dish, Maharani Dhal, held in such respect that its name means 'lentil queen'. Butter (makhni) and cream are continuously added to the black lentils (urid dhal) during the cooking, and tomato provides its distinctive taste and reddish colour. This interpretation is based on a recipe from the highly esteemed London restaurateur Camelia Panjabi. Note that this recipe makes enough for 8–12 people as an accompaniment. This is because of the very long cooking time. Slow cooking is the secret of this dish, and it is more economical to make this quantity then freeze the excess.

Potato & chickpea curry

Serves 8–12 as an accompaniment

225 g (8 oz) whole black lentils (urid dhal)

1.25 litres (2¼ pints) water

40 g (1½ oz) fresh root ginger, finely chopped

2 tablespoons ghee (see page 61)

10–12 cloves garlic, puréed

200 g (7 oz) brown onion paste (see page 61)

1 teaspoon tomato purée

200 g (7 oz) tinned tomatoes, puréed

3 tablespoons garam masala (see page 60)

150 ml (5 fl oz) single cream

150 g (5 oz) unsalted butter

2 teaspoons black Indian rock salt (see page 58)

Masala

2 teaspoons paprika

1 teaspoon coriander seeds, roasted and ground

1 teaspoon cumin seeds, roasted and ground

½ teaspoon chilli powder

1 Soak the lentils in plenty of water for at least 12 hours. Drain and rinse well.

2 To cook the lentils, bring the measured water to the boil in a 2.5 litre (4½ pint) saucepan. Add the lentils and half the ginger. When it returns to the boil, stir to ensure nothing is sticking to the bottom of the pan.

3 Boil for 10 minutes, then reduce the heat to very low and simmer for a further 1 hour or so, stirring from time to time. By this time, the lentils should have absorbed all the water and be soft not al dente.

4 Heat the ghee in a 2.5 litre (4½ pint) ovenproof casserole dish. Add the masala and stir-fry for 1 minute or so. Add the garlic, onion paste and the remaining ginger and stir-fry for a further 2 minutes. Mix in the lentils.

5 Add the tomato purée, tinned tomatoes and garam masala to the lentils. Cook for a further 15 minutes, adding a cupful or two of water as needed so as to retain a pouring consistency.

6 Put the casserole in a preheated oven,

180°C/360°F/Gas 4, and cook for at least 3 hours. Check the consistency of the mixture every 40 minutes or so – adding water to maintain the pouring consistency.

7 On your fourth check, add the cream, butter and salt and give it a final 20 or so minutes cooking in the oven with the oven switched off.

Kuthalam Moong Korma
MILD LENTIL CURRY
Tamil Nadu, south India

This recipe, given to me by the chefs at the Taj Garden Retreat Hotel in Madurai is from the Courtallam region of Tamil Nadu. The use of coconut and milk gives the dish a white-coloured gravy, which the locals say reminds them of the white frothy waters of the nearby Courtallam Falls. This dish is spiced with green chillies and garlic, and is cooked with vegetables and white lentils (moong dhal) in its own juice.

Serves 4 as an accompaniment

3 tablespoons coconut oil

6–8 fresh or dried curry leaves (optional)

40 g (1½ oz) beans, cooked and diced

40 g (1½ oz) carrot, cooked and diced

40 g (1½ oz) small cauliflower florets, cooked

40 g (1½ oz) potatoes, cooked and diced

40 g (1½ oz) fresh peas, cooked or frozen peas, thawed

150 g (5 oz) white lentils (moong dhal), cooked

1 tablespoon mustard-blend oil

salt, to taste

Paste

water and flesh of 1 fresh coconut

2 or 3 cloves garlic, finely chopped or puréed

2.5 cm (1 inch) piece of fresh root ginger, shredded

100 g (4 oz) white onion paste (see page 61)

1 or 2 green chillies, finely chopped
2 teaspoons garam masala (see page 60)
3 teaspoons ground coriander
200 ml (7 fl oz) milk

Masala

2 tablespoons chopped fresh coriander
6–8 fresh or dried curry leaves (optional), fried
4 small dried red chillies, whole
2 or 3 cherry tomatoes, sliced

1 Put all the paste ingredients except the milk in a blender or food processor then 'pulse' using this milk as needed until it is smooth and pourable.
2 Heat the coconut oil in a karahi or wok. Add the above paste and stir-fry, adding water as necessary to keep the mixture loose.
3 After 3 minutes, add the curry leaves, if using, and further water to make a thin sauce. When it is simmering, add the cooked vegetables and lentils. Bring to a simmer – it should be quite runny. Season with salt.
4 Meanwhile, heat the mustard-blend oil in a frying pan. Add the masala and stir-fry for 30 seconds.
5 To serve, take the lentil curry to the table, then garnish it with the hot fried masala, which will sizzle as it comes into contact with the wet curry (see page 189).

Roghani Dhal
BLACK LENTILS WITH RED KIDNEY BEANS
Punjab, north-west India

Black lentils (urid dhal) and kidney beans (rajma) are cooked with ginger and aromatic spices to create this nutritious Punjabi signature dish. No one knows exactly when this dish was first created, but it is probably one of India's earliest, since black lentils, kidney beans and other legumes had been brought to the Punjab area by 7000BC. Indian rock salt is also indigenous to the hills of this area. The dish is a meal in itself or it can be served with breads or plain rice.

Serves 4 as an accompaniment

75 g (3 oz) dried red kidney beans
225 g (8 oz) whole black lentils (urid dhal)
40 g (1½ oz) fresh root ginger, finely chopped
3 tablespoons ghee (see page 61)
200 g (7 oz) brown onion paste (see page 61)
1 teaspoon black Indian rock salt (see page 58)

Masala

2 teaspoons paprika
2 teaspoons garam masala (see page 60)
1 teaspoon cumin seeds, roasted and ground
3/4 teaspoon coriander seeds, roasted and ground
1/2 teaspoon chilli powder

1 Soak the red kidney beans in plenty of water for at least 12 hours. To cook the beans, rinse them well then boil in a saucepan of water for about minutes. Drain and set aside.
2 Soak the lentils in plenty of water for at least 2 hours, then drain.
3 To cook, place the drained lentils and half the ginger in a large saucepan with three times their volume of water. When the water comes to the boil, stir to ensure nothing sticks to the bottom of the pan. Boil for 10 minutes, then simmer for a further 20–25 minutes, stirring from time to time.
4 Heat the ghee in a karahi or wok. Add the masala and stir-fry for 1 minute or so. Add the onion paste and the remaining ginger and stir-fry for a further 2 minutes.
5 Add this to the lentils after their 20–25 minutes of cooking and stir well. Cook for a further 15 minutes. The water will be absorbed into the lentils towards the end of the timing, so keep an eye on it, adding more water if necessary.
6 To test whether they are ready, mash a few lentils

against the side of the pan using the back of a spoon. They're ready if soft enough to mash easily.
7 Add the kidney beans and simmer for 1 further minute or so. The water should be well absorbed but the dish should not be too dry – add a little water at any step during cooking if necessary if it starts to look dry. Season with salt, stir and serve at once.

COOK'S TIP A quicker alternative to soaking and cooking dried kidney beans is to use a 400 g (14 oz) can of kidney beans, although they will not be quite as good as the dried beans. Discard their liquid, rinse them and add them at step 7.

Palak-ka-dala
RAJASTHANI SPINACH DHAL
Rajasthan, north-west Indian desert

The lentils (dala) in this recipe are gram lentils (chana dhal) and oily lentils (toovar/toor dhal). The latter are golden yellow and quite hard and chunky, and marry well with spinach (palak) and the spicing of the desert. This recipe hails from Pushkar, and is a favourite among the camel herders, who gather there for the annual camel fair.

Serves 4 as an accompaniment

50 g (2 oz) split and polished gram lentils
  (chana dhal)
50 g (2 oz) split oily lentils (toovar/toor dhal)
4 tablespoons ghee (see page 61)
100 g (4 oz) brown onion paste (see page 61)
2 or 3 cloves garlic, finely chopped or puréed
300 g (11 oz) baby spinach, chopped
salt, to taste

Masala 1
1 teaspoon turmeric
1 teaspoon ground coriander
1 teaspoon ground cumin
1/4 teaspoon fenugreek seeds, ground
1/2 teaspoon chilli powder

Masala 2
1 teaspoon cumin seeds
1 brown cardamom
5 cm (2 inch) piece of cassia bark
1/2 teaspoon black mustard seeds

Masala 3
2 tablespoons coarsely chopped fresh coriander
1 tablespoon dried fenugreek leaf
2 teaspoons garam masala (see page 60)

1 Mix the lentils together and soak overnight in plenty of water.
2 To cook, place the drained lentils in a large saucepan and simmer in twice their volume of water for about 30 minutes.
3 Add just enough water to Masala 1 to make a paste thick enough to drop sluggishly off a spoon.
4 Heat the ghee in a karahi or wok. Add Masala 2 and stir-fry for about 30 seconds. Add the Masala 1 paste to the pan and stir-fry for about 1 minute. Add the onion paste and garlic and continue to stir-fry for about 2 minutes.
5 Steam, microwave or boil the spinach until cooked.
6 Add the spinach, cooked lentils and Masala 3 to the pan and simmer for about 3 minutes, adding enough water to keep the mixture loose, but not slushy. Season with salt and serve.

Rajasthani spinach dhal

Sambar
TRADITIONAL SOUTH INDIAN SPICY LENTILS
Southern India

Sambar (also called huli and pulusu) is a traditional south Indian lentil dish, the mandatory ingredients of which are toovar lentils, dried red chillies and tamarind. It is usually quite runny and contains vegetables such as gourds, including a variety called drumstick, okra and aubergine. Sambar traditionally accompanies Rasam (gourd soup, see page 68), Masala Dosa (curry-filled rice pancakes, see page 81) and Narial (coconut chutney, see page 231).

Serves 4 as an accompaniment

750 ml (1¹/₄ pints) water
3 tablespoons oily lentils (toovar/toor dhal)
8 drumstick pieces, of 5 cm (2 inch) size (see Cook's tip)
50 g (2 oz) aubergine, cut into bite-sized pieces
1 teaspoon tamarind purée (see page 62)
3 or 4 tablespoons mustard-blend oil
2 or 3 dried red chillies, whole
1 onion, cut into long thin slices
50 g (2 oz) gourd, cut into bite-sized pieces
4 okra, left whole and untrimmed
1 tablespoon coconut milk powder (see page 57)
1 tablespoon frozen peas, thawed
salt, to taste
fresh curry leaves, to garnish

Sambar Masala

1 tablespoon split and polished gram lentils (chana dhal), ground
1 tablespoon whole black lentils (urid dhal), ground
1 tablespoon oily lentils (toovar/toor dhal), ground
1 tablespoon turmeric

Masala

1¹/₂ teaspoons mustard seeds
1 teaspoon black peppercorns
¹/₂ teaspoon coriander seeds
¹/₄ teaspoon fenugreek seeds
¹/₄ teaspoon asafoetida
10–12 fresh or dried curry leaves (optional)

1 Bring the water to the boil in a 3 litre (5¹/₄ pint) saucepan. Add the lentils, drumstick and aubergine pieces and tamarind and simmer for 20 minutes.
2 Meanwhile, add just enough water to the sambar masala to make a paste thick enough to drop sluggishly off a spoon. Heat half the oil in a karahi or wok. Add this paste and stir-fry for about 2 minutes, then add it to the simmering ingredients.
3 Heat the remaining oil. Add the masala and stir-fry for 30 seconds. Add the dried chillies and the onion and stir-fry for a further couple of minutes, then add this to the simmering ingredients.
4 By the end of the 20 minutes simmering – with the items from steps 2 and 3 added – the sambar should be quite runny and soup-like, with everything almost tender. Add the gourd pieces, okra, coconut powder and peas, and season with salt.
5 Simmer for about 5 minutes more until everything is tender. Garnish with a few fresh whole curry leaves and serve.

COOK'S TIP Drumstick (seenai) is a long, thin, hard-skinned gourd, which can grow to 46 cm (18 inches) in length by about 1 cm (¹/₂ inch) in diameter. Drumstick is available fresh or tinned from Asian stores. It needs prolonged boiling, after which the ribbed outer casing remains inedible. The flesh is very soft, and south Indians relish sucking the flesh off the casing. They can be seen in the photograph on page 22, tied in a bundle in the top left of the picture.

7 | rice & bread

Rice

Rice was cultivated in northern India at least 10,000 years ago, yet it did not reach the south until the area became populated in around 1000BC (see page 20). Rice is south India's staple since wheat is not suited to the humid, tropical climate. The plant is a slender grass whose grain forms in thin 'ears' in heavily irrigated 'paddy' fields. The ancient Persian word for rice is 'rijzah', from which is derived the Tamil word for rice, 'arisi', meaning literally 'to separate'. This refers to the process of splitting the grain from the husk to produce 'brown rice'. This must be further hulled to remove its brown bran, in order to produce the familiar white polished grain. The Persian word 'rijzah' was also the basis for the Latin word 'oryza' and the modern Italian 'riso', hence the word 'risotto'. Today, there are over 7,000 varieties of rice, and it is the staple of over two-thirds of the world's population.

Rice has been a Persian staple from as early as 1200BC, when it was known as 'polo'. From this, 'polou' evolved as a dish with rice and meat and/or vegetables, cooked together in a pan until tender. Following Muslim invasions it evolved into Turkish pilav, Greek pilafi, Spanish paella and Indian pullao.

Basmati, meaning fragrant, is India's best quality rice, yeilding long, thin, fluffy grains with a delicate aroma. Adulteration of basmati rice with conventional (cheaper) long-grain rice has become a recent international phenomenon, to the annoyance of the Indian government. Basmati is uniquely Indian and the government wants its name protected in the same way as champagne is in France. The problem has become exacerbated with recent European legislation which states that only 40 per cent basmati is required in each pack.

This explains why price varies so much. The cheapest packs are to be found in supermarkets, each of whom have their own brand priced at well under half that of a specialist rice producer.

Basmati rice cooking timings vary from other types of rice, so to ensure that the recipes given here work, get 100 per cent basmati only.

PLAIN RICE – COOKED BY BOILING

Serves 4

at least 1.75 litres (3 pints) water
1 teaspoon turmeric (optional)
about 250 g (9 oz) pure basmati rice (see rice note, left)

1 Bring the water to the boil in a 2.25–2.75 litre (4–5 pint) lidded saucepan. It's not necessary to salt the water, but if you want the rice to be yellow all over, add the turmeric to the boiling water.
2 Rinse the rice briskly with fresh cold water until most of the starch is washed off. Run boiling kettle water through the rice for its final rinse. Strain it and add it immediately to the boiling water. Cover the pan.
3 When the water returns to the boil (this should take just a few seconds) remove the pan lid and start timing for 8 minutes. Stir gently to prevent rice grains sticking to the pan.
4 After 8 minutes, remove the pan from the stove and quickly strain the rice. Invert the saucepan.
5 Quickly and briskly shake off the excess water from the rice. Transfer the rice back to the saucepan, which should now be hot and dry. The rice itself will still be quite wet (although you can eat it now if you want to).
6 To dry the rice and get fluffy grains, however, put the lid on the saucepan and seal it with plastic wrap. Stand the saucepan in a warm place (near the stove but without applying any heat) and leave for 30–90 minutes. The rice should still be warm – gently fluff it up with a fork and serve. (Note, even if you wish to let the rice go cold for reheating, carry out this step if you want fluffy grains.)

PLAIN RICE –
COOKED BY ABSORPTION

Serves 4

exactly 250 g (9 oz) pure basmati rice (see rice note, opposite)
exactly 450 ml (15 fl oz) boiling water

1 Rinse the rice briskly with fresh cold water until most of the starch is washed off.
2 Choose a lidded saucepan with a capacity at least twice the volume of the uncooked rice. Add the rinsed rice, gently folding it in, then add the boiling water. (Note: if you prefer your rice 'al dente', use slightly less water.)
3 As soon as it starts bubbling, stir to ensure no rice grains are sticking to the bottom of the pan, cover the pan and reduce the heat to less than half. Cook for 8 minutes, but turn the heat right down after 5 minutes or so when all the water will have seemed to disappear.
4 After 8 minutes, check it for dryness, cooking for a little longer if necessary. When the rice is as you like it, turn off the heat.
5 To dry the rice and get fluffy grains, put the lid on the saucepan and seal it with plastic wrap. Stand the saucepan in a warm place (near the stove but without applying any heat) and leave for 30–90 minutes. The rice should still be warm – gently fluff it up with a fork and serve. (Note: even if you wish to let the rice go cold for reheating, carry out this step if you want fluffy grains.)

Pullao
FLAVOURED BASMATI RICE

Pullao rice is simply plain cooked rice, whether cooked by boiling or absorption, flavoured with spices. In its simplest form it comprises just ghee and black cumin seeds, but for a more aromatic flavour you can additionally use any or all of the other spices listed below.

Serves 4

250 g (9 oz) pure basmati rice (see rice note, opposite) and boiling water, quantity determined by your preferred method for cooking the rice (see left)
2 teaspoons ghee (see page 61)
1 teaspoon black cumin seeds

Optional additional flavourings (see above)
2 or 3 bay leaves
5 cm (2 inch) piece of cassia bark
4 green cardamoms
4 cloves
1 brown cardamom
$1/2$ teaspoon fennel seeds
1 star anise

1 Decide whether to cook the rice by the boiling or absorption method and refer to the relevant recipe (see left).
2 If flavouring boiled rice, heat the ghee in a small frying pan. Add the spices and stir-fry for 30 seconds then remove the pan from the heat. Mix these stir-fried spices into the boiled rice at the end of step 5 (see opposite).
3 If flavouring rice cooked by the absorption method, heat the ghee in the saucepan introduced at step 2 on page, then add all the spices and stir-fry for 30 seconds. Add the uncooked rice grains to the saucepan and continue with that recipe.

Khitchri/Khitchdi
RICE WITH LENTILS
Moghul origin, northern India

Khitchri combines rice with masoor lentils. The first written reference to this dish comes from the Moroccan explorer Ibn Battuta in 1342, during his eight-year voyage to India: '*The munj* [moong dhal] *is boiled with rice and then buttered. This is what they call Kishri, and on this they breakfast every day.*'

Serves 4

200 g (7 oz) pure basmati rice (see rice note
    page 206)
50 g (2 oz) split and polished red lentils (masoor
    dhal)
2 tablespoons ghee (see page 61)
1 or 2 teaspoons shredded fresh root ginger
450 ml (15 fl oz) water or fragrant stock (see
    page 59)
salt, to taste
2 tablespoons caramelized onions, to garnish

Masala
1 teaspoon black peppercorns
10 cloves
3 or 4 green cardamoms
6 bay leaves
6 small sticks cassia bark

1 Rinse the rice and lentils separately until the water runs clear.
2 Heat the ghee in a 3.5 litre (6 pint) lidded saucepan. Add the ginger and masala and stir-fry for 30 seconds.
3 Add the rinsed lentils and rice and mix well together. Fry until the lentils and rice have absorbed all the ghee, stirring gently so as not to break the rice grains.
4 Bring the measured water or stock to the boil and add to the pan. Stir well then cover and cook, undisturbed, for 8 minutes. Season with salt and stir well.
5 Reheat the onion tarka and use it as a garnish.

Kodava Pullao
COORG-STYLE RICE WITH MINCED CHICKEN CURRY
Coorg, Karnataka, south India

The Coorgs of Karnataka are unique. Their dress is a little bit Arabic and, to this day, coffee remains their favoured drink. Wild honey is harvested; oranges, sandalwood and rice are exported all around India and abroad. Meat is centrestage, as aptly shown in this unusual pullao with a whiff of orange, which dates back to Tipu Sultan's occupation of Coorg (see page 40). This simplified recipe combines two earlier Coorg recipes.

Serves 8

350 g (12 oz) cooked plain rice (pages
    206–207), cold
1 quantity chicken in a dark pepper sauce (koli
    nallamalu, see page 93)
2 tablespoons freshly squeezed orange juice

Garnish
thinly sliced fresh orange, seeded and quartered
fresh coriander

1 Mix the cooked cold rice with the chicken and enough of its sauce to coat the rice but not swamp it. Drizzle the orange juice over it.
2 Put the ingredients in a 2.25–2.75 litre (4–5 pint) lidded casserole dish. Cover and cook in a preheated oven, 160°C/325°F/Gas 3 for 15–20 minutes, by which time it should be hot right through, with moist, juicy rice.
3 Garnish with slices of orange and fresh coriander and serve.

Meeng Pullao ka Surat
FISH LAYERED WITH RICE
Gujarat, west India

Gujarat is home to more vegetarians (about 70 per cent) than anywhere else in India. Yet it has a significant coast line with a fishing industry to match. This lovely dish was perfected here. First a flat fish is spread with spices, then it is cooked, layered between rice, spread with a tomato sauce and baked in stock. This is the traditional way of cooking a pullao and is a meal in its own right.

Serves 4

2 teaspoons turmeric

2 teaspoons salt

4 tablespoons water

4 cod, haddock or plaice skinned fillets, each weighing about 200–250 g (7–9 oz)

3 or 4 tablespoons ghee (see page 61)

5 or 6 cloves garlic, finely chopped or puréed

2 tablespoons tomato purée

200 g (7 oz) tinned tomatoes, mashed

300 g (11 oz) pure basmati rice (see rice note page 206)

500 ml (18 fl oz) water or fragrant stock (see page 59)

Green Paste

120 ml (4 fl oz) tinned coconut milk

1 teaspoon ground cumin

1 teaspoon salt

1 or 2 green chillies, chopped

4 tablespoons coarsely chopped fresh coriander

1 Mix half the turmeric and the salt with the water in a shallow bowl.

2 Wash the fish fillets. While still wet, coat them all over with the salt and turmeric mixture. Allow to stand for 2 minutes.

3 Put the green paste ingredients in a blender or food processor and 'pulse' using water as needed until it is smooth and pourable. Spread the paste evenly over both sides of the fish fillets.

4 Heat the ghee in a karahi or wok. Add the remaining turmeric and stir-fry for 10 seconds, then add the garlic and stir-fry for 30 seconds. Add the tomato purée and the mashed tinned tomatoes and continue stir-frying for about 3 minutes.

5 Rinse the rice briskly with fresh cold water until most of the starch is washed off. Stir the remaining salt into the water or stock.

6 Choose a shallow oven dish measuring something like 25 x 15 x 7.5 cm high (10 x 6 x 3 inches). Spread half the rice across the bottom. Pour in half the salted water or stock. Place the pasted fish on top of the rice, if possible forming its own layer. Add the tomato stir-fry and its liquid. Spread the remaining rice on top of the fish. Finally, pour in the remaining salted water or stock.

7 Cover the dish with foil and bake in a preheated oven, 190°C/375°F/Gas 5, for 25–35 minutes, or until the rice is tender. Serve straight from the oven dish.

Meen Moplah Biriani
MIXED SEAFOOD RICE
Moplah, Kerala, south India

The Mopillaha or Moplahs are descendants of an isolated Muslim tribe which arrived by sea in Kerala in the eighth century AD. Their style of cooking is also known as Keralan Islamic cuisine. In Kerala they discovered coconuts and a well-established rice-growing tradition. This dish is not unlike Spanish paella. In time-honoured tradition, the fishermen use whatever they catch to this day. Southern India uses mostly round-grain rice, of which there are several types, including slightly sticky varieties. These are rarely available outside India, but paella rice can be substituted for this recipe. Coconut milk lends a silkiness, caramelized onions add a subtle sweetness and cashew nuts bring a crunchiness to the dish.

Serves 4

300–350 g (11–12 oz) round-grain rice, such as paella rice
4 tablespoons vegetable oil
4 raw king prawns, shells on, about 40 g (1¹⁄₂ oz) each
20–24 tiny brown, raw peeled shrimps
4–6 fresh mussels in their shells
8–12 fresh cockles, shelled
100 g (4 oz) monkfish fillet
100 g (4 oz) pomfret fillet
4 rock lobster tails, shelled
2 tablespoons butter
1 teaspoon mustard seeds
1 teaspoon turmeric
3 or 4 cloves garlic, finely chopped or puréed
2.5 cm (1 inch) piece of fresh root ginger, shredded

Mixed seafood rice

100 g (4 oz) fried onions
1 or 2 green chillies, finely chopped
700 ml (24 fl oz) fish stock
pinch of saffron
1 teaspoon salt
4 tablespoons coconut milk powder (see page 57)
10–12 fresh or dried curry leaves (optional)

Masala
4–6 green cardamoms
4–6 cloves
5 cm (2 inch) piece of cassia bark
1 or 2 teaspoons chopped dried red chillies

Garnish
lime wedges
fried curry leaves
20 fried cashew nuts (see page 87)

1 Rinse the rice until the water runs clear. Set aside.
2 Heat the oil in a frying pan then add the king prawns and stir-fry, turning once. After 3 minutes add the other seafood, and continue stir-frying for 3 or 4 more minutes. Set aside with its liquid.
3 Heat the butter in a karahi or wok. Add the mustard seeds and turmeric and stir-fry for 10 seconds. Add the garlic and stir-fry for 30 seconds more, then add the ginger, onions and chillies and stir-fry for 2 minutes. Add the masala and, when sizzling, add the fish stock.
4 When simmering, add the saffron and salt and stir well. Allow this mixture a few minutes to simmer to bring out the colour of the saffron.
5 Run boiling water from the kettle through the rinsed rice, strain well then add the rice to the pan. Add the cooked seafood and its liquid and bring the contents of the pan back to a simmer.
6 Either reduce the heat and let the biriani cook on top of the stove or place it in a shallow casserole dish and cook in a preheated oven,

190°C/375°F/Gas 5, without a lid. Note, if cooking in a karahi or wok, turn off the heat altogether as soon as the water disappears – after 5–6 minutes.

7 Either way do not stir the rice – doing so disturbs the sticky surface of the rice and releases starch, making the dish sticky. Leave it alone for about 20 minutes then test the rice. It should be al dente – cooked, but not brittle. Leave it for a few more minutes, off the heat, then serve in its cooking dish garnished with lime wedges, curry leaves and cashew nuts.

Quas Chawal
RICE FRIED IN GHEE
Kashmir, extreme northern India

This recipe comprises cooked basmati rice, cooked by either boiling or absorption, flavoured with ghee.

Serves 4

250 g (9 oz) pure basmati rice (see rice note page 206) and boiling water, quantity determined by your preferred method for cooking the rice (see pages 206 and 207)
1 or more tablespoons ghee (see page 61)

1 Decide whether to cook the rice by the boiling or absorption method and refer to the relevant recipe.
2 If using boiled rice, heat the ghee in a small frying pan then stir it into the cooked rice at the end of step 5.
3 If using rice cooked by the absorption method, heat the ghee in the saucepan introduced at step 2, then add the uncooked rice grains to the saucepan and continue with that recipe.

Kesar Chaval
SAFFRON RICE

The previous recipe adds butter ghee to the rice. Here the combination is further enhanced by the use of the world's most expensive spice, saffron (kesar). There is no need to simmer the saffron nor simmer it in milk. After the rice is cooked, simply bury the saffron within it and let the rice's moisture release the aroma and colour of the saffron.

Serves 4

250 g (9 oz) pure basmati rice (see rice note page 206) and boiling water, quantity determined by your preferred method for cooking the rice (see pages 206 and 207)
1 or more tablespoons ghee (see page 61)
pinch of saffron

1 As though making rice fried in ghee (see left), decide whether to cook the rice by the boiling or absorption method and refer to the relevant recipe.
2 If using boiled rice, heat the ghee in a small frying pan then stir it into the cooked rice at the end of step 5. At step 6 of that recipe bury the saffron in the rice.
3 If using rice cooked by the absorption method, heat the ghee in the saucepan introduced at step 2, then add the uncooked rice grains to the saucepan and continue with that recipe. At step 5 bury the saffron in the rice.

Qabooli Gosht Biriani
LAMB WITH CHICKPEAS & RICE
Moghul origin, northern India

In this recipe rice is cooked with meat in the time-honoured, traditional way. Biriani derives its name from the Persian word 'berenji', a type of rice, and it was the Moghuls, themselves of Persian ancestry, who developed the dish into a classic. A main ingredient, in this case meat, is parcooked and its gravy reserved. Rice is fried with spices then layered in a dish with the meat (and chickpeas in this recipe) until all the ingredients are used up, ending with rice on top. The reserved gravy is poured in, then the dish is covered and oven-cooked. The word 'qabooli' means acceptable or palatable, and cooked in this traditional way, the result is a myriad of taste and flavour.

Serves 8

4–5 tablespoons ghee (see page 61)

2 or 3 cloves garlic, finely chopped or puréed

2.5 cm (1 inch) piece of fresh root ginger, shredded

300 g (11 oz) fried onions

1 teaspoon salt

1 kg (2¼ lb) lean leg of lamb or 750 g (1½ lb) off-the-bone lamb, diced

300 g (11 oz) pure basmati rice (see rice note page 206)

600 ml (20 fl oz) water or fragrant stock (see page 59)

30 saffron strands, infused in 50 ml (2 fl oz) warm milk

100 g (4 oz) fresh chickpeas, cooked, or drained tinned chickpeas

Masala 1

2 brown cardamoms

6 cloves

1 teaspoon cumin seeds, roasted

1 teaspoon coriander seeds, roasted

¼ teaspoon chilli powder

Masala 2

½ teaspoon turmeric

4–6 bay leaves

4–6 green cardamoms

4–6 cloves

5 cm (2 inch) piece of cassia bark

1 teaspoon fennel seeds

2 star anise

1 Heat half the ghee in a 2.25–2.75 litre (4–5 pint) lidded casserole dish. Add Masala 1 and stir-fry for 30 seconds, then add the garlic and stir-fry for 30 seconds more. Add the ginger and stir-fry for another 30 seconds. Add the onions and salt and continue stir-frying for about 5 minutes.

2 Add the meat and put the casserole dish, lid on, into a preheated oven, 190°C/375°F/Gas 5. Leave it to cook undisturbed for 40 minutes.

3 Meanwhile, start cooking the rice. Rinse the rice briskly with fresh cold water until most of the starch is washed off. Heat the remaining ghee in a lidded saucepan. Add Masala 2 and, when sizzling, add the rice and stir-fry it for the few seconds it takes to absorb the ghee. Add the water or stock and let this cook into the rice, with the lid on, for just 3 minutes. Then set it aside, lid on, until step 5.

4 Remove the meat and any meat gravy from the casserole. Reduce the oven temperature to 180°C/350°F/Gas 4.

5 Place a layer of the rice in the same casserole dish (there is no need to clean it). Add a layer of meat. Add more rice, and the infused saffron, then more meat and the chickpeas. Top with a layer of rice. Add any meat gravy.

6 Cover and cook for 30 minutes, then switch off the oven, leaving the dish undisturbed for at least 10 more minutes.

7 Serve the casserole at the table, not lifting the lid until you are ready to serve.

Tahiri
VEGETABLE BIRIANI SPECIALITY
Hyderabad, central India

Hyderabad is the spiritual home of the biriani, the principles of which are described on the previous page. Tahiri is a vegetarian biriani and is a satisfying meal in itself. Potato, aubergine, cauliflower and peas are the main ingredients, supported by garlic, ginger, yogurt, herbs and spices.

Serves 4

3 tablespoons vegetable oil
200 g (7 oz) aubergine, cut into bite-sized pieces
350 g (12 oz) potatoes, peeled, cooked and cut into small cubes
175 g (6 oz) cauliflower florets
2 tablespoons ghee (see page 61)
50 g (2 oz) yogurt
2 or 3 cloves garlic, finely chopped or puréed
2.5 cm (1 inch) piece of fresh root ginger, shredded
200 g (7 oz) fried onions
1 or 2 green chillies, finely chopped
90 g (3^1/$_2$ oz) fresh peas, cooked or frozen peas, thawed
1 quantity cooked plain rice, cooked by absorption (see page 207)
fresh coriander, whole
a few mint leaves, chopped
juice of 1 or 2 lemons
salt, to taste

Masala 1

1 teaspoon turmeric
^{1}/$_2$ teaspoon asafoetida

Masala 2

2 teaspoons poppy seeds
2 teaspoons sesame seeds
2 teaspoons coriander seeds
1^1/$_2$ teaspoons cumin seeds
1 teaspoon black mustard seeds
^{1}/$_4$ teaspoon fenugreek seeds

1 Heat the oil in a karahi or wok. Add Masala 1 and stir-fry for 30 seconds. Turn off the heat and add the aubergine, potatoes and cauliflower, stirring to coat the vegetables with the mixture so that they look golden.
2 Place these vegetables in an oven tray, so that they are closely packed together, one layer deep. Bake in a preheated oven, 190°C/375°F/Gas 5, for 15–20 minutes. Reduce the oven temperature to 160°C/325°F/Gas 3.
3 Meanwhile, heat the ghee in a karahi or wok. Add Masala 2 and stir-fry for 30 seconds. Add the yogurt, garlic, ginger, onions and chillies and continue stir-frying for 1 further minute or so. Add this mixture and the peas to the vegetables in the oven tray.
4 Place the cooked rice over the vegetables and sprinkle coriander, mint and lemon juice over the top. Cover the oven tray with foil and bake for 15–20 minutes then serve.

Vegetable biriani speciality

Puli Saadam
TAMARIND RICE
Chennai, Tamil Nadu, south India

In this recipe – a favourite dish in Chennai (Madras) – rice is flavoured with tamarind, peanuts and spices. Accompany it with a dhal of your choice from Chapter 6 in order to create a nutritious, delicious and economical meal.

Serves 4

2 tablespoons mustard-blend oil
at least 1.75 litres (3 pints) water
about 250 g (9 oz) pure basmati rice (see rice note page 206)
1 tablespoon tamarind purée (see page 62)
2 tablespoons peanuts, pan-roasted (see page 86) and crushed

Masala
1 teaspoon mustard seeds
1 teaspoon cumin seeds
1 teaspoon whole black lentils (urid dhal)
1 teaspoon split and polished gram lentils (chana dhal)
1/2 teaspoon asafoetida
2 green chillies, finely chopped
a few fresh or dried curry leaves (optional)

1 Heat the oil in a karahi or wok, add the masala and stir-fry for 30 seconds.
2 To cook the rice, follow the recipe for boiling rice on page 206. At step 6 of that recipe add the above stir-fried spices to the cooked rice in the saucepan, then add the tamarind and peanuts and proceed to the end of the recipe.

Sewian Ki Khichri
NOODLES WITH RICE
Andhra Pradesh, south-east India

In the 2,000 years since the Chinese invented noodles, they have never really caught on in India. Unlike in the south-east Asian countries, the Chinese were never present in India in sufficient numbers. None the less, there are a few Indian noodle dishes. This recipe, from Andhra Pradesh, combines rice noodles with rice and spices. Note the use of the bottled brinjal (aubergine) pickle, available from Asian stores.

Serves 4

100 g (4 oz) dried wheat noodles
3 tablespoons ghee (see page 61)
2 teaspoons panch phoran (see page 62)
3 or 4 cloves garlic, finely chopped
4–6 spring onions, bulbs and leaves, chopped
2 tablespoons coarsely chopped fresh coriander
1 green chilli, chopped
1 tablespoon chopped bottled brinjal (aubergine) pickle
2 teaspoons garam masala (see page 60)
2 or 3 tablespoons freshly squeezed lemon juice
250 g (9 oz) baby spinach, chopped
200 g (7 oz) tinned sweetcorn kernels, plus 4 tablespoons juice from the tin of sweetcorn
250 g (9 oz) cooked plain rice
salt, to taste

Masala
1 teaspoon ground coriander
1/2 teaspoon ground cumin
1/2 teaspoon turmeric

1 Cook the noodles in a large saucepan of boiling water for about 3 minutes, or until as al dente as you wish. Drain and set aside.
2 Heat the ghee in a karahi or wok. Add the panch

phoran and stir-fry for about 10 seconds. Add the masala and stir-fry for 15 seconds. Add the garlic and continue stir-frying briskly for a further 30 seconds.

3 Add the spring onions, coriander, green chilli, brinjal pickle, garam masala and lemon juice, and enough water to keep the mixture loose. Stir-fry for about 2 minutes, then add the spinach, sweetcorn and its liquid. The spinach will soon soften down into the mixture – just keep stirring gently until it does.

4 Add the cooked rice, stir very gently until the ingredients are heated right through. Add the cooked noodles and again stir until everything is hot right through.

5 Season with salt and serve as a meal in itself accompanied by mango chutney (see page 224) and a raita from Chapter 8.

BASIC UNLEAVENED DOUGH

This is a basic but very necessary and simple recipe, which uses wholemeal high-gluten Indian wheat flour (ata).

Makes 450 g (1 lb) dough

450 g (1 lb) wholemeal high-gluten Indian
  wheat flour (ata)
warm water for mixing

1 Tip the flour into a large ceramic or glass bowl. Add warm water, little by little, and work it into the flour using your fingers to create a lump of dough.
2 Remove the dough from the bowl and knead it with your hands on a floured board until it is cohesive and well combined.
3 Return it to the bowl and leave to rest for 10 minutes, then briefly knead the dough once more. It is now ready to use.

Aloo Dolma Puri
POTATO-STUFFED FRIED BREAD
Bengal, north-east India

In Bengal, these little breads are made in a flash. Ping-pong-sized balls of unleavened dough are deftly rolled, a thumb jabs a hole down the centres, the potato stuffing is inserted and the balls are hand-slapped into discs and deep-fried.

Makes 16

450 g (1 lb) wholemeal high-gluten Indian
  wheat flour (ata)
warm water for mixing
2 tablespoons ghee (see page 61)
vegetable oil for deep-frying

Stuffing

3 tablespoons mashed potato
1 teaspoon cumin seeds
$1/2$ teaspoon garam masala (see page 60)

1 Combine the stuffing ingredients together in a bowl.
2 Use the flour and warm water to make the basic unleavened dough as described opposite, adding the ghee to the flour along with the water.
3 Divide the dough into 4 then divide each quarter into 4 to give 16 similar-sized pieces. Shape each piece into a ball then make a hole in each using your thumb. Fill the hole with the potato stuffing then pull and press the dough back over the hole.
4 Roll each ball into a thin disc on a floured board.
5 Heat the oil in a deep frying pan to 190°C/375°F (chip-frying temperature). Add one disc at a time to the hot oil. It should sink to the bottom and rise to the top immediately, puffing up. Remove the disc from the pan after 30 seconds, shake off the excess oil and drain on absorbent kitchen paper. Repeat until all the puris are cooked, then serve at once before they deflate.

Bathuway Ka Roti
SPINACH-LAYERED BREAD
Punjab, north-west India

This paratha-type (layered unleavened) bread comes from the Punjab. The dough mixture is kneaded with spinach and spices, before being rolled in layers and shallow-fried.

Makes 4

450 g (1 lb) wholemeal high-gluten Indian
   wheat flour (ata), plus extra for sprinkling
100 g (4 oz) ghee (see page 61), plus
   4 tablespoons for frying
warm water, to mix

Filling
6 tablespoons mashed potato
100 g (4 oz) fresh spinach, shredded
2 tablespoons frozen peas, thawed
1 green chilli, chopped
1 tablespoon chopped fresh coriander
$1/2$ teaspoon salt
$1/2$ teaspoon coriander, ground
2 teaspoons white cumin seeds, roasted

1 Combine the filling ingredients together in a bowl.
2 Tip the flour into a large ceramic or glass bowl. Add most of the ghee and some warm water, little by little, and work them into the flour using your fingers to create a lump of dough.
3 Remove the dough from the bowl and knead it with your hands on a floured surface until it is cohesive and well combined. Return it to the bowl and leave it to rest for 10 minutes, then briefly knead the dough once more.
4 Divide the dough into 8 balls then roll these out to 8 thin discs about 15 cm (6 inches) in diameter – you will need a pair of discs for each paratha.

Spinach-layered bread

5 Lightly spread 2 tablespoons of filling over 4 of the discs, leaving clear 2 cm (1 inch) around the edge. Brush this area with the remaining ghee then place another disc on top and press the 2 discs together to seal. Sprinkle with flour and roll out lightly to create a disc about 20 cm (8 inches) in diameter.
6 Fry the parathas one at a time. Melt 1 tablespoon of the ghee in a frying pan and fry for about 2 minutes on each side, until golden brown. Shake off the excess oil and serve the parathas hot.

Thar ke Batti Chupatti
RAJASTHANI DRY UNLEAVENED BREAD DISCS
Rajasthan, north-west Indian desert

An age-old culinary myth tells that Rajasthani warriors used to bury uncooked discs of unleavened bread in the intense heat of the Thar desert sands (batti), in marked locations. The warriors would later return, dig out the now-cooked discs, spread them with ghee and tuck in. Quite why the local desert-dwelling wildlife did not get there first is unexplained, but it is a good yarn. We can replicate this without the desert by dry-frying our discs, when of course they are known as chupattis.

Makes 8

1 quantity unleavened dough (see page 217)
ghee, to serve (optional)

1 Divide the dough into 8 equal-sized balls. Roll these out on a floured board to make 8 thin discs.
2 Heat a frying pan or tava until very hot. Place a chupatti on the pan and cook for 1–2 minutes, then turn and cook the other side.
3 Make the other chupattis in the same way. Serve them immediately, spread with ghee, if liked.

Khatta Puda
SAVOURY GRAM FLOUR PANCAKES
Gujarat, west India

A key ingredient in this favourite Gujarati breakfast and snack recipe, gram flour is near impossible to make into a dough because, without blending it with wheat flour, it simply breaks up. As a pancake batter helped by cornflour, however, it is easily made into a cohesive disc. Also called cheela, this thickish pancake is eaten as you would bread. Serve it with raita, pickles and mango chutney from Chapter 8.

Makes 4

4 tablespoons vegetable oil
4 or 5 cloves garlic, finely chopped or puréed
2 onions, finely chopped
2 fresh red chillies, finely chopped
6 cherry tomatoes, quartered
2 tablespoons chopped fresh coriander
4 teaspoons ghee (see page 61)

Batter
1 egg
25 g (1 oz) gram flour (besan)
1 tablespoon cornflour
1 tablespoon natural yogurt
1/2 teaspoon turmeric
1/4 teaspoon bicarbonate of soda
1/2 teaspoon cumin, ground
1 teaspoon salt
1 1/2 tablespoons water

1 Heat the oil in a karahi or wok, add the garlic and stir-fry for 30 seconds. Add the onions, red chillies, tomatoes and coriander and continue stir-frying for about 5 minutes. Set aside.
2 Whisk all the batter ingredients together to make a thick pourable mixture.
3 Heat 1 teaspoon of the ghee in a frying pan of

about 20 cm (8 inches) diameter. Spread one-quarter of the tomato and chilli mixture across the frying pan.
4 Pour one-quarter of the batter into the frying pan. Twist the pan deftly and swiftly so that the batter rolls right around it and covers the base of the pan quickly.
5 Fry over a medium heat for 1 or 2 minutes until just firm. Turn the pancake over and cook for 1 further minute. Slide it out of the pan and serve the pancake flat, not folded.
6 Make 3 more pancakes in the same way.

Papadom
LENTIL FLOUR WAFER

Whichever way you spell 'papadom' – and there are plenty of options, from 'papard' to 'puppuddum' – it is an unparalleled piece of south Indian culinary magic, which has been around for a long time. Each papadom is made by hand from a lentil flour dough ball, which is deftly slapped into a thin flat disc and laid out on huge trays to dry in the sun. This is usually done by women who have spent a lifetime learning the skill. When the papadoms are hardened, they are put into packets in dozens or twenties and it is in this form that most people buy them. At this stage, the papadom is about as edible as a disposable plastic plate! The magic comes about when they are cooked, whereupon they become light, crisp, crunchy wafers. At the restaurant, papadoms are served as appetizers in much the same way as the Anglo-French bread roll, Italian grissini or Chinese prawn cracker, to fill a gap while customers place their orders.

Papadoms range in size from mini to large, and their flavours vary from plain and unspiced to those spiced with black pepper, cumin seeds, chilli and whole lentils. There are three ways of cooking them: deep-frying, grilling or microwaving.

Deep-frying

Preheat the oil to 170°C/340°F. Deep-fry one papadom at a time in the hot oil for about 5 seconds. Remove from the oil using tongs and shake off the excess oil. Allow to cool, but keep in a warm, damp-free place for a few hours until each papadom is crispy and oil-free.

Grilling

Preheat the grill to about medium-high. Grill 1 or 2 papadoms at a time, for about 10 seconds, with the grill tray in the midway position. Ensure that the edges are cooked. Being oil-free, grilled papadoms can be served at once or stored until ready.

Microwaving

Papadoms can also be microwaved, although their flavour is not as good as when they are grilled. Most microwaves are power-rated at 650 watts. Place a papadom on a plate and cook for about 30 seconds on full power. Inspect and apply more heat if necessary. Serve at once or store in airtight containers .

Kochuri, or Dhal Puri
DEEP-FRIED BENGALI PUFF BREAD
Bengal, north-east India

A puri is a small flat unleavened wholemeal flour dough disc, which is deep fried and, if you're lucky, puffs up into a crispy balloon. In this Bengali version, cooked lentils (moong or masoor) are added to the unleavened dough mix before the puri are rolled out.

Makes 16

450 g (1 lb) wholemeal high-gluten Indian
  wheat flour (ata)
warm water for mixing
2 tablespoons ghee (see page 61)
4 tablespoons cooked masoor lentils
vegetable oil for deep-frying

1 Use the flour and warm water to make the basic unleavened dough as described on page 217, adding the ghee and the cooked lentils to the flour along with the water.
2 Divide the dough into 4 then divide each quarter into 4 to give 16 similar-sized pieces. Shape each piece into a ball.
3 Roll each ball into a thin disc, 7.5–10 cm (3–4 inches) in diameter, on a floured board.
4 Heat the oil in a deep frying pan to 190°C/375°F (chip-frying temperature). Add 1 disc at a time to the hot oil. It should sink to the bottom and rise to the top immediately, puffing up. Remove the disc from the pan after 30 seconds, shake off the excess oil and drain on absorbent kitchen paper. Repeat until all the puris are cooked, then serve at once before they deflate.

Roat
DRY SWEET BREAD

Andhra Pradesh, south-east India

A speciality bread from Andhra Pradesh, this sweet bread can be eaten at breakfast or tea time, or as a pudding with or without cream or ice cream. It is also eaten with savoury dishes. Similar to peshwari naan, where the leavened dough is stuffed with sugar, almonds and raisins, in the case of roat, the dough is mixed with dissolved sugar, grated coconut, poppy seeds and toasted almond flakes.

Makes 4

450 g (1 lb) wholemeal high-gluten Indian
    wheat flour (ata)
warm water for mixing
4 teaspoons white granulated sugar
1 tablespoon grated fresh coconut flesh or
    desiccated coconut
2 teaspoons white poppy seeds
2 tablespoons almond flakes, toasted and
    crushed

1 Use the flour and warm water to make the basic unleavened dough as described on page 217, adding the sugar, coconut, poppy seeds and almond flakes to the flour along with the water.
2 Divide the dough into 4 equal-sized balls. Roll these out on a floured board to make 4 thin discs.
3 Heat a frying pan or tava until very hot. Place a roat on the pan and cook for 1–2 minutes, then turn and cook the other side.
4 Make the other roats in the same way. Serve immediately.

8 | chutneys
& pickles

Bottling sauces, pickles and chutneys

Keep any jam jars with their lids. Wash thoroughly and sterilize them as follows before placing your own homemade pickles in them.

1 Place cleaned and rinsed jars into the dishwasher or in the hottest water you can.

2 Let them drain on absorbent kitchen paper without wiping them.

3 When they are dry place them in a preheated oven, 120°C/250°F/Gas ½, for 30 minutes or use an oven that has just been switched off and is cooling down after use.

4 Preferably while they are still hot, fill the jars with your hot chutney or pickle, pushing out air cavities, but not cramming in the chutney. Take care to handle the outsides only.

5 Cap the jars and shake the chutney down, leaving a small space at the top.

6 Heat some vegetable oil in a small pan. Carefully pour it into each jar, so that it covers the filling. You may need to repeat this after the oil has settled. This is called 'sealing'. Screw the cap on tightly.

7 Inspect the jars after a couple of days, ensuring that there is at least 1 cm (½ inch) oil above the chutney or pickle to prevent it moulding on top. If not, heat some more oil and pour in.

8 Leave for at least a month before serving.

Am Chaatni
SWEET MANGO CHUTNEY
Bihar, north-east India

In this recipe from the north-eastern Indian state of Bihar, fresh mangoes are simmered in palm sugar (jaggery) with ginger, garlic and spices to make a sweet chutney which, when bottled, will keep in the fridge for several weeks. This is a version of the mango chutney pioneered by J. H. Sharwood in India in 1889 for export to Britain, and which has become the ubiquitous chutney found at every Indian restaurant around the world.

Makes about 1 kg (2¼ lb)

1.5 kg (3 lb) ripe mangoes, peeled and the flesh sliced, retaining all juices
675 g (1 lb 6 oz) palm sugar (jaggery) or white sugar
175 g (6 oz) cloves garlic, finely chopped
175 g (6 oz) fresh root ginger, finely chopped
100 g (4 oz) sultanas
100 g (4 oz) raisins
salt, to taste

Spices
1 tablespoon ground cumin
1 tablespoon ground coriander
1 tablespoon chilli powder
1 teaspoon ground cloves

1 Put the mangoes and their juice in a 2.25–2.75 litre (4–5 pint) lidded saucepan. Add enough water to cover the fruit, then stir in the sugar, garlic, ginger and spices. Bring to the boil.

2 Once boiling, reduce the heat to low and let the ingredients simmer gently for about 1 hour while the liquids reduce, stirring regularly.

3 When the mixture has the consistency of jam, add the sultanas and raisins and season with salt.

4 Put the hot chutney into sterilized bottles or jars. Seal when cool and store in the fridge.

Balchao Camararo
PRAWN PICKLE
Goa, Indian west coast

The Portuguese introduced this recipe, also known as balichao and balichow to Goa. Fish, large prawns, pork or, as here, tiny shrimps (galmo) ground in palm feni (the local brew) are pickled with a hot masala. The pickle is used as a relish or as a cooking base (see page 135), and variations appear in Malaca, Macau and Burma.

Makes about 1.75 kg (4 lb)

1 litre (1¾ pints) distilled malt vinegar
1 litre (1¾ pints) vegetable oil
1 kg (2¼ lb) cooked prawns, any size
1.75 kg (4 lb) small hard tomatoes, chopped
1 tablespoon palm sugar (jaggery) or brown
  sugar
12 cloves garlic, finely chopped
6–8 fresh red chillies, chopped
1 tablespoon salt

Masala 1

2 tablespoons paprika
1½ tablespoons ground coriander
1½ tablespoons ground cumin
1 tablespoon chilli powder
1 tablespoon mango powder
1 tablespoon turmeric

Masala 2

1 tablespoon cumin seeds
1 tablespoon mustard seeds

1 Add a little of the vinegar to Masala 1 to make a paste. Let it stand for a few minutes.
2 Heat about 6 tablespoons of the oil in a karahi or wok and fry Masala 2 for about 1 minute.
3 Add the Masala 1 paste to the pan and fry for 10 minutes, adding some more oil to maintain a good paste-like texture. Keep stirring.
4 Add the prawns, tomatoes, sugar, garlic, chillies, salt and the remaining vinegar and stir-fry for 10 minutes.
5 Put the pickle and remaining oil in a large lidded casserole dish, then cook, lid on, in a preheated oven, 190°C/375°F/Gas 5, for 1 hour.
6 Put the hot pickle into sterilized bottles or jars, seal and cap (see bottling note opposite). It will keep indefinitely.

Choti, or Murabba
MATURE SWEET MANGO PICKLE
Bengal, north-east India

This is a sweet mango pickle (as opposed to chutney). I first came across it at a friend's house in Sylhet. It is sweet with a hint of sour (from tamarind) and is very mature and dark in colour. This recipe creates a good chutney, which I'm sure will liven your palate at any time.

Makes about 1 kg (2¼ lb)

900 g (2 lb) sweet mangoes, preferably slightly
  underripe, weighed after removing the stones
300 ml (10 fl oz) water
450 g (1 lb) molasses sugar
8 cloves garlic, very finely chopped
2–4 fresh red chillies, chopped
2 tablespoons tamarind purée (see page 62)

Masala

2 or 3 bay leaves
5 cm (2 inch) piece of cassia bark
10 cloves
4 green cardamoms, crushed

1 Wash (but don't peel) the mangoes, then cut the flesh into large chunks. Scrape as much flesh off the stones as you can and set aside.
2 Bring the water to the boil. Add the mango stones and the masala and simmer for 20 minutes. Discard the solids but keep the water simmering.
3 Add the molasses and allow to dissolve completely, stirring all the time.
4 Add the mango flesh and the remaining ingredients, and bring to the boil.
5 Immediately reduce the heat to produce a gentle rolling simmer. The mixture will seem very watery at first, as the mangoes go to pulp, but it will quickly reduce and begin to caramelize. It is cooked after about 20 minutes when it will have set to a solid

syrupy texture. During this 20 minutes, inspect and stir the mixture 3 or 4 times.

6 Put the hot pickle into sterilized bottles or jars, seal and cap (see bottling note page 224). It will keep indefinitely.

Nimbu Achar
LIME PICKLE
Throughout India

This classic lime pickle is tart, hot and delicious. The recipe also works with lemon, green mango, aubergine or green chillies instead of lime. Use the same quantities, weighing them after preparation. Remove the stone and chop the flesh of mangoes and remove the stalks of aubergines and chillies.

Makes about 900 g (2 lb)

225 ml (15 fl oz) vegetable oil
10 large cloves garlic, chopped
450 ml (12 fl oz) distilled malt (white) vinegar
1 tablespoon salt
1 tablespoon sugar
625 g (1 lb 5 oz) limes or lemons, quartered
120 g (4 oz) green chillies

Masala
1 teaspoon turmeric
1 teaspoon ground cumin
1 teaspoon chilli powder
1 teaspoon garam masala (see page 60)
2 teaspoons paprika

1 Add just enough water to the masala to make a paste thick enough to drop sluggishly off a spoon.
2 Heat 3 tablespoons of the oil in a karahi or wok. Add the masala and stir-fry for 2 minutes. Add the garlic and stir-fry for 1 further minute. Set aside.
3 Put the vinegar, salt and sugar in a large saucepan and bring to a simmer. Add the fruit and simmer, stirring occasionally, for about 30 minutes,

during which time the vinegar will reduce.
4 Add the masala paste and the rest of the oil and cook gently until the vinegar boils out and the oil comes to the top.
5 Put the hot pickle into sterilized bottles or jars, seal and cap (see bottling note page 224). It will keep indefinitely.

Khuttar Mitha Sabzi ka Achar
SWEET & SOUR VEGETABLE PICKLE
Gujarat, west India

Root vegetables and cauliflower are the main ingredients in this Gujarati pickle. The vegetables are first baked to dry them out as well as cook them, then finished off in hot oil flavoured with the sweet and sour tastes of tamarind and jaggery.

Makes about 1.5 kg (3 lb)

200 ml (7 fl oz) vegetable oil
6 cloves garlic, finely chopped
5 cm (2 inch) piece of fresh root ginger, shredded
400 g (14 oz) carrots, peeled and halved
400 g (14 oz) white radish (mooli), chopped
400 g (14 oz) parsnip, peeled and cut into thick rings
400 g (14 oz) cauliflower florets
250 g (9 oz) fried onions
6–8 dried red chillies, chopped
75 g (3 oz) tamarind purée (see page 62)
75 g (3 oz) palm sugar (jaggery)
120 ml (4 fl oz) vinegar
2 tablespoons salt

Masala
1 1/2 tablespoons chilli powder
1 1/2 tablespoons mustard powder

Lime pickle

1 Heat the oil in a karahi or wok. Add the masala and stir-fry for 30 seconds, add the garlic and ginger and stir-fry for 30 seconds more. Switch off the heat and add the vegetables to the pan, stirring to coat them with the mixture.

2 Place the vegetables in an oven tray so that they are packed together, one layer deep, and coat with some of the oil from the pan. Bake in a preheated oven, 190°C/375°F/Gas 5, for 15–20 minutes.

3 Meanwhile, add the fried onions, chillies, tamarind, palm sugar (jaggery), vinegar and salt to the karahi or wok. Bring to a simmer then add to the cooked vegetables and their oil and mix well.

4 Put the hot pickle into sterilized bottles or jars, seal and cap (see bottling note page 224). It will keep indefinitely.

Cachumber ki Mirchi
SPICY ONION CHUTNEY
Throughout India

A popular Indian garnish is to serve thinly sliced onion, lime wedges and whole green chillies with the main course. This salad is a variation on this.

Makes about 500 g (1 lb 2 oz)

1 large red or white onion, thinly sliced
2 green chillies, thinly sliced
1 tablespoon coriander, freshly chopped
1 tablespoon fresh lime juice
1 teaspoon tamarind purée (see page 62)
1 teaspoon ground cumin
1 teaspoon bottled mint sauce
$1/2$–1 teaspoon chilli powder
black salt (kala namak) or white sea salt, to
   taste (see page 58)

1 Combine all the ingredients in a bowl. Serve at once or cover and refrigerate overnight, during which time it will become more translucent. It will keep for a few days in the fridge.

Saboot lal Mirchka Achar
CHILLIES STUFFED WITH CHILLI PICKLE
Throughout India

You need some chilli pickle for this recipe – you can buy it at Asian stores or else make your own. The recipe for chilli pickle below was given to me by Trevor Pack, who attended one of my cookery courses and was kind enough to bring some bottles of his homemade chilli pickle. It has a haunting sweetness and is quite delightful used on its own or as the stuffing ingredient for this recipe. Ramiro chillies are at least 15 cm (6 inches) long, bright red and quite mild. In their absence, any large red chilli or red pepper is suitable for stuffing.

Makes about 1 kg (2¼ lb) pickle

Trevor's Chilli Pickle
300 ml (10 fl oz) vegetable oil
6 cloves garlic, minced
5 cm (2 inch) piece of fresh root ginger, grated
450 g (1 lb) green chillies, chopped
450 g (1 lb) onions, chopped
300 ml (10 fl oz) distilled malt (white) vinegar
1 tablespoon salt
1 tablespoon muscovado sugar

Masala
4 tablespoons ground cumin
2 tablespoon turmeric
1 tablespoon curry powder

4 ramiro chillies for stuffing

1 First make the chilli pickle. Add just enough water to the masala to make a paste thick enough to drop sluggishly off a spoon.

2 Heat 4 tablespoons of the oil in a karahi or wok. Add the garlic and ginger and stir-fry for

30 seconds. Add the masala paste and stir-fry for 3 or 4 minutes until the colour changes and the oil floats. Set aside.

3 Heat the remaining oil in a 2.25–2.75 litre (4–5 pint) lidded saucepan. Add the green chillies and the onions and stir-fry for 10–15 minutes, adding water from time to time to prevent sticking.

4 Add the contents of the karahi to the saucepan, together with the vinegar, salt and sugar and simmer, stirring occasionally, for 10–15 minutes, or until the mixture thickens and darkens in colour.

5 Put the hot pickle into sterilized bottles or jars, seal and cap (see bottling note page 224). It will keep indefinitely. Alternatively, allow some of the pickle to cool then use it to stuff the ramiro chillies as follows.

Stuffing the chillies

1 Steam, microwave or blanch the chillies for 3 or 4 minutes until parcooked yet crisp. Dry them using absorbent kitchen paper.

2 Using a small sharp knife, carefully cut a slit along half the length of one side of each chilli, taking care not to cut through to the other side. Carefully scoop out and discard the pith and seeds.

3 Carefully stuff the chillies with the chilli pickle. (If the chillies are reluctant to close enough to retain their stuffing, use small rubber bands or twine as a temporary measure to hold them together.)

4 Put the chillies into cold sterilized bottles or jars, seal with cold oil and cap (see bottling note page 224). They will keep indefinitely.

Churri
HERBAL YOGURT CHUTNEY
Hyderabad, central India

From the word 'choor', to chop, this Hyderabadi relish made from yogurt, coriander, mint and chilli goes with everything, but is the traditional accompaniment to birianis (see pages 213 and 214). It is called pachhri in India's deep south.

Makes about 500 g (1 lb 2 oz)

250 g (9 oz) plain Greek yogurt
200 g (7 oz) finely chopped onion
1 tablespoon coriander, finely chopped
1 teaspoon mint leaves, finely chopped
1 or 2 green chillies, finely chopped
1/2 teaspoon chilli powder
1/2 teaspoon garam masala (see page 60)
black salt (kala namak), to taste (see page 58)

1 Mix all the ingredients together and serve chilled. The chutney will keep in the fridge for a few days, but does not freeze.

Hara Podina
GREEN PURÉED CHUTNEY
Throughout India

This chutney is found with minor variations across the length and breadth of India. Hara means 'green', podina means 'mint leaf'. However, by far the most prevalent ingredient is fresh coriander. It is a most refreshing chutney.

Makes about 500 g (1 lb 2 oz)

200 g (7 oz) fresh coriander and their soft
   stalks, coarsely chopped
4 tablespoons chopped fresh mint
3 green chillies, finely chopped
1 teaspoon bottled mint sauce
2 tablespoons coconut milk powder (see
   page 57)
juice of 1 lemon
1 teaspoon salt

1 Put all the ingredients in a blender or food processor and 'pulse' using water as needed until it is smooth and pourable. This chutney will keep in the fridge for a few days and freezes well.

Chuk

BEETROOT & CUCUMBER CHUTNEY

Bengal, north-east India

Introduced into India by the British during the 18th century, beetroot (chukander in Hindi) likes a moderate temperature and so grows happily in the Indian hills. It is not a widely used ingredient in Indian cooking. Cucumber (kakari, kheera or ssasha) ia a member of the gourd family. It was native to northern India by at least 1000BC, and is believed to have been taken westwards following Alexander the Great's Greek incursion into India in 323BC (see page 14). This Bengali combination of raw beetroot and cucumber offers an interesting colour and taste. It is delicious with Kakrar Chop (crab & chilli rissoles, see page 78).

Makes about 350 g (12 oz)

1 unvinegared, cooked peeled beetroot, thinly
  sliced
5 cm (2 inch) piece of cucumber, peeled and
  thinly sliced
5 cm (2 inch) piece of leek, sliced
5 or 6 mint leaves, chopped
1 teaspoon nigella (wild onion) seeds, crushed
juice of 1 fresh lime
salt, to taste

1 Cut the slices of beetroot into quarters. Do the same to the cucumber.
2 Press out the slices of leeks to produce rings.
3 Mix all the ingredients in a bowl and refrigerate for at least 6 hours. The chutney will keep in the fridge for a few days, but does not freeze.

Imli Gajar

TAMARIND & CARROT CHUTNEY

Throughout India

Also known as the Indian date, tamarind (imli) is a souring agent widely used in southern Indian cooking. The tamarind tree bears pods of about 15–20 cm (6–8 inches) long, which become dark brown when ripe. These pods contain seeds and pulp, which are preserved indefinitely for use in cooking by compression into 300 g (11 oz) rectangular blocks (see page 62). Whereas carrots in the west are bright orange, there are yellow, red and purple varieties in the Third World. The Indian variety, for example, is a deep, almost beetroot-coloured red, its colour coming from large amounts of carotenoid in the vegetable. Tamarind and carrot are combined here to make this sweet and sour chutney, which is adored throughout India.

Makes about 500 g (1 lb 2 oz)

3 or 4 large carrots, shredded
350 g (12 oz) Sweet & Sour Brown Tamarind
  Chutney (see page 70)
salt, to taste

1 Mix the shredded carrots with the chutney, mixing well so that all the carrot is covered by the liquid. Season with salt.
2 Place in a serving bowl and refrigerate for at least 6 hours.
3 Serve when ready. This chutney will keep in the fridge for a few days. Alternatively, it freezes well.

Narial
COCONUT CHUTNEY
Southern India

In this recipe coconut is cooked with milk, mustard seeds, chillies and curry leaves. Served cold, it traditionally accompanies Rasam (gourd soup, see page 68), Masala Dosa (curry-filled rice pancakes, see page 81) and Sambar (spicy lentils, see page 204), but it is really good with any curry.

Makes about 500 g (1 lb 2 oz)

2 tablespoons coconut or vegetable oil
1 green chilli, finely chopped
1–2 teaspoons chopped dried red chillies
200 g (7 oz) flesh of 1 fresh coconut or
    150 g (5 oz) desiccated coconut
4–5 tablespoons milk
$1/2$ teaspoon salt

Masala

2 teaspoons black/brown mustard seeds
1 teaspoon yellow mustard seeds
10–12 fresh or dried curry leaves (optional)

1 Heat the oil in a karahi or wok. Add the masala and stir-fry for 30 seconds, then add both the fresh and the dried chillies and stir-fry for 30 seconds more. Add the coconut and continue stir-frying for about 2 minutes.
2 Add the milk to give the chutney a thick but moist texture. Keep stirring and, once the coconut starts to brown slightly, transfer the chutney to a cold bowl to prevent it cooking further.
3 Season with salt. When cool, refrigerate the chutney for at least 6 hours. It may need a few more spoonfuls of milk to loosen it before serving. This chutney will keep in the fridge for a few days. Alternatively, it freezes well.

Podina ka Raita
MINT & YOGURT DIP
Modern chef's recipe

The celebrated yogurt dip is here lightly sweetened with two surprising ingredients in a recipe developed by Indian chef Lodue Miah.

Makes about 300 g (11 oz)

250 g (9 oz) natural yogurt
1 teaspoon bottled mint sauce
1–2 teaspoons mango chutney, puréed
1 tablespoon pineapple juice
$1/2$ teaspoon turmeric

1 Mix all the ingredients together and store in the refrigerator. The raita does not freeze – its shelf life is dictated by the yogurt.

Kakari ka Raita
CUCUMBER & YOGURT DIP
Throughout India

Couple cucumber with chilled yogurt and you have the ultimate cooler and a great antidote to the heat of chilli. Adding a little chilli powder to this recipe, however, makes it really exciting!

Makes about 350 g (12 oz)

5 cm (2 inch) piece of cucumber, peeled if liked
250 g (9 oz) natural Greek yogurt
$1/2$ teaspoon black salt (kala namak) or white
    sea salt, to taste (see page 58)
$1/2$ teaspoon chilli powder (optional)
$1/2$ teaspoon garam masala (see page 60)

1 Cut across the cucumber in half to give 2.5 cm (1 inch) lengths, then cut each piece lengthwise into matchsticks.

2 Mix all the other ingredients together. Add the cucumber then place in a serving bowl and refrigerate for at least 6 hours before serving. The raita will keep in the fridge for a few days, but does not freeze.

Pachadi
MANGO & GOURDS IN BEATEN CURD

Tamil Nadu, south India

The mango originated in the East Indies and has been cultivated in India for over 6,000 years. So revered in India that it is called the 'Queen of Fruit'. Mango is also used as a vegetable, particularly in pickles and chutneys. The fruit grows to an average of 30 cm (12 in) long and may be round, oval, kidney- or even heart-shaped. Skin colours range from green, through yellow to pink, maroon and purple. Mangoes are coupled here with gourd to make this yogurt-based chutney, a delightfully refreshing dish from southern India. It can be eaten on its own or as a chutney.

Serves 4

4–6 firm ripe mangoes, any type
450 g (1 lb) gourd flesh, any type
4 tablespoons mustard-blend oil
1 tablespoon black/brown mustard seeds
2.5 cm (1 inch) piece of fresh root ginger, finely sliced
2–4 green chillies, chopped
150 g (5 oz) natural yogurt
salt, to taste
4 tablespoons whole green lentils (moong dhal), roasted, to garnish

1 Halve the mangoes, remove the stones and scoop out small balls of flesh using a melon baller. Use any pulp or odd shapes as well. Discard the skins and stones.

2 Boil or bake the gourd for about 10 minutes until tender. Leave it to cool enough to enable you to cut open and cut the flesh into cubes. Discard the seeds, pith and skin.

3 Heat the oil in a karahi or wok. Add the mustard seeds and stir-fry for 1 minute, add the ginger and chillies and stir-fry for 1 minute more.

4 Beat the yogurt briskly with a fork or whisk. Add it to the karahi or wok, stirring rapidly to prevent it from curdling. Immediately add the gourd flesh and, when simmering, add the mango. Add a little water if needed to prevent sticking and season with salt. When heated through, serve the chutney garnished with the roasted lentils. This chutney will keep in the fridge for a few days.

Am ka Raita
MANGO & YOGURT DIP

Throughout India

Mango is widely regarded as India's 'Queen of Fruit', both for its flavour and for its role as an export crop. Here mango juice and yogurt are combined to make a superb cool dip.

Makes about 375 g (13 oz)

250 g (9 oz) natural Greek yogurt
2 tablespoons finely chopped mint
100 ml (3$\frac{1}{2}$ fl oz) mango juice
1 green chilli, finely chopped
1 teaspoon finely chopped ginger
1 teaspoon very finely chopped garlic
$\frac{1}{2}$ teaspoon salt

1 Mix all the ingredients together. Place in a serving bowl and refrigerate for at least 6 hours before serving. The raita will keep in the fridge for a few days, but does not freeze.

Mango & yogurt dip

Tamatu Loncha

DOMINIQUE'S SWEET & HOT TOMATO CHUTNEY

Mumbai, western India

In the Maharashtran Mumbai (Bombay) area a sweet cooked tomato chutney is popular. I put a variation of this recipe, belonging to my wife Dominique, into my first cookbook. By the careful selection of spices, Dominique has honed her recipe to create an attractive, clear russet-red chutney, which tastes as good as it looks.

Makes 600 g (1 lb 4 oz)

150 ml (5 fl oz) water
225 g (8 oz) sugar
450 g (1 lb) tomatoes, skinned (optional) and chopped
1 clove garlic, finely chopped
2–3 bay leaves
150 ml (5 fl oz) distilled malt (white) vinegar
1½ teaspoons nigella (wild onion) seeds
1½ teaspoons chilli powder

1 Put the water and sugar in a 1.5 litre (2½ pint) non-stick saucepan and heat gently until the sugar has completely dissolved.
2 Increase the heat, add all of the remaining ingredients and bring to a boil, then reduce the heat again and leave to simmer. The mixture will initially appear watery, but the water will reduce over about 30–45 minutes. Stir occasionally at first, but as the water reduces, the syrup becomes predominant. When this happens stir the chutney almost continuously to prevent sticking. Stop cooking as soon as you judge that the water has totally reduced out.
3 Put the hot chutney into sterilized bottles or jars,

Dominique's sweet & hot tomato chutney

seal and cap (see bottling note page 224). It will keep indefinitely.

COOK'S TIP If you wish to skin the tomatoes, briefly steam, microwave or blanch them so that you can remove the skins easily without making the tomatoes too mushy.

Takkali Thoviyal

TOMATO CHUTNEY

Kerala, south India

Fresh tomatoes, lentils and tamarind combine to give this chutney of Keralan origin a chunky texture and sour flavour. The black salt, an acquired taste, provides an authentic touch.

Makes about 500 g (1 lb 2 oz)

3 tablespoons mustard-blend or vegetable oil
25 g (1 oz) split and polished gram lentils (chana dhal)
1 teaspoon whole black lentils (urid dhal)
2 tablespoons finely chopped garlic
1 or 2 green chillies, finely chopped
450 g (1 lb) tomatoes, any type, chopped
1 teaspoon tamarind purée (see page 62)
black salt (kala namak) or white sea salt, to taste (see page 58)
2 tablespoons caramelized onions (see page 61), to garnish

Masala

10–12 fresh or dried curry leaves (optional)
1–2 teaspoons chopped dried red chillies
2 teaspoons mustard seeds
1 teaspoon turmeric
½ teaspoon asafoetida
½ teaspoon ground cumin
½ teaspoon ground coriander

1 Heat half the oil in a karahi or wok. Add the gram and black lentils and stir-fry for 30 seconds. Add the masala and stir-fry for another 30 seconds. Remove 2 tablespoons of this mixture and set aside for use in steps 4 and 5.
2 Heat the remaining oil in another karahi or wok. Add the garlic and green chillies and stir-fry for 30 seconds. Add the tomatoes, reduce the heat and continue stir-frying for about 5 minutes.
3 Combine the contents of the two pans and stir in the tamarind and salt. Place the chutney in a serving bowl and refrigerate for at least 6 hours.
4 Just before serving heat the reserved 2 tablespoons of mixture from step 1 with the onion tarka and stir-fry for 30 seconds.
5 To serve, take the cold chutney to the table, then garnish it with this hot tempering masala, which will sizzle as it comes into contact with the wet chutney.
6 This chutney will keep in the fridge for a few days. Alternatively, it freezes well.

Seb
APPLE CHUTNEY
Kashmir, extreme northern India

Juicy cooking apples are harvested during the summer in Kashmir, and when cooked and combined with spices, palm sugar (jaggery) and garlic, make a splendid chutney for Kashmiris to eat during the winter. I was given this recipe by chef M. Raman, the training chef of India's Sheraton hotels.

Makes about 900 g (2 lb)

200 ml (7 fl oz) water
300 g (11 oz) palm sugar (jaggery)
1 kg (2¼ lb) cooking apples, peeled, cored and grated
3 tablespoons golden sultanas
2 tablespoons lime juice
2 tablespoons salt

2 or 3 cloves garlic, finely chopped
2.5 cm (1 inch) piece of fresh root ginger, shredded
50 g (2 oz) spring onions, finely chopped
350 ml (12 fl oz) white wine vinegar

Masala
1½ teaspoons cloves
1 teaspoon chilli powder
3 or 4 bay leaves

1 Heat the water in a 2.25–2.75 litre (4–5 pint) saucepan, add the palm sugar (jaggery) and stir until dissolved.
2 Add the masala and, when simmering, add the remaining ingredients.
3 Simmer, stirring frequently, until the chutney has the consistency of jam.
4 Put the hot chutney into sterilized bottles or jars, seal and cap (see bottling note page 224). It will keep indefinitely.

9 | desserts & sweet treats

Ambya cha bhat
MANGO-FLAVOURED SWEET RICE
Bengal, north-east India

Think of India and you will probably think of mangoes and rice. So here they are in tandem, using tinned products for an effortless sensual pudding.

Serves 4

200 g (7 oz) tin mango slices in syrup
400 g (14 oz) tin creamed rice
10–12 saffron strands
1 tablespoon sugar
$^1/_2$ teaspoon green cardamom seeds, ground
freshly grated nutmeg, to decorate

1 Put the mango slices and their syrup in a blender or food processor and 'pulse' to a purée.
2 Combine all the ingredients and allow to stand for at least 1 hour in the fridge, while the saffron infuses.
3 Serve in individual bowls with a sprinkling of freshly grated nutmeg on top to decorate.

Gajjar Halva
CARROT PUDDING
Throughout India

Halva are sweets and the word derives from the Arabic for sweets, 'hulw'. By the seventh century, Arabs were making a mixture of dates and milk. They later incorporated the Persian sweet-making techniques of frying syrup and wheat flour in ghee. The Arabs took their hulw to India, where it became halva, and so important that cooks who specialize in it are called 'halvais'. Indian halva is easily made from sugar, ghee and vegetables, fruit or semolina (sujee). Its colours depend on the

Mango-flavoured sweet rice

ingredients used, for example orange (carrot), green (pistachio), yellow (mango), red (water melon), brown (fig), dark brown (date) and buff-coloured (semolina). This recipe uses carrot, which will remain a glorious orange colour providing you use white sugar. Served cold, the halva solidifies and can be cut into small squares. Alternatively, it is delightful served soft and warm. It is worth making this large batch as you can freeze any spare.

Serves 12

500 g (1 lb 2 oz) carrots, scrubbed and finely
  grated
1 litre ($1^3/_4$ pints) milk
150 g (5 oz) white granulated sugar
4 tablespoons ghee (see page 61)
a few drops rosewater
1 teaspoon cardamom seeds, ground
25 g (1 oz) almonds
25 g (1 oz) pistachio nuts
25 g (1 oz) golden sultanas (optional)

1 Place the grated carrot in a large non-stick saucepan with the milk, and simmer, stirring from time to time, over a medium heat until the mixture turns thick and dry. This will take about 45 minutes. Towards the end of cooking, as it dries out, stir frequently and watch carefully as it burns easily. When you can pull the mixture away from the bottom of the pan easily, with no liquid running, it is ready.
2 Add the sugar and stir until it has dissolved and been absorbed. Adding the sugar will make the mixture runny again, so repeat the simmering and stirring technique of step 1, although it will take only about 10 minutes to dry out this time.
3 Add the ghee and stir-fry for a few minutes until the mixture goes a pleasant dark orange-brown colour.

4 Stir in the rosewater, ground cardamom, nuts and sultanas, if using.

5 Serve the halva hot, or tip it into a shallow greased baking tin, smooth the surface and leave it to set for at least 6 hours. Before the halva is completely set, mark it into little squares using a sharp knife. When solidified, turn the halva out onto a board and cut it up into the bite-sized pieces.

Double ka Mitha
INDIAN BREAD & BUTTER PUDDING
Moghul origin, northern India

Bread and butter pudding began life as poor people's food as a way of enlivening stale bread with dairy products, sugar and spices. The dish can be traced as far back as medieval times in England and Europe, and there is an erstwhile Egyptian version called *um m'ali*, which uses stale filo pastry, although there is no mention of it in Ancient Egypt. As you might expect, no one perfected this dish better than the Moghuls. Called double ka mitha, or shahi tukre, the recipe involves frying fresh bread in ghee then baking it in reduced sweetened milk, spiced with cardamom, saffron, vanilla and rosewater. After baking it goes firm and golden. The ultimate touch is a decoration of vark (edible silver or gold leaf) with pistachio nuts and toasted almonds.

Serves 4

plenty of ghee (see page 61) for frying
8 slices white bread, crusts removed
1 litre (1³/₄ pints) milk
250 ml (8 fl oz) sweetened condensed milk
pinch of saffron strands
a few drops vanilla essence
¹/₂ teaspoon green cardamom seeds, ground
a few drops rosewater

Decoration
1 tablespoon almond flakes, toasted
1 tablespoon pistachio nuts, crushed
4 sheets edible silver or gold leaf (vark) (see note on page 120)

1 Heat the ghee in a frying pan then fry the bread slices on one side until golden. Turn them over, add more ghee as necessary and repeat. Remove the fried bread from the pan and drain on absorbent kitchen paper.

2 Bring the milk to the boil in a 2 litre (3¹/₂ pint) non-stick saucepan. Reduce to a simmer, add the condensed milk and cook for 15 minutes, stirring occasionally.

3 Add the saffron, vanilla essence and green cardamom and remove from the heat.

4 Arrange 4 of the fried bread slices over the base of an oven tray or shallow dish, then place the other slices on top. Pour the milk mixture over the bread, ensuring that the bread is thoroughly soaked.

5 Place the tray immediately in a preheated oven, 190°C/375°F/Gas 5, and bake for 15 minutes. Remove and leave to cool. It will set quite firmly.

6 When cold, cut into 4 portions, place on individual serving plates and decorate with the nuts and/or the vark.

Indian bread & butter pudding

Gulab Jaman
SYRUP-DRENCHED GOLDEN GLOBES
Bengal, north-east India

Gulab jaman literally means a rosy plum and refers to its fragrance and shape, not its ingredients. It is a dessert of cake-like texture, conceived in Bengal but now enjoyed all over India. It comprises spheres (about 3 cm/1¼ inches in diameter) of paneer (Indian cheese), flour and milk powder, moulded to plum shapes (although they can be round), and fried to a golden colour before being steeped in saffron-flavoured syrup. The dessert is usually served cold, but it can be served warm, and even flambéed with brandy (see below). Bengal's sweet makers (moiras) took to paneer (called chhana in Bengali) as ducks to water, using it as a new ingredient for their sweetmeats.

Makes 8

225 g (8 oz) paneer (see page 62)
3 tablespoons milk powder
up to 3 tablespoons cornflour
300 ml (10 fl oz) water
900 g (2 lb) white granulated sugar
2 or 3 tablespoons rosewater
vegetable oil for deep-frying
pinch of saffron strands

1 Knead the paneer in a bowl with the milk powder and just enough cornflour to create a smooth, pliable dough, adding a little water as necessary.
2 Divide the dough into 8 and form the pieces into balls or plum shapes.
3 To make the syrup, bring the water to the boil in a saucepan then add the sugar. Simmer until you get a runny syrup, stirring often. Remove from the heat. Add the rosewater and set aside.
4 Heat the oil in a deep frying pan to 190°C/375°F (chip-frying temperature). Add the balls of paneer to the hot oil, one at a time, so as to maintain the oil

temperature. Fry for 2 or 3 minutes until they are golden. Remove from the pan, shake off the excess oil and drain on absorbent paper.
5 Put the hot fried balls and the saffron into the syrup and simmer for 18–20 minutes.
6 Serve warm or cold.

COOK'S TIP To make a flambé with gulab jaman, ensure the balls are not swamped by too much syrup.

Jalebi
SYRUP-DRENCHED CRISP SPIRALS
Throughout India

Indians love their sweets really sweet, and this jalebi is no different. A creamy batter is squeezed into deep-frying oil to produce crisp golden rings or spirals. While still warm, the rings or spirals are immersed in thin syrup, which they absorb.

Makes 4–6

225 g (8 oz) plain flour
2 tablespoons plain yogurt
pinch of saffron strands
300 ml (10 fl oz) water
225 g (8 oz) white sugar
½ teaspoon rosewater
oil for deep-frying
2 tablespoons pistachio nuts, chopped

1 Combine the flour and yogurt with a little warm water to make a thickish batter. Add the saffron and stand the batter in a warm place for 12–24 hours to allow the yogurt to ferment.
2 To make the syrup, bring the measured water to the boil in a saucepan then add the sugar. Simmer until you get a runny syrup, stirring often. Remove from the heat. Add the rosewater and leave the syrup to cool.
3 Stir the batter well. Add a little water if necessary but keep it quite thick. Heat the oil in a deep-frying

pan to 190°C/375°F (chip-frying temperature).

4 Fill a clean plastic bag with the batter. Very carefully, cut off one corner of the bag to make a tiny hole no more than 3 mm (¹/₈ in) in diameter.

5 Maintaining a short continuous flow of batter, squeeze a small amount of the batter, about the size of a golf ball, through the hole in the bag into the hot oil. Make a jalebi by 'piping' overlapping squiggles to make a disc about 7.5 cm (3 inches) in diameter. Make more jalebi in the same way until the surface area of the pan is full.

6 The jalebi will set firmly as they cook – use tongs to turn them. When they are golden brown all over – this takes about 2 minutes – remove them from the pan, shake off the excess oil and drain on absorbent kitchen paper. Cook another batch of jalebi in the same way.

7 Place the cooked jalebi in the syrup and serve hot, or leave them for an hour or so to absorb the syrup and then serve cold.

Pothittu
CRÊPES FILLED WITH SWEET CHEESE
Bagada, Karnataka, southern India

These pancakes with a sweet sauce come from the Badaga tribe of the Nilgiri hills district of south India. The distinctive filling includes coconut milk, palm sugar (jaggery) and sesame seed. Malpoa is a Bengali variant with a creamy filling. This dish is very rich so I suggest you make only 4 pancakes, although the batter mixture will make more.

Serves 4

Pancakes
50 g (2 oz) plain white flour
25 g (1 oz) butter, melted, plus a little extra for greasing
1 egg, beaten
150 ml (5 fl oz) milk, warmed

1 teaspoon white sugar
2 or 3 drops vanilla essence
120 ml (4 fl oz) maple syrup, to serve

Filling
100 g (4 oz) soft cream cheese
50 g (2 oz) thick sour cream
2 tablespoons thick coconut milk
1 teaspoon palm sugar (jaggery) or white sugar
1 teaspoon white sesame seeds
¹/₂ teaspoon ground cardamom
¹/₄ teaspoon freshly grated nutmeg

Decoration
icing sugar
freshly grated nutmeg
lime wedges

1 First, make the pancakes. Sift the flour into a bowl and stir in the melted butter, beaten egg, warm milk, sugar and vanilla essence. Beat well and leave to stand for about 10 minutes. The batter should be of a pouring consistency.

2 Heat a little butter in a very hot pan. Pour in enough batter to make a thin pancake when swirled around the pan. Cook until set, then turn over and briefly cook the other side. Turn it out. Use the remaining batter to make 3 more pancakes in the same way. Allow the pancakes to go cold.

3 Mix the filling ingredients together in a bowl and mash until smooth. Spread one-quarter of the filling along the central line of one pancake, then roll the pancake into a cylinder. Fill the other 3 pancakes in the same way.

4 To serve, dust the cold pancakes with icing sugar and nutmeg and serve with the warmed syrup and a wedge of lime.

COOK'S TIP Pancakes of any type can be cooked in advance, stored between layers of foil and refrigerated for a day or frozen. If frozen, thaw, remove the foil and reheat in an oven or microwave.

Am Pall
SIEVED MANGO WHIPPED WITH CREAM
Throughout India

Simple to make, fruit fools consist of cooked and cooled fresh fruit pressed through a sieve then blended with an equal quantity of rich cream. The dish dates as far back as 17th-century England. Alan Davidson in *The Oxford Companion to Food* attributes the derivation of the word 'fool' to the French 'fouler', meaning to mash. It is not surprising to find that the dish had evolved independently in 17th-century Moghul India. What is surprising, however, is the coincidental similarity of the name – the Hindi word for fruit is pall, phaal or phul. Using tinned fruit and the blender avoids the chore of sieving. Mango (am) is a popular choice for a fruit fool, but apple, banana, gooseberry, redcurrant, rhubarb and orange work equally well. This dish is quite rich so the portion sizes are relatively small.

Serves 4

400 g (14 oz) tin mango slices in syrup
1/2 teaspoon ground cinnamon
3 or 4 tablespoons icing sugar (optional)
300 ml (10 fl oz) whipping cream

1 Put the mango slices and their syrup, the cinnamon and icing sugar, if using, in a blender or food processer and blend to a smooth purée.
2 Whip the cream in a large mixing bowl until at least doubled in volume. Gently fold the mango purée into the cream – the folding technique retains air and keeps the fool light.
3 Cover the bowl and refrigerate for 1–2 hours before serving.

Sieved mango whipped with cream

Shrikand Kesar
SAFFRON YOGURT SYLLABUB
Gujarat, west India

From Maharashtra and Gujarat comes this syllabub of whipped yogurt and thick cream, sweetened with white sugar and fragranced with finely ground green cardamom seeds and saffron, then dusted with freshly grated nutmeg. A little syllabub goes a long way. It is particularly attractive served in stemmed glasses, straight from the fridge. The shrikand will keep in the fridge for a few days, but does not freeze.

Serves 4

1 tablespoon natural yogurt, strained
150 ml (5 fl oz) whipping cream
1 teaspoon ground almonds
1 teaspoon white sugar
1/8 teaspoon ground cardamom
6–10 saffron strands
freshly grated nutmeg, to decorate

1 Simply whisk all the ingredients together and place into serving bowls or stemmed glasses. Refrigerate for at least 6 hours – after this time, the lovely orange-gold marbling effect of the saffron is apparent.
2 Just before serving, decorate with freshly grated nutmeg.

Sil Datte Moyra
BANANA PUDDING
Goa, Indian west coast

This deliciously simple recipe comes from the town of Moyra in Goa, where plump sweet bananas are grown. You can use ordinary bananas or, better still, miniature or apple bananas. The sauce from the raisins, golden sultanas, chopped mixed nuts, ghee, sugar and sherry or rum can be made well in advance as it preserves like jam.

Serves 4

1 tablespoon raisins
3 tablespoons golden sultanas
1 tablespoon chopped mixed nuts
2 tablespoons ghee (see page 61)
2 tablespoons water
4 tablespoons palm sugar (jaggery) or brown
  sugar
2 tablespoons sherry or rum
4 large fresh bananas

1 Place the raisins, sultanas and nuts in a blender or food processor and coarsely grind with a little water.
2 Heat the ghee and the water in a 2 litre (3¹/₂ pint) saucepan. Add the sugar and stir well. When simmering add the ground raisin mixture. Simmer for a while so that the sauce thickens enough for the water to reduce out.
3 Add the sherry or rum then remove from the heat. Peel and chop the bananas. Pour the hot sauce over them and serve at once with a dollop of sour cream or vanilla ice cream.

Pall Satay
SKEWERED GRILLED FRUIT
Modern chef's recipe

When we think of satay, we usually think of thin strips of skewered, grilled peanut-marinated meat. However, satay simply means 'cooking on skewers'. One of my favourite food writers, Jennifer Brennan states that the word *'originated in Java, Indonesia... and was developed from the Indian kebab brought there by Muslim traders. Even India cannot claim its origin, for there it was legacy of Middle Eastern influence.'* This is my wife Dominique's invention and it has become her signature dish. Taking the word literally, she came up with skewering not meat but fruit and she has cooked her fruit satays for many of our Indian friends. It makes a great dessert for barbecues or dinner parties. Use only firm fruit with contrasting colours. The recipe works particularly well with apple, nectarine, peach, mango, banana and kiwi fruit. If possible, use star fruit for dramatic effect.

Serves 4

20–24 chunks of fruit (see above)
fresh mint, to decorate

Syrup
120 ml (4 fl oz) white granulated sugar
175 ml (6 fl oz) water
¹/₂ teaspoon ground cinnamon

1 Soak 4 bamboo or wooden skewers overnight in water to minimize the chances of them burning during cooking.
2 To make the syrup, bring the sugar and water to the boil in a saucepan, then simmer for about 5 minutes. Add the cinnamon and keep stirring

Banana pudding

until the syrup clings to the back of the spoon.

3 Thread 5 or 6 fruit chunks onto each skewer. Brush the fruit with the syrup using a pastry brush.

4 Place the skewers on a rack in a grill pan, and cook under a preheated medium grill for 2 or 3 minutes – make sure you watch them in case the sugary fruit catches fire. Turn the skewers and cook for another 2–3 minutes.

5 Serve the fruit still skewered, decorated with mint leaves.

Kulfi
INDIAN ICE CREAM
Moghul origin, northern India

In Moghul days large blocks of ice were carried by runners from the Himalayas to wherever the Moghuls were at court. Keeping the blocks huge meant the ice could reach the lowland cities of Delhi, Agra and Lahore. By then the blocks were smaller, but they were a necessary Moghul court luxury to keep their rooms cool. Fifteenth-century air-conditioning was achieved by having man-made waterfalls trickling down serrated walls in every room in the Moghul household. Ice was only fed into the waterfall of the room where the emperor was present, and the cool air was circulated by fan-pulling servants (punka wallahs). There was no shortage of punka wallahs, nor ice, and it is not surprising that Moghul chefs got hold of it. They already made a spicy sweet cream. It did not take much evolution to mix crushed ice with the spiced cream mixture to make kulfi. No stirring took place, and the mixture was put into special conical kulfi moulds (which enabled the kulfi to slip easily out of the mould before serving). The moulds were then packed in ice-filled boxes and the kulfi frozen solid.

Serves 4

2.25 litres (4 pints) whole milk
150 g (5 oz) sugar
4 drops vanilla essence
pinch of green cardamom seeds, ground
pinch of salt
50 ml (2 fl oz) double cream
grated nutmeg, to decorate

1 Pour the milk into a large saucepan. Bring to the boil then cook over a low heat, stirring constantly, until it has reduced to one-third of its volume.

2 Add the sugar, vanilla essence, ground cardamom and salt and stir well. For a flavoured kulfi add your chosen flavouring at this stage (see below) and stir well to combine.

3 Transfer the kulfi mixture to a freezer container and let cool before placing in the freezer for 30 minutes. Stir in the cream then pour into 4 kulfi moulds or yogurt pots and return to the freezer overnight.

4 To serve, remove the kulfi from the moulds by running the moulds under hot running water for a few seconds, and sprinkle with grated nutmeg.

KULFI FLAVOURINGS
Chocolate: 150 g (5 oz) dark bitter chocolate, broken into pieces
Pistachio: 90 g ($3^1/_2$ oz) chopped pistachio nuts, plus $1/_8$ teaspoon green food colouring (optional)
Mango: 100 ml ($3^1/_2$ fl oz) thick mango pulp
Almond: 90 g ($3^1/_2$ oz) toasted and chopped almonds

10 | drinks

Anardana
POMEGRANATE DRINK
Northern India

Pomegranates (anardana) grow on deciduous trees up to 7 m (23 feet) tall with deep green leaves and vermillion flowers. Cutting the pomegranate open reveals its neat package of translucent, bright crimson flesh, encasing numerous seeds with a unique taste combination of astringent, sour, bitter and sweet. Today, pomegranate grows in India, particularly in the Himalayan foothills, where the seeds of wild pomegranate called daru yield the best anardana.

Serves 4

175 ml (6 fl oz) pomegranate syrup
175 ml (6 fl oz) water
pinch of salt
2–3 cupfuls crushed ice
4 mint leaves, to decorate

1 Mix the syrup, water and salt together in a large jug. Refrigerate for at least 2 hours.
2 To serve, put the crushed ice into 4 tall tumblers. Pour in the juice and decorate with the mint leaves.

Am Ka Ras
SPICY MANGO DRINK
Rajasthan, north-west Indian desert

Camels are to be seen everywhere in Rajasthan – pulling carts, carrying huge loads and even ploughing. They are also indispensable to the tribes in the vast tracts of the Rajasthani deserts. So important are they that once a year their breeders and thousands of camels come together for the annual November camel fair in Pushkar. I have been to it once, and amidst the bedlam of the haggling and camel grunting, boys were selling this refreshing savoury spiced mango juice drink.

Serves 4

175 ml (6 fl oz) unsweetened mango pulp
600 ml (20 fl oz) cold water
1/2 teaspoon tamarind purée (see page 62)
1 teaspoon ground cumin
1/2 teaspoon chilli powder
1/2 teaspoon mango powder
pinch of mustard powder
salt, to taste

1 Mix all the ingredients together in a large jug. Refrigerate for at least 2 hours before serving.

Kahwah
GREEN TEA
Kashmir, extreme northern India

Kashmiri green tea, always served at the end of a wazwan (feast), contains almonds, saffron, cardamom, green tea and sugar. Kashmiris make the process elegant by serving tea from the samovar. Kahwah (or cha, char or chai) is served throughout India at all times of day or night.

Serves 4

750 ml (24 fl oz) water
2 teaspoons green tea
4 green cardamoms
1 cinnamon stick
3 or 4 peeled almonds
pinch of saffron
sugar, to taste

1 Bring the water to the boil in a 2 litre (3 1/2 pint) saucepan. Add all the other ingredients and simmer for 5 minutes.
2 Pour the tea into a preheated teapot, using a tea strainer to remove the solid matter. Serve at once.

Green tea

Komal
SAVOURY YOGURT
& COCONUT DRINK

Gujarat, west India

This Gujarati drink of spiced yogurt and coconut milk may seem like an unusual combination, but it tastes exquisite if you can use home-made yogurt and fresh coconut milk. Most of us will have to make do with factory-made yogurt and tinned coconut milk but, even then, it is superbly satisfying, especially if spiked with chilli.

Serves 4

2 tablespoons mustard-blend oil
225 g (8 oz) natural yogurt
200 ml (7 fl oz) tinned coconut milk
1 tablespoon chopped coriander
1 or 2 green chillies, slit lengthwise, seeds
    removed if liked
1 teaspoon sugar
$1/2$ teaspoon salt

Masala

$1/2$ teaspoon cumin seeds
$1/4$ teaspoon asafoetida
6–8 curry leaves

1 Heat the oil in a frying pan. Add the masala and stir-fry for 30 seconds. Set aside.
2 Mix the remaining ingredients together in a jug and refrigerate for at least 6 hours.
3 To serve, pour the drink into stemmed wine glasses and decorate with the reserved masala.

Lhassi
SAVOURY OR SWEET
YOGURT DRINK

Kashmir, extreme northern India

This is a mixture of yogurt and crushed ice, plus water, too, if liked. For centuries, it has been a favourite drink in northern India and Kashmir, where ice is available for much of the year. Both the savoury and the sweet version of lhassi are refreshing at any time of day, especially breakfast.

Lhassi Namkeen
SAVOURY YOGURT DRINK

Serves 1

1 cupful crushed ice
225 g (8 oz) natural Greek-style yogurt
up to 300 ml (10 fl oz) water (optional)
$1/2$ teaspoon ground white pepper
$1/3$ teaspoon chilli powder (optional)
salt, to taste

1 Put the ice in a tall glass.
2 Put all the remaining ingredients in a blender and blend together. Pour over the crushed ice in the glass, and serve.

Lhassi Meethi
SWEET YOGURT DRINK

Serves 1

1 cupful crushed ice
225 g (8 oz) plain Greek-style yogurt
up to 300 ml (10 fl oz) milk (optional)
a few drops rosewater or orange flower water
sugar, to taste

1 Put the ice in a tall glass.
2 Put all the remaining ingredients in a blender and blend. Pour over the crushed ice and serve.

Nimbu Pani
LIME JUICE WITH WATER
Throughout India

Fresh limes (nimbu), which grow prolifically all over the country, are used to make India's most refreshing and delicious cold drink.

Serves 1

2–3 fresh limes
1/2 cupful crushed ice
salt or sugar, to taste

1 Squeeze the limes, discarding any pips. Put the lime juice into a tall glass.
2 Add water to the lime juice, to fill three-quarters of the glass. Top up with crushed ice. Add salt or sugar to taste.

Punch
MULLED WINE
Throughout India

Hindus have no proscription on drinking. The Portuguese brought wine to India and the British brought whisky. The Raj combined them in this warm beverage, which was particularly enjoyed in the wintery hills stations when it was really cold. It was called punch because it contains five ingredients (wine, spices, sugar, orange peel and whisky), and panch is the Hindi word for 'five'.

Serves 4

750 ml (24 fl oz) red wine
4 green cardamoms
1 cinnamon stick
sugar, to taste
8 cloves
5 x 2 cm (2 x 1/2 inch) piece of orange peel
50 ml (2 fl oz) whisky

1 Heat all the ingredients except the whisky in a 2 litre (3 1/2 pint) saucepan and bring to a gentle rolling simmer – don't allow to boil or the alcohol will evaporate.
2 Add the whisky, then pour the punch into a prewarmed glass serving jug, using a strainer to remove the solid matter, and serve hot.

Mulled wine

index

Akhni 59
Al Yakkhn 156
All-India recipes 82, 84, 86, 87, 88, 162, 182, 186, 226, 228, 229, 230, 231, 232, 239, 242, 245
allergies 64
Aloo Chole 199
Aloo Chop 82
Aloo Dolma Puri 217
Aloo Ghobi Methi 156
Am Chaatni 224
Am ka Raita 232
Am ka Ras 250
Am Pall 245
Ambya Cha Bhat 239
Anardana 250
Andaman Islands 42; recipe 136
Andhra Pradesh 38–39; recipes 216, 222
apple 170, 236
Apple Chutney 236
Arabs in India 15
Aromatic Roast Lamb 124
Aryans 11–13
Assam: recipes 91, 169
aubergine 158, 183
Avial 157

Bahn Morog Shikari 103
Baigan Burtha 158
Baigan ka Salan 158
Baked Chicken Legs 99
Baked Herb Pomfret 152
Baked Lamb Chops 113
Baked Marinated Beef 115
Bakra Dahi Wala 110
Balchao Burra Camararoa 135
Balchao Camararoa 224
Bamboo Shoot Curry 159
bamboo shoots 159, 181
Banana Pudding 246
Bathuway ka Roti 219
Batter-coated Potato Balls 82
Bean & Chickpea Salad 71
beans 71, 186, 201
beansprouts 192

beef 73, 77, 111, 115, 117
Beef Coconut-fry 111
Beef Tomatoes Stuffed with Cheese & Spinach 184
Beetroot and Cucumber Chutney 230
Bemla Kauvery 159
Bendakka 160
Bengal 33; recipes 70, 83, 102, 103, 105, 145, 153, 171, 180, 217, 221, 225, 230, 239, 242
Bhoona Murgh 90
Bihar: recipe 224
Bindi 160
Black Lentils with Red Kidney Beans 201
Bom Chount 170
Bombay Duck 88
Bommaloe Macchli 88
Bonda Mysori 82
bread: basic unleavened dough 217
    Deep-fried Bengali Puff Bread 221
    Dry Sweet Bread 222
    Lentil Flour Wafer (Papadom) 220
    Potato-stuffed Fried Bread 217
    Rajasthani Dry Unleavened Bread Discs 219
    Savoury Gram Flour Pancakes 220
    Spinach-layered Bread 219
Broccoli Stems 172
Brown/White Onion Paste 61
Butter Chicken 96

cabbage 190
Cachumber ki Mirchi 228
Cafreal 90
Caranguejos Konkani 135
cardamom 47
Carrot Pudding 239
cashew nuts 56, 87, 166
Casseroled Tamarind Fish 142

cauliflower 156
celery 169
Chachchori Morog 93
Champ Bukhari 113
Charu 66
Cheese Cubes Fried in Ghee 88
Cheese Cubes Fried in Sweet Chilli Dipping Sauce 88
chefs, modern: Anand, Sanjay 102
    Gomes, Stephen 175
    Gopal, Pital 95
    Prasaad, Alfred 113
    Saraswat, Arvin 77
    Sarkhell, Udit 78
    Shriram, Aylur 140
    Singh, Hardeep 106
    Singh, Kuldeep 88
    Sunderam, Vikram 160
    Todiwallah, Cyrus 169
Chemeen Manga Charu 140
chicken 77, 90–102, 208
Chicken Cooked with Cumin 102
Chicken in a Dark Pepper Sauce 93
Chicken Fried in Egg Batter 91
chickpeas 71, 199
Chilli-hot Pork & Offal 128
Chilli Paneer Tikka 88
Chillies Stuffed with Chilli Pickle 228
Chopped Turkey Stir-fry 106
Choti 225
Chowgra 163
Chuk 230
Churri 229
chutneys and pickles 70, 71, 224–231
Coconut Chutney 231
Coconut, Yoghurt & Mango Mixed Vegetables 157
Cod in Yoghurt Sauce 143
Coorg 40; recipes 66, 93, 122, 159, 208
Coorg-style Rice with Minced Chicken Curry 208

Coquiero Caldine 170
crab 78, 135
Crab & Chilli Rissoles 78
Creamy Brown Lentils 199
Creamy Chicken Pieces 77
Crêpes Filled with Sweet Cheese 243
Crisp, Chewy Street Food 70
Crisp-fried Wild Salmon 152
Crisp Okra 160
Crisp Spiced Whitebait 147
Cucumber Yoghurt Dip 231
Cumin Water 66
Curried Beansprouts 192
Curry-filled Rice Pancakes 81
Curry Soup 66

Dahi Batata Pava 70
Dakshini Salat 73
Dandal 172
Deep-fried Bengali Puff Bread 221
Deep-fried Chicken Drumsticks 94
Deep-fried Fritters 87
Delhi 24, 35 (see also Mughals); recipe 172
Desert Barbecued Quail 108
Devilled Fried Cashews 87
Devilled Squid Rings 149
Dhaaba Wallah Ande ka Tarkari 162
Dhal Bukhara 199
Dhal Doyi Jhol 70
Dhal Puri 221
Dhansak 114
Dilruba Sabzi 166
Do Peeaza Chukander 113
Dominique's Sweet & Hot Tomato Chutney 235
Dopeyaja Harsh 103
Dosa 80
Double ka Mitha 240
Dravidians 9–10
Dry Sweet Bread 221
duck 103, 106
Dum Pukht ke Titaar 104

Egg & Pea Curry 162

eggs 74, 162, 181
Erachi Olathiathu 111
Europeans in India 27–32

Fenugreek-flavoured Potato
& Cauliflower 156
Fenugreek & Spinach-
flavoured Chicken 101
Festival Vegetables 179
Fihunu Mas Lebai 136
Filled & Fried Pastry Balls
86
Filowri 83
Fish Layered with Rice 209
Fish in a Spicy Sauce 146
Foogath 166
Fragrant Stock 59
Fragrantly Simmered Fish
153
Fried or Barbecued Sardines
146
Fried Fish with Spinach 138
Fried Trout in a Yoghurt
Sauce 139
fruit 56–57

Gaijar Halva 239
Galouti Kebab 77
Garam Masala 60
garlic 58–59
Ghee 61
Ghee Paneer Tikka 88
ginger 59
Goa 38; recipes 87, 90, 128,
131, 132, 135, 149, 150, 154,
166, 170, 191, 224, 246
Goan Crab Curry 135
Goan Mild Vegetable Stew
or Curry 170
Goan Mushrooms 191
Goat Curry Cooked in
Yoghurt 110
Gosht Tikkea Malai ke
Bohris 115
Gourd, Plantain & Cashew
Curry 166
Gourd Soup 68
gourds 68, 166, 182, 232
Gram Flour Vermicelli
Noodles in a Tangy Tomato
Gujarati Curry Sauce 187
Greeks in India 14–15
Green Beans with Lentils
179
Green Puréed Chutney 229
Green Tea 250

Green Vegetarian Rissoles 78
Grilled Garlic Red Mullet
136
Grilled Mackerel 138
Gujarat 36; recipes 66, 115,
143, 178, 183, 187, 195,
208, 220, 226, 245
Gujarati Five-Vegetable Stew
195
Gulab Jaman 242

Haakh Gadh 138
Hara Kebab 78
Hara Podina 229
Haryana 33; recipe 172
Herbal Yoghurt Chutney 229
herbs 46, 56
Horin Kofta 116
Hot Green Chutney 71
Hot, Sour & Spicy Pork
Curry 122
Hot & Sour Vegetables
167
Hot, Sweet & Sour Prawns
140
Hot-tempered Tomato Curry
189
Huggo 138
Hyderabad 38–39; recipes
146, 158, 163, 174, 214,
229
Hyderabadi Spiced
Aubergine 158

Imli 70
Imli Gajar 230
Indian Bread & Butter
Pudding 240
Indian Ice Cream 248
Indus Valley Civilization
10–11

Jal Jeera 66
Jalebi 242
Jungle Meat 118
Jungli Maas 118

Kachori 86
Kadhi Shorba 66
Kahwah 250
Kaju 87
Kakari ka Raita 231
Kakrar Chop 78
Kalia 105
Kanne 66
Kari or Karikal 164

Karnataka 39–40; recipes 95,
138, 146, 148, 181, 189,
243
Kashmir 33; recipes 96, 110,
116, 123, 124, 138, 139,
156, 170, 212, 236, 250,
251
Kashmiri Curried Apple 170
Keema 117
Kerala 41–42; recipes 83, 94,
111, 153, 157, 182, 211,
235
Keralan Soured Kingfish
Curry 153
Khara Soti Boti Kebab 74
Khatta Puda 220
Khatti Machi Dum 138
Khumbi 169
Khuttar Mitha Sabzi ka
Achar 226
kingfish 153
Kobiraji 91
Kochuri 221
Koli Nalla Malu 93
Kolmino Patio 140
Komal 251
Kootu Kazhani 167
Kori Gassi 95
Kosumbri 71
Kozambhu 142
Kozhi Varattiyathu 94
Kulfi 248
Kurass ke Phul 169
Kuthalam Moong Korma
200

lamb 73, 74, 77, 113, 114,
118, 122, 123, 124, 132,
213
Lamb with a Cashew &
Coconut Paste 132
Lamb with Chickpeas &
Rice 213
Lamb with Onion &
Beetroot 113
Lamb Shank 122
Leek, Potato & Cashew
Soup 68
Lentil Dumplings with
Vegetables 178
Lentil Flour Wafer 220
lentils 70, 73, 114, 148, 179,
180, 199–204
Lhassi 251
Lhassi Meethi 252
Lhassi Namkeen 251

Lime Juice with Water 252
Lime Pickle 226
lobster 135
Looki Kalia 171
Lucknow 35; recipes 68, 104,
122

Maacher Jingha Sorse Jhol
145
Maachi Jhol 153
Maasah 95
Macchi ka Salan 146
Macchi Kadhi 143
mackerel 138
Madhya Pradesh 37; recipe
86
Maharaja recipes 100, 106,
113
Makhani Murgh 96
Mangalorean Chicken Curry
95
mango 224, 225, 232, 239,
245, 250
dried 55
Mango-flavoured Sweet Rice
239
Mango & Gourds in Beaten
Curd 232
Mango & Yoghurt Dip 232
Marinated Veal Escalope 119
marinating 77
Masala Dosa 81
Mashed Potato Rissoles with
a Spicy Centre 82
Mathi 146
Mattar Valor 172
Mature Sweet Mango Pickle
225
Mauryan Empire 15–16
Meat Simmered with Lentils
& Vegetables 114
Meat & Sweet Potato Stew
127
Meen Moplah Biriani 211
Meeng Pullao ka Surat 209
Methi Gosht 118
Milagu-tannir 67
Mild Chicken Curry 90
Mild Lentil Curry 200
Min Tikka 147
Minced Beef Curry 117
Mint & Yoghurt Dip 231
Mirchi ka Salan 174
Mirchwangan Korma 96
Mixed Seafood in Coconut
Sauce 148

Mixed Seafood Rice 211
Mixed Vegetable Curry 164
modern recipes 77, 78, 88, 95, 102, 106, 113, 140, 160, 169, 175, 184, 246
Moghuls 24–27, 35; recipes 73, 77, 96, 99, 100, 103, 119, 121, 124, 166, 174, 208, 213, 240, 248
monkfish 145
Mooli Cheemen 148
Moonfali Tava 86
Mumbai 37; recipes 70–71, 88, 235
Murgh Malai Tikka 77
Murgh Masala 100
mushrooms 169, 191
Muslims in India 19–20, 24 (see also Mughals)
mussels 154
Mustard-spiced Prawns & Monkfish 145
Mysore 39; recipe 82

Narial 231
Navrattan Korma 174
Nehari 122
Nimbu Achar 226
Nimbu Pani 252
Nine-Jewel Vegetable Curry 174
Niramish Butta 175
noodles 187, 216
Noodles with Rice 216
nuts 56

oils 57–58
okra 160
Omelette-wrapped Meat Chunks 74
onion 59, 61, 228
Onion Masala Sauce 61
Onion-sweetened Duck 103
Oonbharlu 177
Orissa 37; recipes 66, 90, 158
Oven-cooked Marinated Chicken 90

Pachadi 232
Pakora 87
Palak-ka-dala 202
Pali Satay 246
Pan-roasted Peanuts 86
Panch Phoran 62
Pandi 122

Paneer 62
Papadom 220
Papri 178
Parpu Konjan 148
Parsee Potatoes 184
Parsee Roast Root Vegetables 177
Parsees 20, 37; recipes 74, 114, 127, 140, 152, 177, 181, 184
partridge 104
Pasanda 119
Pasanda Kebab 73
Patrani Machli 152
Payari Moong Upkari 179
Pea & Green Bean Curry 172
peanuts 56, 86
Peixe Reachado 150
Pepper Soup 66
Pepper Water 67
Persians in India 13–14
Pheasant in a Thin Red Sauce 105
Piri Piri Diabole Mankyo 149
Podina ka Raita 231
Pomegranate Drink 250
pomfret 152
Porial Bagada Ottakuddi 181
Porial Kadama 179
pork 122, 128, 131
Poro Mirchi 181
potato 82, 156, 192, 199, 217
Potato & Chickpea Curry 199
Potato-stuffed Fried Bread 217
Pothittu 243
Prawn Pickle 224
prawns 140, 145, 148, 224
Prawns with Mango 140
Prawns or Shrimps in Lentils 148
Pullao 207
Puli Saadam 216
Pumpkin Curry 171
Punch 252
Punjab 33; recipes 101, 117, 118, 156, 172, 192, 199, 201, 219
Punjabi-style Fenugreek-flavoured Meat Curry 118
Qasuri methi ke Sag Murgh 101
quail 108

Raan 124
Raan-e-Murgh 99
Railway Station Vegetable Curry 182
Rajasthan 35–36; recipes 108, 118, 186, 202, 219, 250
Rajasthani Dry Unleavened Bread Discs 219
Rajasthani Spinach Dhal 202
Rajasthani String Beans with Berries 186
Ramus 152
Rangalu Kanchalaldom 180
Rasa Karela Chi-bhaji 182
Rasam 68
Ravaiya 183
Red Hot Chilli Chicken Korma 96
red mullet 136
Rezala Morgh 102
Ribs in a Rich Sauce 123
rice 206
    basmati 207
    Boiled 206, 207
    Fried in Ghee 212
    Pullao 207
    Saffron 212
Rice, Lentil & Coconut Salad 73
Rice with Lentils 208
Rice Pancake 80, 81
Rice Pizza 81
Rice-stuffed Roasted Whole Chicken 100
Rich-tasting Hot Chicken 102
Roat 222
Roghan Josh Gosht 124
Roghani Dhal 201
Romans in India 18–19

Saboot lal Mirchka Achar 228
Saffron Rice 121
Saffron Yoghurt Syllabub 245
Sag Mattar Paneer 186
Sakarand ka Gosht 127
salmon 152
Salnoo 184
salt 58
Sambar 204
Samosas 84
Sangri Kair 186
sardines 146

Savoury Yoghurt & Coconut Drink 251
Savoury Yoghurt Drink 251
Sealed Partridge 104
Seb 236
Sevian Tamatar 187
Sewian ki Khichri 216
Shikar ki Buttuck 106
Shorba Nawabi 68
Shredded Bamboo Shoots 181
Shredded Cabbage & Carrot with Coconut 190
Shrikhand Kesar 245
Sieved Mango Whipped with Cream 245
Sikkim: recipe 129
Sil Datte Moyra 246
Silk Road 16–18
Sindhi Potato 192
Skewered Grilled Fruit 246
Slow-cooked Aromatic Meat Dish 124
Smoky Aubergine Purée 158
Soola ka Battar 108
Sorportel 128
Sour Lentil & Yoghurt Soup 70
South Indian Vegetable Curry 196
Southern India 39–42; recipes (see also individual areas) 68, 71, 80, 81, 179, 190, 192, 196, 204, 231
Spiced Stuffed Peppers 95
spices: to grind 45
    ground 55–56
    to store 56
    whole 47–55
Spicy Grilled Escalopes 73
Spicy Mango Drink 250
Spicy Onion Chutney 228
Spicy Stuffed Fish 150
Spicy Tamarind Cooler 66
Spinach-layered Bread 219
Spinach with Peas & Cheese 186
Split Pea Rissoles 83
squid 149
Stir-fried Celery 169
Stir-fried Chicken Curry 93
Stuffed Baby Aubergine 183
Sufaid Korma ke Khada Masle 121
Sular Shikaari ke Lepcha 129
Sweet Mango Chutney 224

Sweet Potato & Green Banana 180
Sweet & Sour Brown Tamarind Chutney 70
Sweet Yoghurt Drink 252
sweetcorn 175
Syrup-drenched Crisp Spirals 242
Syrup-drenched Golden Globes 242

Tabak Maz 123
Tahiri 214
Tak-a-Tan 106
Takkali Thoviyal 235
tamarind 57, 62, 66, 216, 230
Tamarind & Carrot Chutney 230
Tamarind Purée 62
Tamarind Rice 216
Tamarta, Bhare Sag Palak 184
Tamatu Loncha 235

Tamil Nadu 42; recipes 67, 73, 142, 147, 148, 160, 164, 167, 179, 189, 200, 216, 232
Tamil Stir-fried Okra 160
Tangy Lobster Curry 135
Tasty Fried Bitter Gourd 182
Tempered Mussels with Tendim 154
Thakkali Chugander 189
Thakkali Mulakittathu 189
Thar ke Batti Chupatti 219
Thoran 190
Tomato & Beetroot 189
Tomato Chutney 235
tomatoes 184, 187–189, 235
Tondak 191
Took Aloo 192
Traditional South Indian Spicy Lentils 204
Triangular Filled & Fried Pastries 84
trout 139

Turkari 196
turkey 106
Ugavela Moong 192
Undhui 195
utensils 44–45
Uthappam 81

veal 74, 119, 121
Veal in a White Creamy Aromatic Sauce 121
Vegan Sweetcorn Curry 175
Vegetable Biriani Specialty 214
vegetables 156, 157, 163, 164, 166, 167, 170, 174, 177, 179, 182, 195, 196, 214
Vegetables in a Creamy Sauce 166
Velvety Smooth Minced Meat Rissoles 77
Venison Meat-balls 166

Vevichathu Surmai 153
Vindaloo 131

weights & measures 64
whitebait 147
Wild Boar Curry 129
Wild Duck 106
Winter Vegetable Curry 156

Xacutti 132

yoghurt 70, 139, 143, 157, 163, 229, 231, 232, 245, 251, 252
Yoghurt-based Vegetable Curry 163

Zawb Tempeirada 153
Zeera 54
Zeera Murgh 102

acknowledgements

India Food and Cooking is a book I have long yearned to write, and I sincerely thank New Holland's Rosemary Wilkinson for giving me my opportunity to do so.

I chose the 200 recipes that would give the reader the widest range of ingredients, tastes and methods, with all the principal signature dishes of each region included. All the recipes have been tested, and for such diligence I am indebted to my chef-wife Dominique, who cooks my recipes to the letter and forbids me to help, because I will lose confidence in them and inevitably add a bit here or there and change things. Because of her, they do work, resulting in authentic dishes which Indian householders would be proud to offer to their family and friends.

I particularly enjoyed writing the food history chapter. As far as I know, it has never been done chronologically in one complete work. It involved hundreds of fascinating hours of research. Authors can get precious about their opus, and when I did Clare Sayer, my editor, who put in many hours herself, tactfully and gently helped me to cut away the dead wood.

No book is the work of one person, and the other talented members of the team who have helped in the production of this beautiful book all need a mention: Stuart West the photographer, Stella Murphy the food stylist and Roger Hammond the designer. There is no substitute for holding a good book in your hands and I pay tribute to the skill of all those involved.